MANGA ART

MANGA ART

BEN KREFTA

Ben Krefta is a UK-based freelance illustrator and graphic designer whose unique, unconventional designs are primarily targeted at edgy, tech-savvy, video-game-playing, manga-reading teens and young adults. He has worked on a number of art and design projects for web sites, game developers, and magazines and has delivered digital art demonstrations for clients such as Hitachi and Wacom. He is also the author of a number of bestselling how-to-draw manga books. For more information, visit his personal homepage, www.benkrefta.com

Arcturus

This edition published in 2018 by Arcturus Publishing Limited
26/27 Bickels Yard, 151–153 Bermondsey Street,
London SE1 3HA

ISBN: 978-1-78828-300-7
AD006055US

Printed in China

Contents

INTRODUCTION

Manga is a term which describes comics produced by Japanese "mangaka" (cartoonists) primarily for a Japanese audience. The style was developed in Japan during the mid to late 19th century and draws heavily on influences from Western and American comics combined with ideas taken from Japanese art and wood-block prints. In the West, the term is often used to describe a particular style of Japanese drawing and art as well as a type of Japanese comic.

What Is Manga?

"Manga—it's just a fad, isn't it?" said one of my art tutors at university. He would perhaps be surprised to see how this particular fad has exploded in popularity in the West. Manga art, games, movies, comics, fashion, and other aspects of Japanese culture now have a loyal and growing following. Comic and pop culture shows and conventions are often attended by devoted fans sporting costume play ("cosplay") outfits of their favorite manga and game characters.

How to Recognize Manga

Most character artists start with line art, which they then color and render in the style they like best. Many modern manga-style artists fuse a variety of Western styles into their artwork. They also use idiosyncratic coloring styles, such as a flat-tone "cel" effect and a soft airbrush style, together with more traditional painterly effects. (A cel, or celluloid, is a transparent sheet on which characters and props are hand-drawn or painted for 2D animation and cartoons.) Many digital manga artists produce a soft, shaded style of coloring which has an airbrushed look to it. Japanese artists sometimes refer to this as manga CG (computer graphics). Some opt for a painterly style to mimic watercolors, markers, or acrylics.

Manga Styling

The manga style has gradually evolved over the last century, but in the 1960s–80s it really seemed to commit to the visuals that many fans are familiar with to this day. These often include the following characteristics:

- Large eyes (especially for female and younger characters)
- Small noses, usually simplified as a dot or an L-shaped line
- Flat-looking faces and angular chins
- A wide range of hair and eye colors
- Overstated hairstyles
- Lean body types
- Exaggerated breast size
- Emotion indicators, such as an oversized sweat drop or cruciform vein on the head
- Simplified line work
- Background effects such as speed lines or patterned tones

Manga styles should be adapted as you prefer. In this book I use a range of different styles and themes, including digital media, to illustrate how to draw various manga creations. Over the years I have developed my own way of doing things and this will undoubtedly be evident in the artwork here. If you want to experiment with adapting any of the characters to be, for example, even more cute and "chibi," go for it! Or if you prefer dark, moody schemes, don't feel you need to stick with the bright and colorful tones I use.

Your Manga Artist Journey

Drawing is a skill that takes a lot of time to master. It's a neverending process of development that can deliver a massive sense of achievement, fun and excitement, but it can make you feel defeated if things aren't going quite right. Remember that whether you're 13 or 30 you can already draw, and the more you practice the better you'll be.

Before embarking on the tutorials in this book, think about where you are right now. Design yourself a character—just make it up in your head. This is your starting point. After a few weeks of practice and working through the tutorials, try doing the same thing again and seeing how much you've improved.

It's a good idea always to date your work, either on the paper itself or on a labeled folder on your computer. Every few months, take out all your drawings and lay them out in sequence or post them on your wall. Notice where you've improved and see if you can identify areas that need more work. Try turning your drawing upside down or looking at it in a mirror—areas that aren't working will jump out at you. The idea is to be your own critic, but be kind to yourself at the same time. Take pleasure in your achievements and if you feel you haven't progressed as much as you'd hoped, use that as an incentive to improve rather than beat yourself up about it.

If you're halfway through a drawing and feeling frustrated that it doesn't seem to be going well, don't give up and throw it in the bin. Take a break and come back to it later. Set some drawing goals—a series of sketches, some inked drawings, or full-color artwork. Then set aside some time to complete them. Maybe tackle one task a day, or complete a full-color work each week.

Carry a sketchbook at all times and draw whenever you have a moment to yourself or when inspiration hits you. Make use of tablet or phone apps for drawing and painting. Keep your art gear close at hand so that you can start straightaway.

Read manga, watch anime, play video games and generally immerse yourself in whatever you love to fuel your passion. Remember to analyze what you like and don't like about the artwork. Make notes and keep a record of your ideas. Perhaps join an art class so that you can draw or paint with other students, all learning from one another. Alternatively, enter the online realm to collaborate with others around the world. Copy, trace, draw from photos and life—as long as you are drawing, you are improving. Ultimately, I hope you'll be able to apply your developing skills to creating your own style of manga characters. Draw a lot, experiment widely, and—most importantly—have fun!

TOOLS AND MATERIALS

You can start creating artwork with just a pencil, an eraser, and some paper. But I recommend experimenting with different media to discover what suits your style, be it colored pencils, paint, markers, or one of the many digital software packages available.

A well-arranged workspace is essential. Some people are happy to draw in a sketchbook or a tablet on their lap, and that's fine, but it will take hours of practice to reach a good standard so you'll need a working environment that is comfortable for long stretches of time. An ergonomic chair is useful for lengthy drawing sessions, and a clean, tidy environment can help to unclutter your mind. However, it's still useful to have reference books close at hand, or access to images on your computer, for those times when you need a little extra inspiration or guidance.

When you are working with color, natural light is best so that you can see a realistic range of hues, but a lamp and overhead lights will help to reduce eyestrain on dull days. You can buy daylight bulbs with a color temperature that most closely reproduces natural light.

Typically, modern manga artwork will start out as a pencil sketch which is later refined by using black ink pens and then applying color or tone. I've created artwork using pencil, ink, and digital color for many years, but I increasingly use digital media to draw and paint. Of course, any artist needs to be able to draw with just a pencil and paper, but an understanding of digital and traditional artwork creation methods is also important today.

The basic tools required to create awesome manga artwork are set out in the following pages.

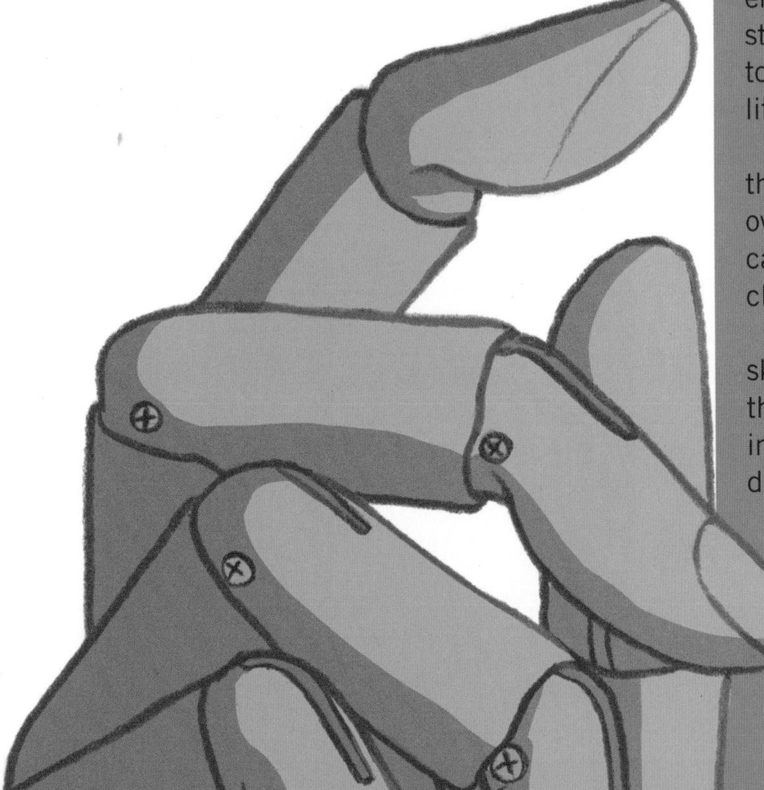

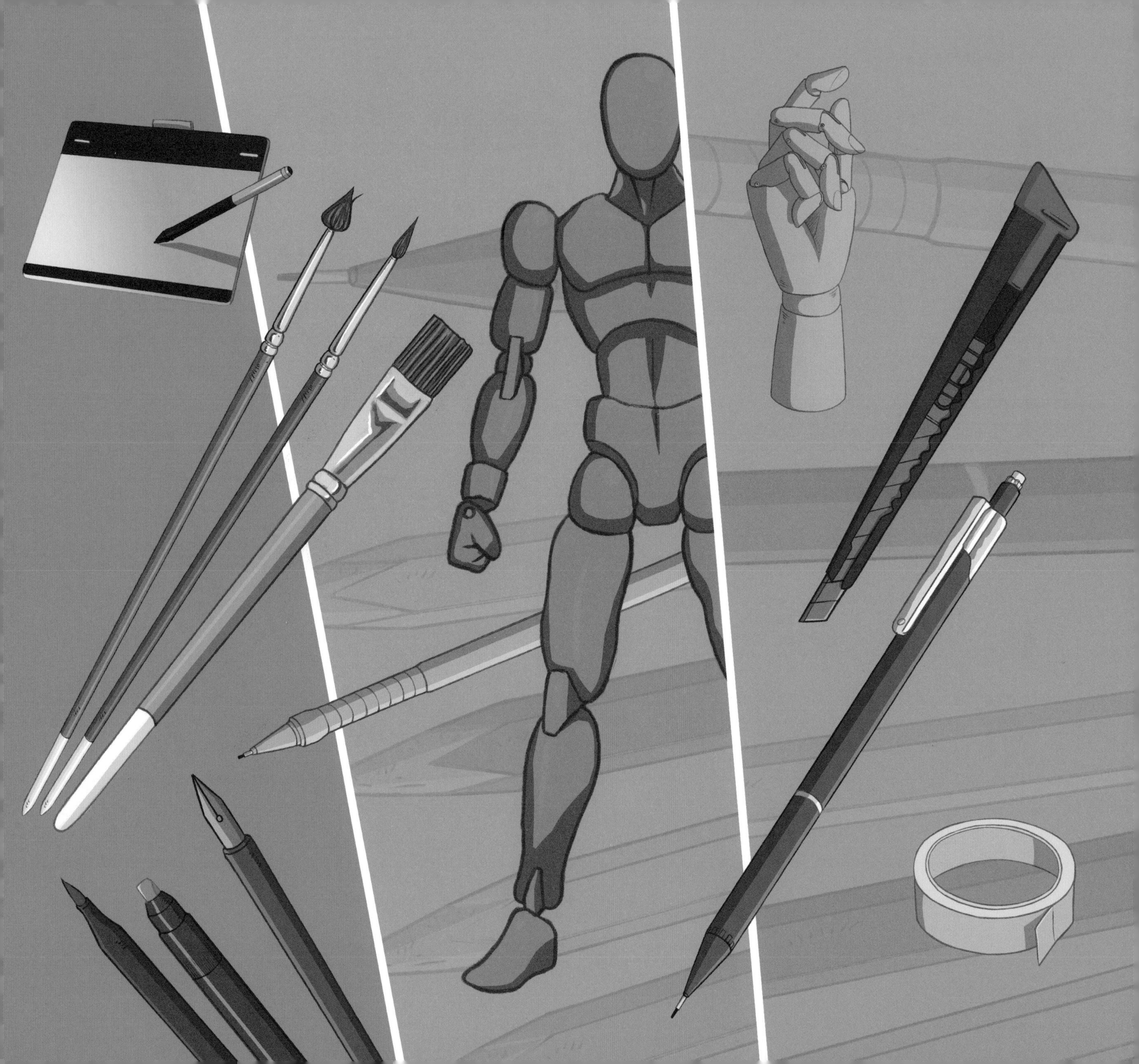

BASIC DRAWING EQUIPMENT

PENCILS

Practice drawing with pencils as much as you can, either for quick sketches, layouts, or fully shaded illustrations. If you plan to shade your work, you'll need a selection of pencil grades. Most manufacturers offer a range from 6H (the hardest) to 6B (the softest), with HB in the middle. Like many comic-book artists, I tend to draw with a 2H grade as this allows me to keep my guidelines light, smooth, and clean. If I want to define my lines I can use either a darker B grade pencil or ink.

Pencil marks softer than 2B will smudge, so it's best to reserve the softer grades for shadows and shading. Place a tissue under your drawing hand to prevent smudges, or use a smudge guard which covers the parts of your hand and fingers that rest against the paper.

I prefer a mechanical pencil to a wooden one. This means I don't have to spend time sharpening it and the tip stays at a constant thickness; the Pentel brand I use allows for the eraser tips to be replaced when they are worn out.

I may sketch with other colors before drawing lines with a darker graphite pencil, especially if I want to avoid using an eraser. Yellow, light blue, and light green work well for preliminary guidelines and shapes, while darker red or purple can be used to refine these lines. By pressing lightly with your colored pencil, you can create delicate or subtle color combinations; by pressing harder, you can create more vibrant, solid tones. To blend colors, add a second color on top of the first. You can create a variety of tones by gradually building up colors in this way. After scanning your art, you can use digital software to delete specific, unnecessary colors such as a preliminary blue pencil under-sketch.

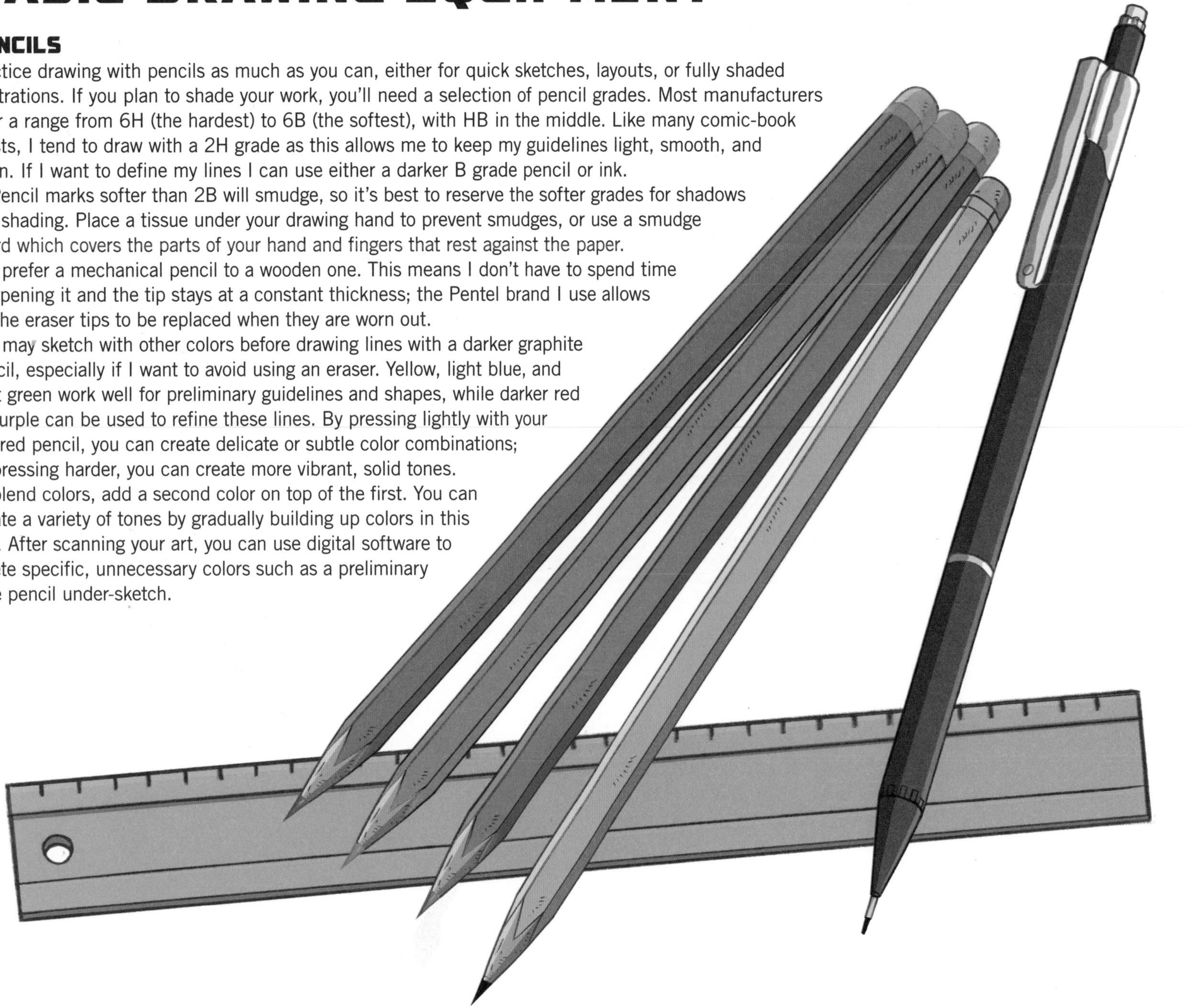

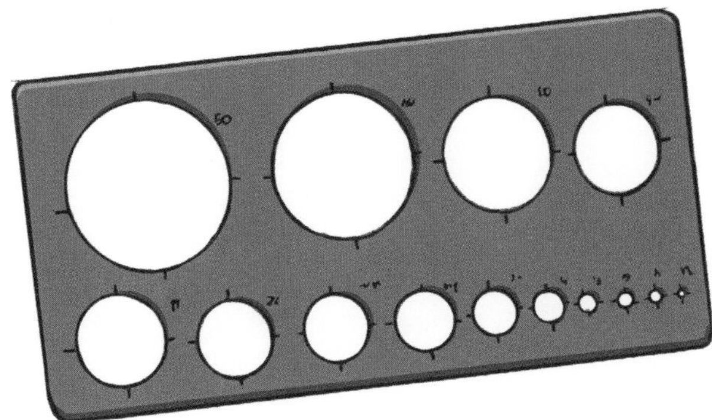

Templates and Rulers

For drawing circles, templates are preferable to compasses as the latter can leave marks or holes. French curves are handy for smooth, accurate line work, especially when drawing mechanical objects. I often sketch shapes using rough pencil lines then use the curves to correct the shapes, pressing harder to commit the lines to paper.

A ruler or straight edge is essential for drawing anything mechanical or for action lines, borders, and buildings. I create backgrounds—such as streets, cities, interiors, and other perspective drawings—using rulers.

When using templates and rulers to ink your work, be careful not to slide them around on the page as you may smear an inked line. Either wait for each inked portion to dry or lift the template or ruler and place it down before continuing. Use a tissue or rag to wipe down the edges to keep your work clean.

Erasers

A good eraser is essential. Find one that removes graphite pencil with ease. I use three: a small, thin one on the end of my mechanical pencil which gets into small spaces; a larger one for when I need to remove lots of lines in one hit; and a putty or kneadable eraser.

A putty eraser is great for getting rid of smudges cleanly and can be shaped to get into small areas. It can also be used to "wipe" lightly over pencil art, effectively lightening parts of your drawing and allowing you to refine your line work further with less mess. The best way to clean it is to rub away the dirty edges on a sheet of paper.

With soft pencils, be careful not to smudge your work when wiping away pieces of eraser left on the paper—and when you're erasing pencil lines after inking, take care to give the ink some time to dry to avoid smudging.

Surfaces

Artists have their own preferences when it comes to paper. Traditionally, comic-book artists use smooth sheets of Bristol board, though some opt for a more rough-textured, cartridge paper sketchbook.

Other Useful Tools

A manikin (see page 11) can be useful for reference. Traditional wooden hands are also good anatomical aids. A scalpel is useful for trimming paper.

INK, MARKERS, AND PAINT

Inking is the process of converting pencil work to a high-contrast black and white as seen in manga comics. Ballpoint or fine-line pens can be used to give a consistent line thickness; they come in various widths for both bold and fine linework.

Variations in line weight and thickness aren't as common in manga as they are in Western comics, but it's still important to give your line work some depth, for example by using tapering lines or making background lines thinner. Brush pens or quill nib pens, which can be dipped into black Indian ink, work very well for this.

If you look closely at manga art, you'll notice that weight and thickness often diminish towards the end of a line. In order to taper lines in this way, apply less pressure toward the end of a stroke—this is an important technique that will make your work look more fluid and professional.

Successful inking is a skilled process and requires a different technique to penciling. Practice by inking several sketches before applying ink to your finished pencil drawing, just to familiarize yourself with the medium. If you're feeling confident enough, you can bypass the pencil stage entirely and go straight to ink. You can correct any mistakes with white correction fluid.

Markers are used to add color or tone to finished inked work. They dry slowly and bleed into one another, making it possible to create smooth color blends. You can buy double-ended markers with a chiseled tip for technical application and a thin tip for details. Brush-tip markers are fantastic to work with, as they're like a paintbrush with a constant flow of color. I like to use a set of six gray brush markers in different tones to create monochromatic work with multiple layers of depth.

Advantages

- ***A simple ballpoint pen, or biro, is easy to use like a pencil.***
- ***Inking makes your work look solid, bold, and clear; it is then ready for you to apply color or tone at a later stage.***
- ***Markers are a quick, convenient solution for adding saturated color or tone and remove the need to mix paint or wash brushes.***

Disadvantages

- ***Ink cannot be removed without spoiling your paper and drawing.***
- ***Markers require thicker paper that will not wrinkle or allow inks and dyes to bleed through.***

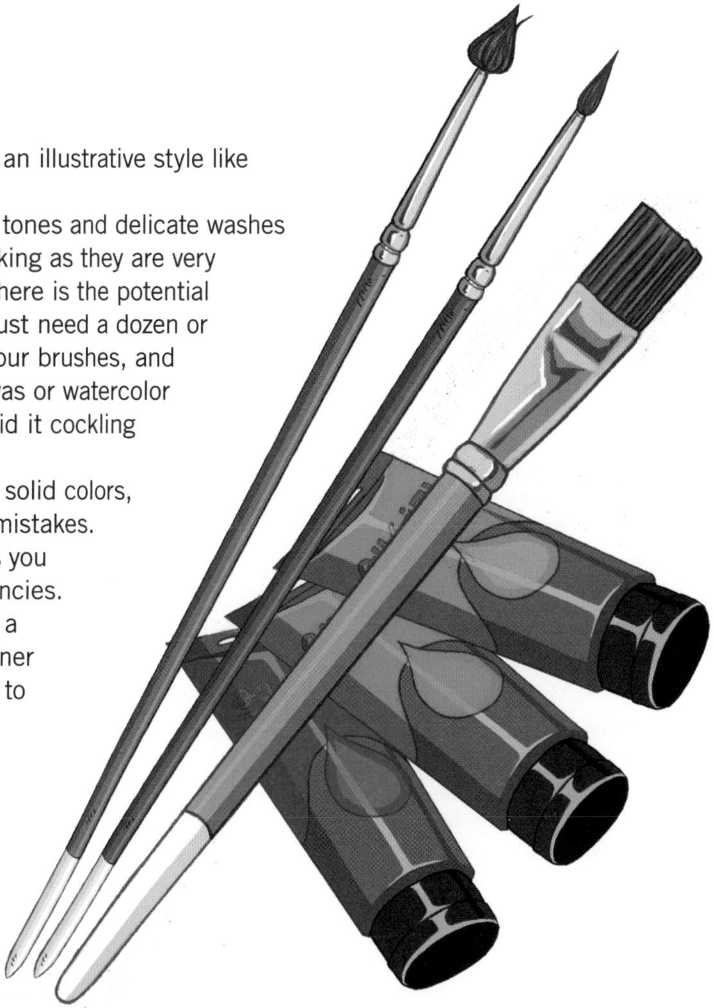

PAINTS

After penciling or inking your artwork, you can bring it to life by painting it. With an illustrative style like manga, you will probably wish to use watercolor and/or acrylic as your media.

While markers give a bold, graphic effect, watercolor painting provides subtle tones and delicate washes that will give your work a loose, fluid feel. Watercolors suit a fine-art style of working as they are very organic in the way they are applied to and appear on the paper—that is to say, there is the potential for the paint to run, bleed, and disperse across the canvas. To start with, you'll just need a dozen or so colors, a few brushes of different sizes, water to dilute your paint and clean your brushes, and a palette or a saucer on which to mix your paints. You can paint direct onto canvas or watercolor paper. Make sure you use paper of a minimum weight of 140lb (300gsm) to avoid it cockling (developing an uneven surface) when wet.

The advantages of acrylic paints are that they are quick-drying, provide deep, solid colors, and can be applied in opaque layers to build up colors, refine details or correct mistakes. A beginners' set of ten or more tubes of color should be enough to start with. As you develop your skills, you might like to experiment with acrylics of varying consistencies. You'll also require water and a paper towel for cleaning and, as with watercolors, a palette to mix on and different-sized brushes. Once transferred from their container to a palette, acrylic paints dry rapidly so you might like to buy a stay-wet palette to delay this.

Start painting with a large brush and work on bigger areas of color before focusing in on details with a smaller brush. Acrylic is quite a thick paint and can be watered down if necessary to achieve thin washes or watercolor-like effects. It's very versatile and as long as you avoid oily or waxy surfaces you can apply it to paper, canvas, glass, wood, metal, or plastic.

Advantages

- ***Paint offers more texture and natural fluidity than ink.***
- ***It is more hands-on and tactile than pencils, pens, or a computer.***
- ***Traditional media, such as watercolor and acrylics, create a tangible piece of artwork that has more value if you want to sell it.***

Disadvantages

- ***Paint can be difficult to control and requires practice before you can handle it well.***
- ***It is messy and requires additional time to set up and clean down.***
- ***Mistakes are easier to make and much harder to correct than with digital media.***

DIGITAL

In recent years, the production of artwork has shifted toward the use of computers and image-making software, as this technology has made the job of creating, coloring, editing, and reproducing artwork fast and easy. You probably already own a laptop, desktop computer, tablet, or smartphone and, with some practice and perseverance, you will be able to create beautiful digital art on all these devices.

Typically, manga and comic artists draw their characters or pages in pencil, ink them by hand, then scan them and complete the color stage using the computer and a graphics tablet. But artists are increasingly moving toward wholly digital creation from start to finish. The industry standard graphics software is Adobe Photoshop. It's a versatile program for modern-day photographers and artists alike and I've been using it for my art and illustration projects for many years. PaintTool SAI, Clip Studio Paint, Gimp, and Painter are low-cost alternatives that are also worth considering.

LAYERS

While you may already be familiar with basic Photoshop functions, unleashing Photoshop's full potential will take some practice. Once you master it, however, the results can be incredible! After familiarizing yourself with the Photoshop interface, you'll need an understanding of how layers work. These are a fundamental part of digital art, and work like a stack of acetate or clear plastic sheets. The lines you paint on one layer won't affect another layer in the Layers panel. If you paint on a layer above, you'll cover up the layer underneath, but you won't paint over it. By painting different colors on different layers, you can shade each one without adding, say, unwanted hair color on a girl's face or skin tone on a boy's jacket. Each layer can then be edited individually at any time.

The second half of this book shows you how to use Photoshop as a tool for creating and coloring your artwork. It will help you explore your full potential by showing how to combine your existing hand-drawn artwork with the latest graphics software to create fully rendered character designs.

STEP 1
Set up and sketch

STEP 2
Ink then add flat tones

STEP 3
Flat shading

STEP 4
Soft rendering

STEP 5
Complete the rendering

STEP 6
Finesse and add background

DRAWING HEADS

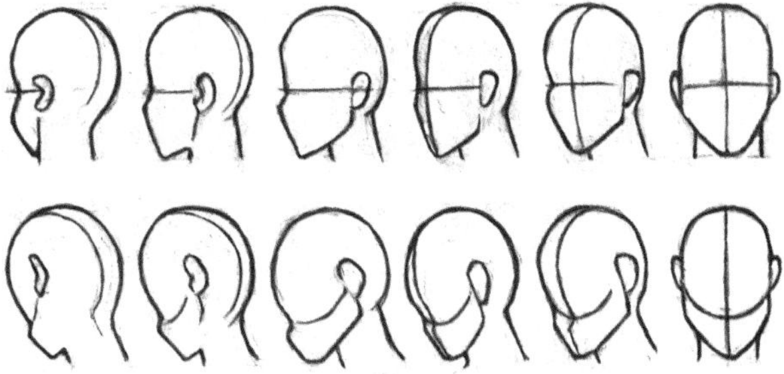

Heads come in various shapes and sizes determined by the character's age, gender, and physique or simply by the many different manga styles we can use. To construct a head, start by drawing a circle for the top part and straighter lines for the jaw.

The size of the head is arguably one of the most important parts of any manga artwork as it will determine the amount of detail you can add to the face, as well as the size of the torso, and of other characters or objects in the illustration.

I always start by drawing a rough circle or oval. This helps to work out where on the page I'm going to draw the head and how big it should be. I can see how much room I have to play with and if I'm not happy with that it's very easy to erase the guide circle and draw one a little bigger or smaller, depending on what's required.

This chapter includes step-by-step construction methods for front, three-quarter and side view male and female heads, along with a selection of angled manga heads for reference.

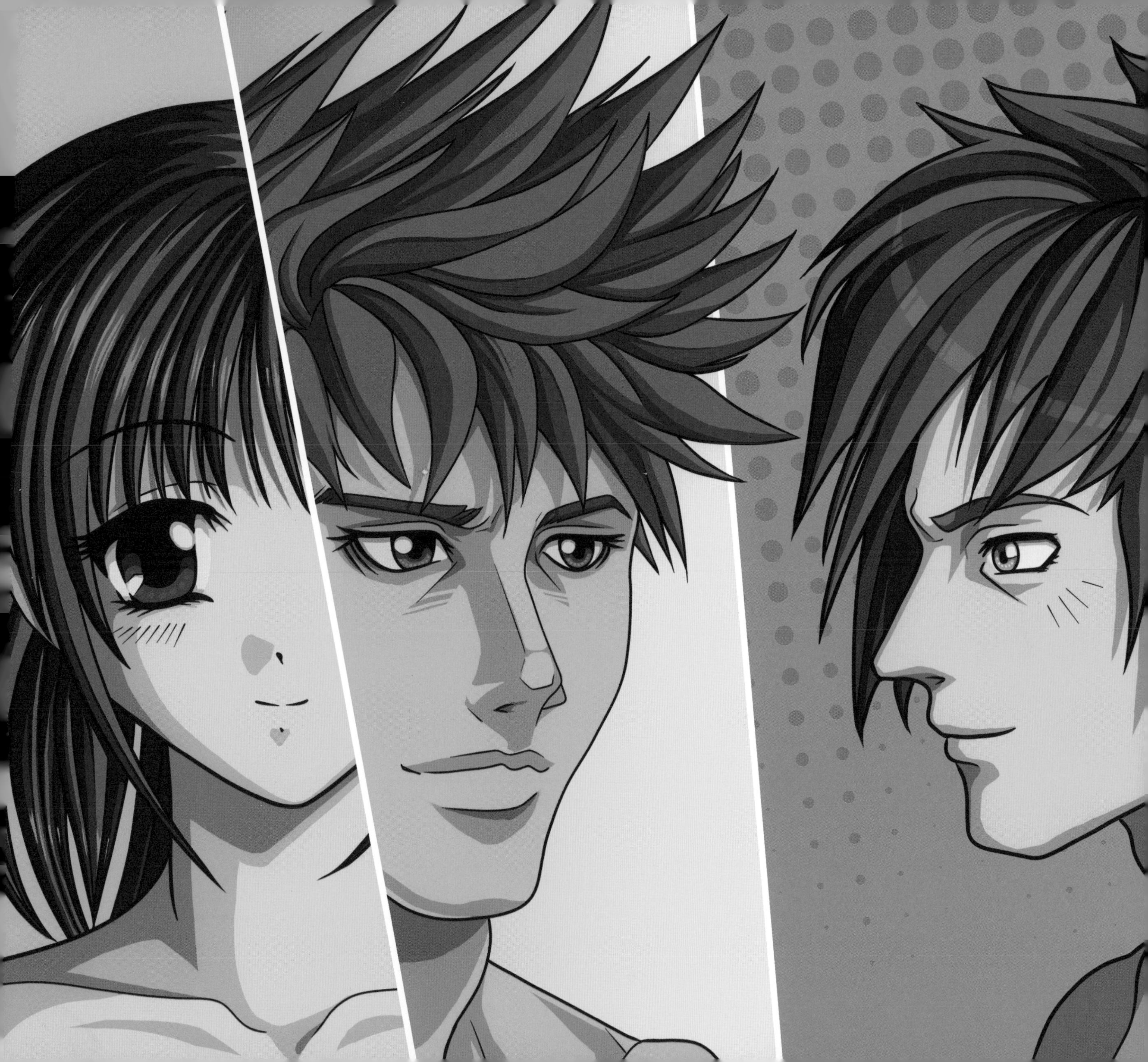

HEADS FROM DIFFERENT ANGLES

If you're a beginner, I recommend you start drawing heads from a front view. This will allow you to work out facial proportions, such as the distance between the lips and chin, or the gap between the ears and eyes. Keep your initial head circle guidelines light so that they can be erased easily. Of course, people's features vary widely and they are exaggerated in manga. Look at the examples on this page: consider the size of a character's eye, then use it to measure the other proportions of the face. For example, a character's head might be the width of four eyes in a horizontal line, or the distance from the top of the eye to the top of the head might be the same as the bottom of the eye to the bottom of the chin.

Once you feel comfortable with drawing the front view, try drawing the head at an angle. Most artwork you create will illustrate characters facing toward the viewer. Introducing angled heads can make your drawing more dynamic. Often, if drawing a front view of a head, I will angle the body a little so that the pose doesn't look so rigid.

Heads and faces are among the trickiest things to draw, but they are also one of the most rewarding aspects of character creation. Here I've drawn different styles of heads from various angles for you to use as reference.

If the head is tilting downward, the facial features move down, while the height of the ears moves up. More of the top of the head is shown.

Eyebrows are around the same height as the top of the ears.

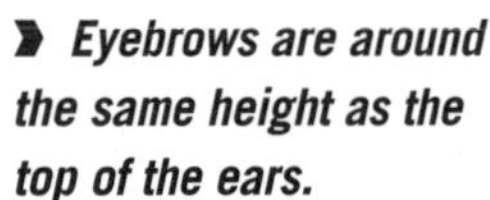

When the head is tilted upward the facial features move up while the height of the ears moves down. More of the chin and underside of the jaw are visible.

Note the subtle curves at the side of the face—there's a slight indent next to the eye socket.

The further the head turns away from the viewer, the smaller and narrower the eye on the far side of the face will look.

You can make the head wider to accommodate larger eyes.

If the head is tilted upward in a three-quarter view, the features should be drawn at a diagonal angle.

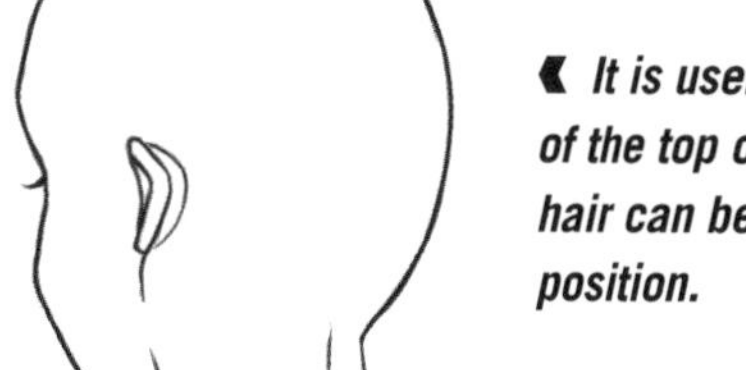

It is useful to know the shape of the top of the head so that hair can be added in the correct position.

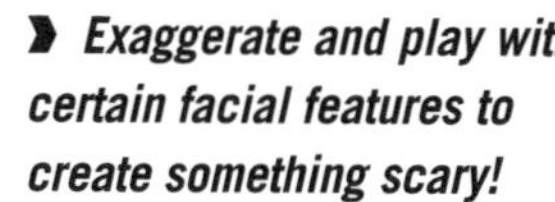

Exaggerate and play with certain facial features to create something scary!

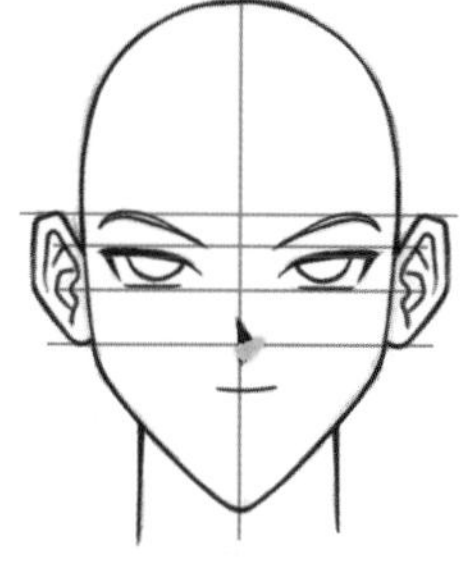

Remember to use guidelines! Horizontal parallel lines will help give consistency to eyes and ears. These guides can be erased when you finalize the artwork.

For a cute, childlike effect, make the head larger in proportion to the torso.

The ear size and shape are often similar to reality, although they may be enlarged and simplified.

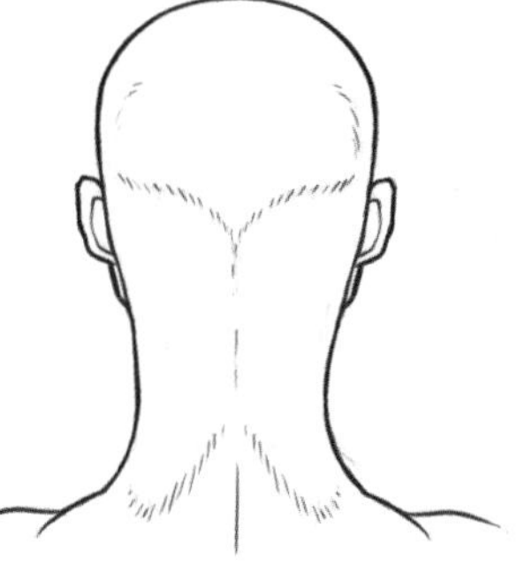

The rear of the head should be an identical shape to the front, with the obvious exception of the facial features.

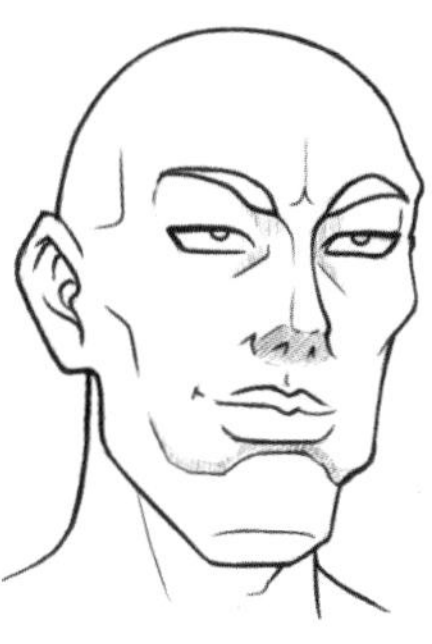

Manga characters tend to have big eyes and small noses, but this isn't always the case, especially with male characters. Lumps, bumps, and facial contours are more prominent on older manga characters, villains and muscular types.

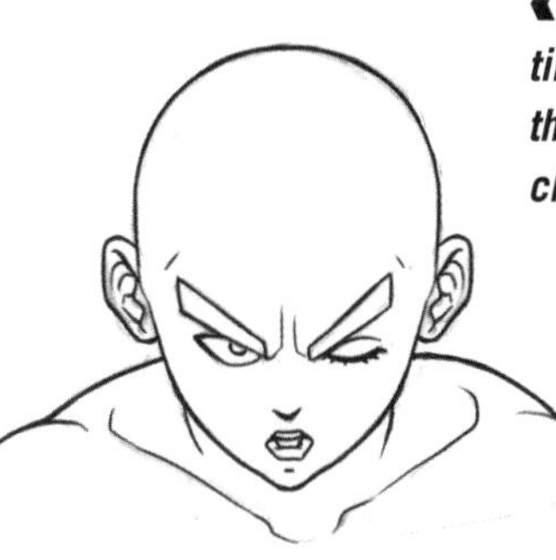

When the head tilts downward, the eyebrows are closer to the eyes.

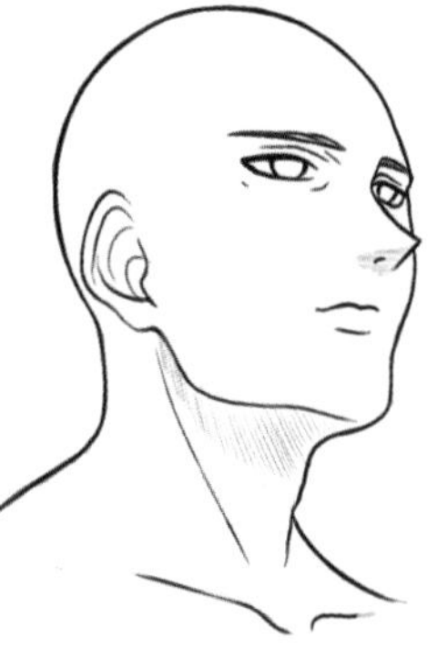

When the head tilts upward, the tip of the nose is closer to the eyes.

THE FEMALE HEAD: FRONT VIEW

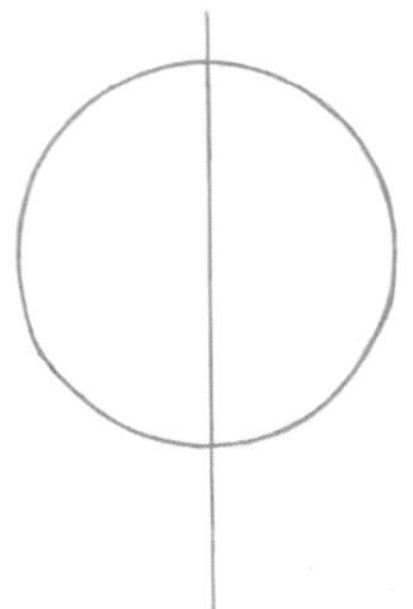

STEP 1
Start by drawing a faint circle and a vertical center guideline. Continue the line beyond the circle.

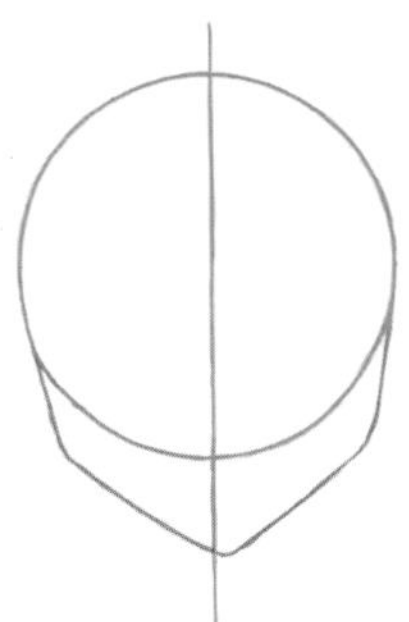

STEP 2
Draw the jawlines, which should meet at the center guideline. Round off any angles to reduce the look of sharp corners.

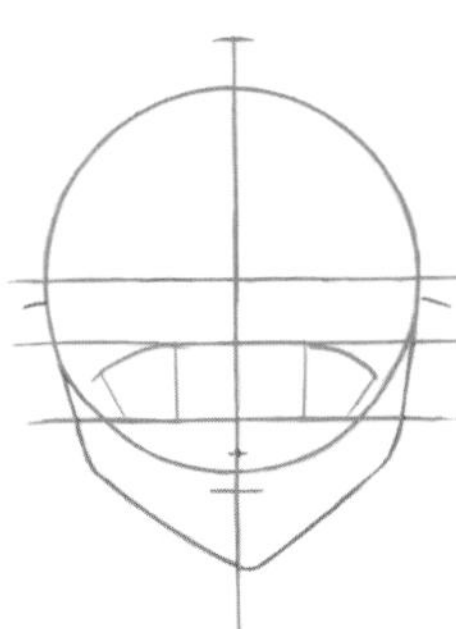

STEP 3
Add guidelines to indicate where the eyes, top of the eyebrows, nose, and mouth will be positioned.

STEP 4
Refine the eyes, adding ears and a single curved line for each eyebrow. The neck aligns with the middle of the eyes. Add shoulders and collarbone.

STEP 5
Erase the guidelines and add the hair. Instead of drawing individual strands, group it into long spikes. These should be roughly the same length for the bangs, getting longer at the side of the head. Taper each spike toward the bottom. The ears will be mostly covered with hair.

STEP 6
This step shows the final pencil drawing. I've added detail to the eyes, smaller strands of hair and "blushie" lines under each eye. You can add shading to increase the detail, but I haven't as the drawing will be inked and colored.

STEP 7
Clean up the drawing by inking over the top of it, either by tracing it onto a fresh sheet of paper and redrawing it with a pen or by scanning it and going over it using a graphics tablet and digital software.

STEP 8

Next, choose your color scheme. The way you build up your colors will depend on which medium you choose to work with; if you're using paint or digital, the first step is laying flat tones before shading. Alternatively, you might want to start with the lightest colors before introducing increasingly darker shading and shadows, as in steps 9 and 10. Hair color can hint at a character's personality—in this case I've gone for green, which, along with the cute big eyes, means she's a trustworthy, easy-going, kind-hearted character. Conversely, green hair with a long face and narrow eyes could indicate a greedy, selfish character.

STEP 9

Using a darker tone, and with a right-hand light source in mind, place shadows on the left-hand areas of the skin and hair. The head will cast shadow under the chin and on the neck. The cheeks don't have a lot of shadow. Each spike of hair needs shading to give a 3D effect.

STEP 10

A second round of darker shading on the hair and skin helps to add more depth to the features. I've given the hair two curved bands of lighter tone for a glossier look. To finish, I put some extra-subtle shading and highlights in the eyes.

THE MALE HEAD: ANGLED VIEW

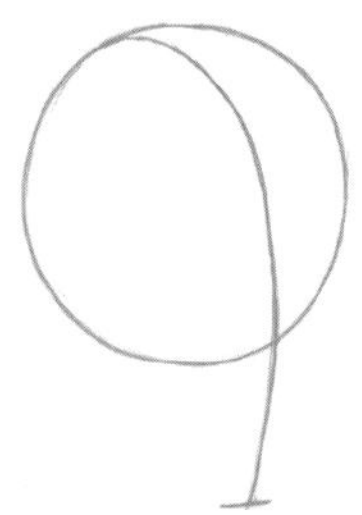

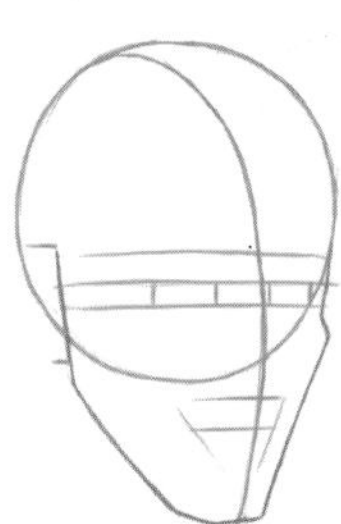

STEP 1
Draw a circle and a curved guideline. The head is angled toward the right, so the line sits a third of the way from the right. Indicate where the bottom of the chin will be.

STEP 2
Extend the sides of the face down to meet the chin line. Add the jawline on the left. The ear will be placed to the left of this line.

STEP 3
Add guidelines for the eyes, top of the eyebrows, nose, mouth, and ears. The bottom of the eyes will be about halfway between the top of the head and the chin.

STEP 4
Add the nose on the right of the guideline, drawing the eyes in the guideline boxes and adding the eyebrows and ear. Draw the neck and shoulders. Add marks for the hairline.

STEP 5
Erase the guidelines and add the hair. Draw thick, triangular spikes roughly the same length. Define the ear and lips, as shown. Add slanted lines on the neck to show the tendons and collarbone.

STEP 6
For the final pencil drawing, I've continued to add detail to the eyes and hair and smoothed out some of the edges. If you aren't going to color it, you could add some hatching (closely drawn parallel lines) and shading here or there.

STEP 7
Clean up the drawing by inking over it, either by tracing it onto a fresh sheet of paper and redrawing it with a pen or scanning it and using a graphics tablet and digital software.

STEP 8
Decide on which colors to go with, laying flat tones before shading. Or you might wish to start with the lightest colors first before adding progressively darker shading and shadows, as in steps 9 and 10 below.

STEP 9
Using a darker tone, and with a right-hand light source in mind, place shadows on the left-hand parts of the skin and hair. The head will cast a lot of shadow under the chin and on the neck, and there will be a lesser degree of shadow on the face, cast by the hair. Each spike of hair needs shading and the left side of the hair will be darker.

STEP 10
A second round of darker shading on the hair and skin helps to add more shape and contour to the features. The eyes have also been given subtle shading and highlights.

THE MALE HEAD: SIDE VIEW

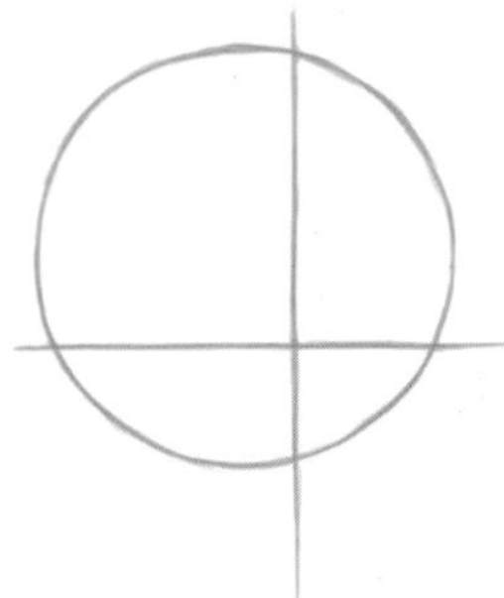

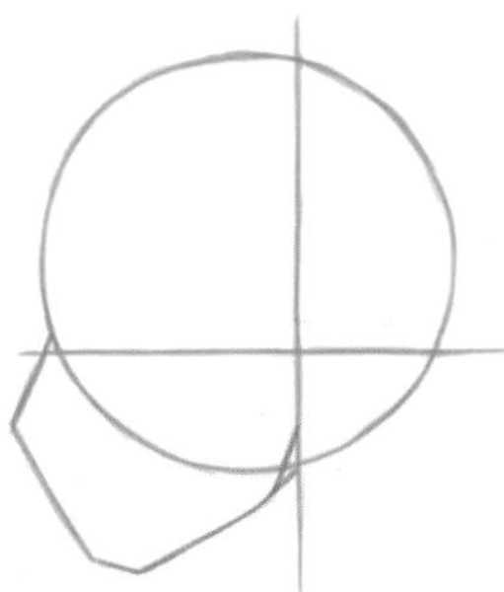

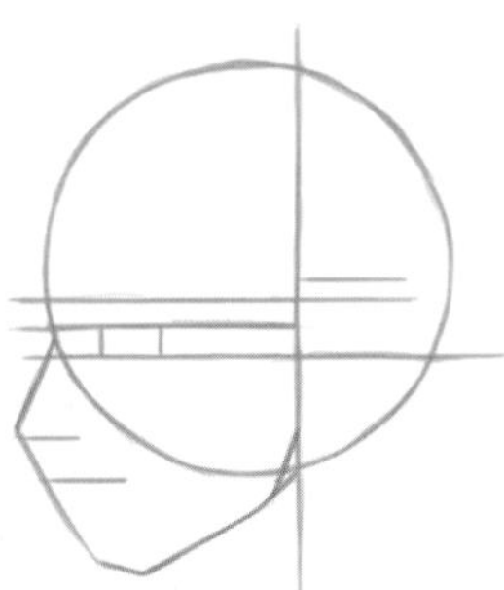

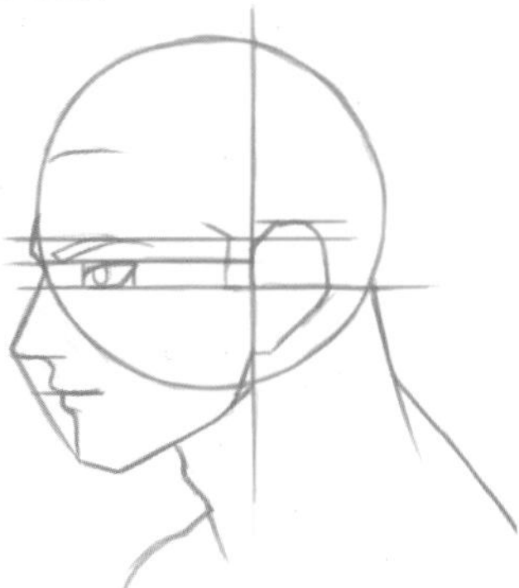

STEP 1
Draw a circle. This character will face left, so pencil in an off-center "crosshair" toward the bottom right. These guidelines will be used to position the eye and ear.

STEP 2
Draw a box-like shape toward the bottom left. This will house the nose, mouth, and chin. The blue lines indicate the portions you want to keep—the top of the nose and the jaw.

STEP 3
Add guidelines to indicate where the eyes, top of eyebrows, nose, and mouth will be positioned. The bottom of the nose will line up with the bottom of the ear.

STEP 4
Refine the eye as an almond shape and draw the brow and ear. The top of the ear will be a little higher than the eyebrow. Draw in the nose, mouth, neck, chin, and hairline.

STEP 5
Erase the guidelines and begin adding the hair, sectioned into large shapes. These overlap the face without obscuring the eye. Add a neck tendon and collarbone.

STEP 6
Divide the hair into smaller portions to illustrate flow and direction. Add detail to the eye and ear. Include a little shading if you don't intend to ink or color the image.

STEP 7
Ink the drawing in the method described on page 22. In this example, I have inked using the software PaintTool SAI.

STEP 8

Build up your colors using your preferred method. I wanted my character to be the adventurous leader type, so I've chosen a strong shade of red for his hair.

STEP 10

To finish, make a second round of darker shading on the hair and skin to help add more depth to the features and give some extra-subtle shading and highlights to the eyes.

STEP 9

Using a darker tone, and with a right-hand light source in mind, place shadows on the left-hand areas of the skin and hair. The head will cast a lot of shadow under the chin and on the neck and chest; add a little more shading on the face. Each spike of hair needs shading, especially the left side, which will be darker.

Drawing Faces

In real life, faces have a range of shapes, sizes, and characteristics. In manga, these varieties are usually exaggerated. By redrawing the proportions of facial features you can illustrate a character's qualities—whether they are old, young, male, female, good or evil, for example—as well as subtler personality traits.

If needs be, the style and shape of the face allows for a wide range of exaggerated expressions to convey a character's mood. Large, round eyes and simple noses and mouths represented by just a few dashes and curves may sound easy to draw, but there are still right and wrong ways to draw the features outlined in this section.

EYES

Manga faces revolve around the eyes. They're the key component to give your characters emotion, personality, and a unique style. Eyes are lots of fun to practice and experiment with, but can be tricky to get right as they need to be balanced, symmetrical and placed correctly. They're usually positioned halfway down the head and spaced one eye's width apart. If the eyes are quite large, you'll need to draw the head a little wider to accommodate them.

How detailed you choose to make your characters' eyes is a matter of personal taste. Since there's not a lot of focus on manga characters' noses and mouths, some artists like putting a lot of details, colors, lighting effects, and flares in or around the eye to create a focal point on the face.

While large, saucer eyes are often found in manga, eyes can come in a variety of shapes and sizes that still adhere to the manga aesthetic. I've drawn some examples here.

The shiny look is achieved by using a ball of light reflection.

The eyelid covers the top of the iris unless the eyes are wide open with surprise.

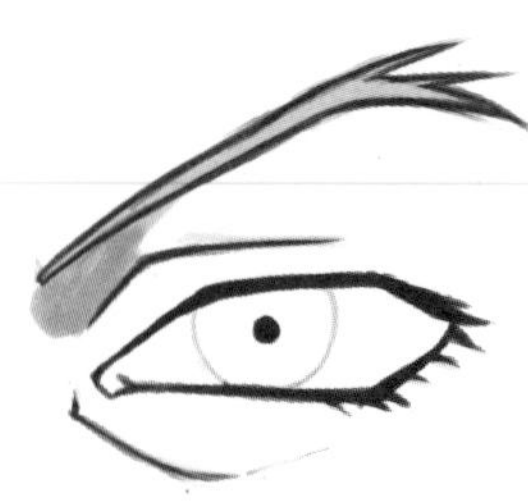

Villains tend to have small dot-like pupils. This can also be used to denote shock and surprise.

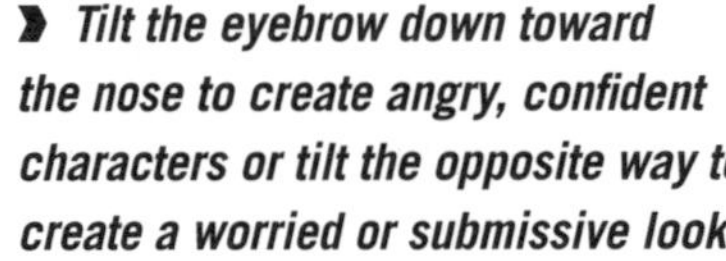

Tilt the eyebrow down toward the nose to create angry, confident characters or tilt the opposite way to create a worried or submissive look.

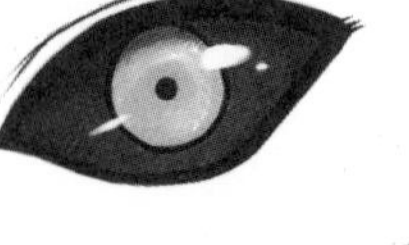

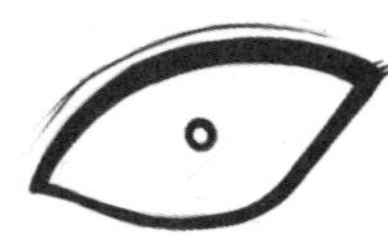

Adjusting the iris, pupil and color schemes can create villains and demons.

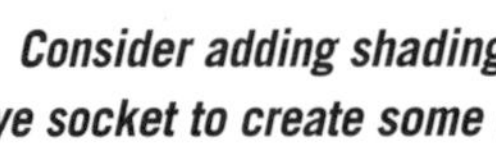

Closed eyes means the top lash is lowered to meet the bottom.

Consider adding shading around the eye socket to create some depth.

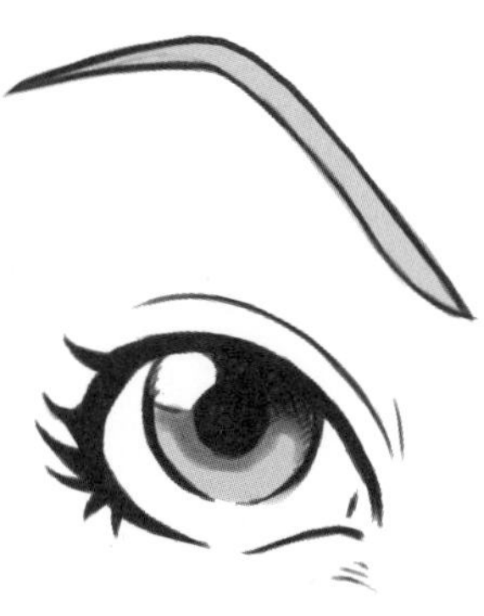

Simplified eyelash spikes can be placed toward the outside top lash—more or bigger lashes create a feminine look.

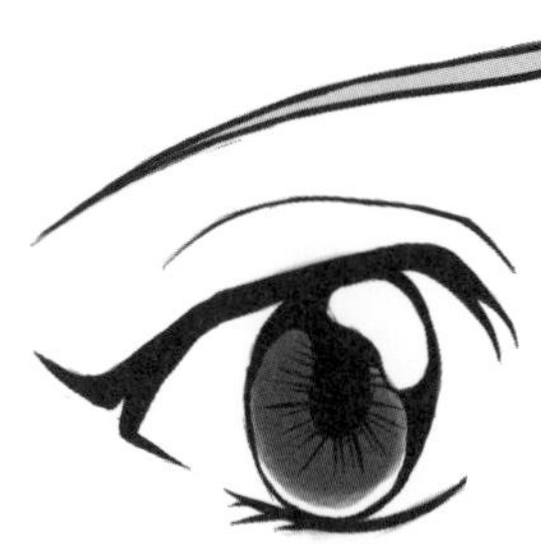

Use a large white oval or bean-shaped reflection to make big eyes look cute and sparkly.

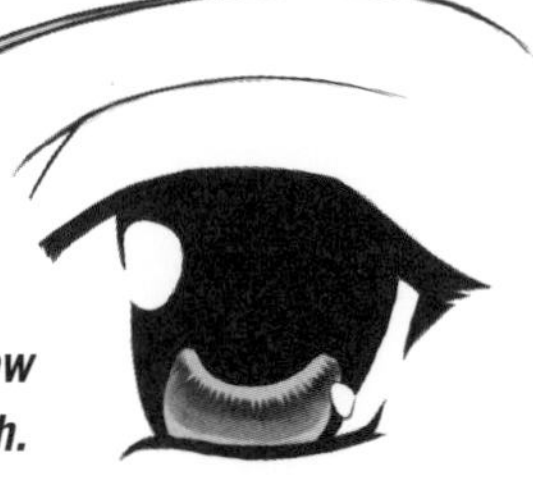

Larger pupils show innocence and youth.

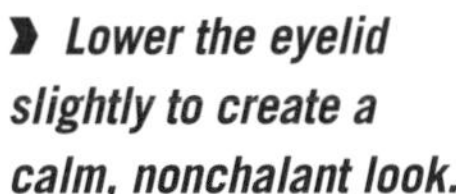

Lower the eyelid slightly to create a calm, nonchalant look.

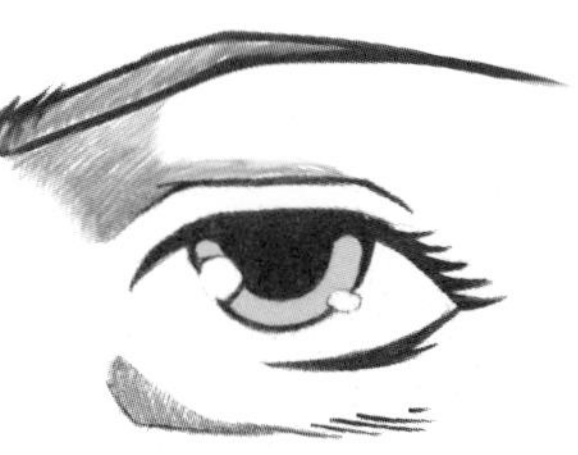

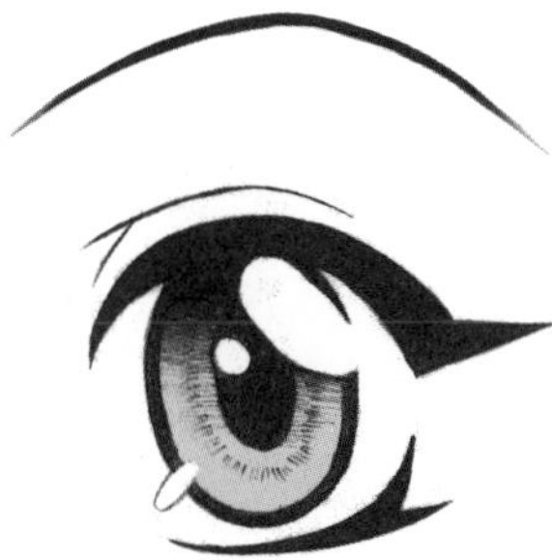

Eyebrows, especially for females, are often like a thin, curved blade of grass.

Irises are shaded dark at the top and lighter at the bottom, either for effect or to show the eyelashes are casting a downward shadow on the eye.

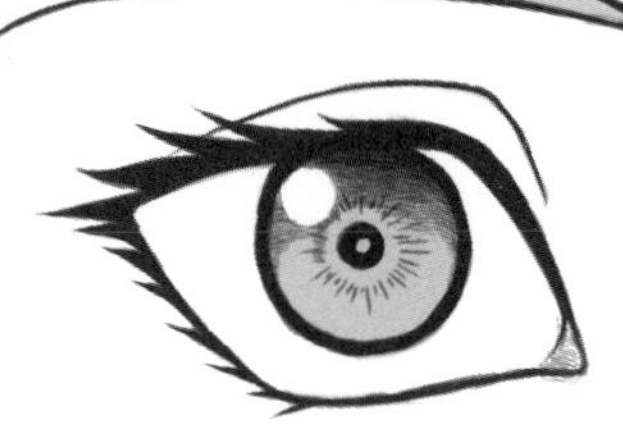

Most eyes are variations on almond, diamond, oval, and circle shapes.

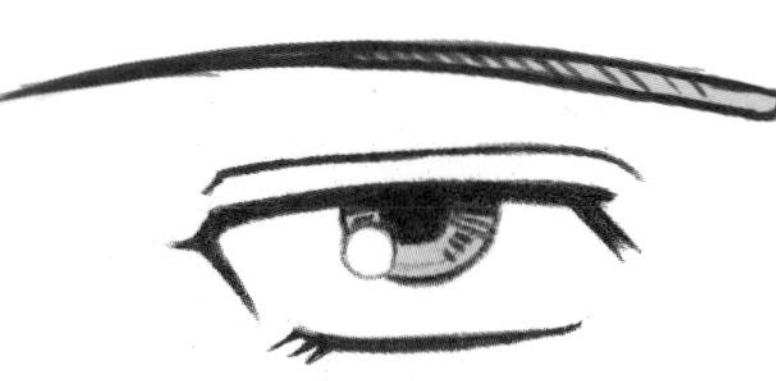

Male eyes are usually narrower and more angular than female ones.

Eyelashes are usually simplified as a thicker line around the eyes.

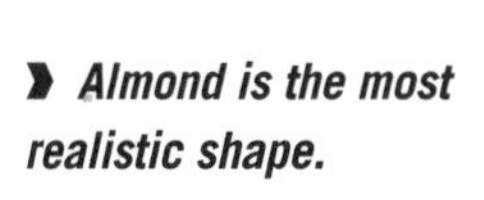

Almond is the most realistic shape.

CONSTRUCTING THE EYES

STEP 1
Starting with the left eye, draw V-shaped guidelines. Inside these lines, draw two opposing curves for the top and bottom of the eye, with the top line ending a little bit lower on the left.

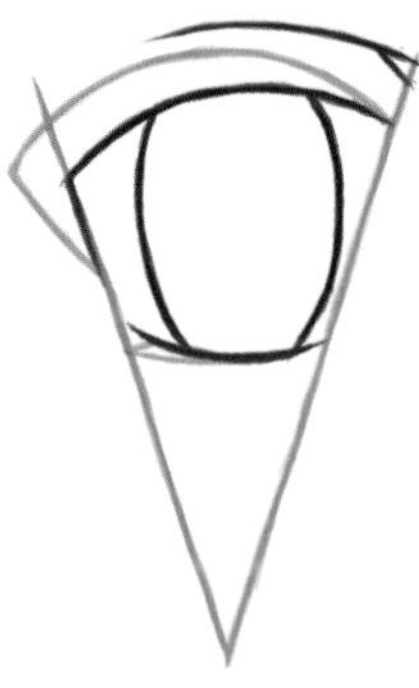

STEP 2
Draw in the iris, and draw a curve parallel with the top of the eye for the eyelid. The right side of this ends in a "y" shape. Lightly draw in where the eyelashes will be—indicated in blue.

STEP 3
Give the eyelashes some detail. Draw the eyebrow line above. As this is a female eye, a central, thin "blade of grass" is sufficient for the eyebrow.

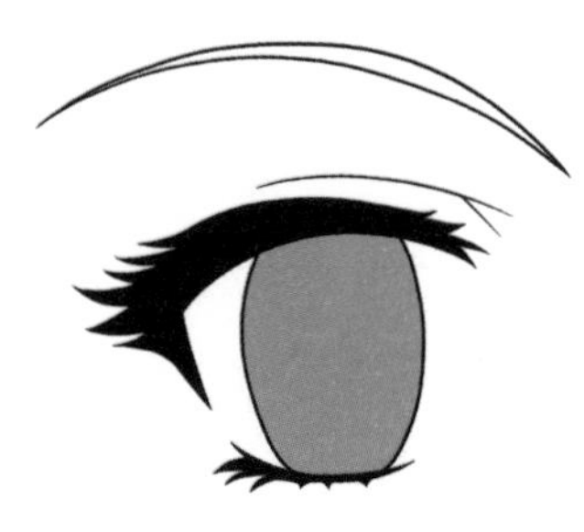

STEP 4
Ink over the top to make the lines a little smoother. Now it's time to consider colors—the fun part! Pick a base color. I've gone for blue in this example.

STEP 5
Fill the pupil and add shadow to the top portion. Use an off-white tone (blue, purple, or gray) for the eye white. Add shadow at the top of the eye white. Fill in the eyebrow.

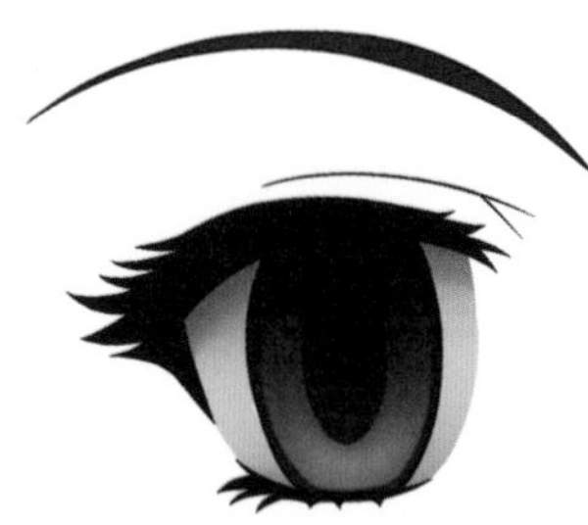

STEP 6
Begin to blend in the darker tones. Try to create a graduation effect with the iris, from black at the top, with the lightest color toward the middle-bottom.

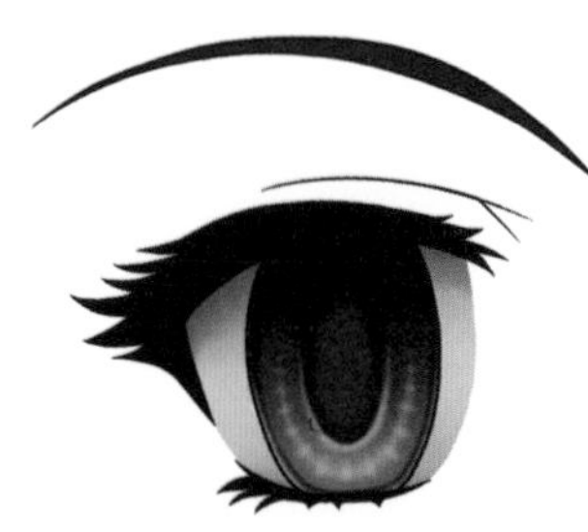

STEP 7
Add highlights to create a luminous effect, and a thin lighter tone to the iris edge and around the pupil. Add lighter lines in the middle between the iris and pupil.

STEP 8
Add round highlights. These can be solid white or can contain a hint of shading toward the top as shown.

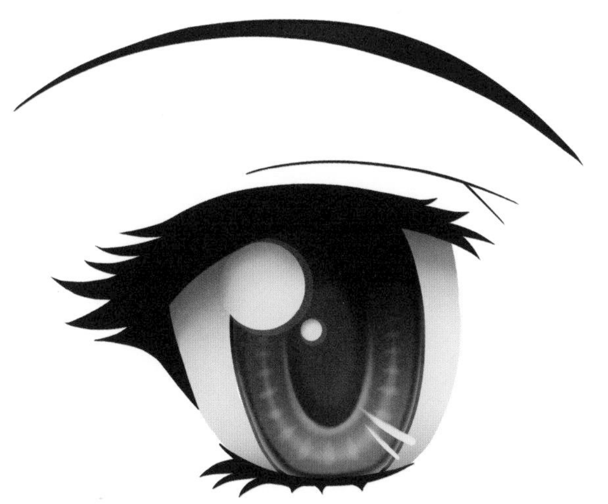

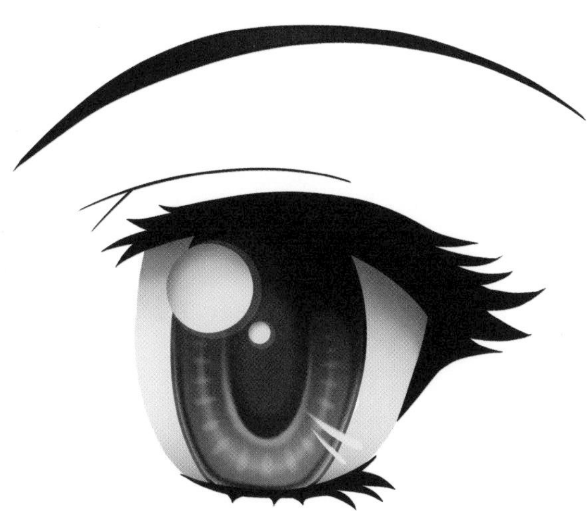

STEP 9

Here the main highlights consist of one big circle toward the corner, a smaller circle diagonally beneath it, and one or two lines in the opposite corner. Now draw the other eye. Since a left-hand light source is generating the round highlights, remember to add a left highlight to the left side of the other eye. If you're using digital media, a simple copy, paste and flip won't do!

STEP 10

By tilting the eyes and coloring them green instead of blue it's possible to create a more confident, headstrong character. Or perhaps she's just green with envy?

NOSES, MOUTHS, AND EARS

While generally not as much emphasis is placed on noses, mouths, and ears as on eyes in manga, they are still key components needing careful consideration. There is an art to making a few simple mouth lines look as if they belong. A triangular bit of shading may be all that's required to indicate a nose, but the distance between it and the mouth, or other parts of the face, will determine if a character has convincing proportions or simply looks odd!

Forward-facing views, in particular, allow artists to use minimal lines or shading to show a nose and a mouth. Lots of lines or shading to show where a realistic face would contort with a smile or a frown aren't needed in manga, unless you are drawing aged characters.

I've included a number of examples of noses, mouths, and ears from different angles to show how to create a manga look.

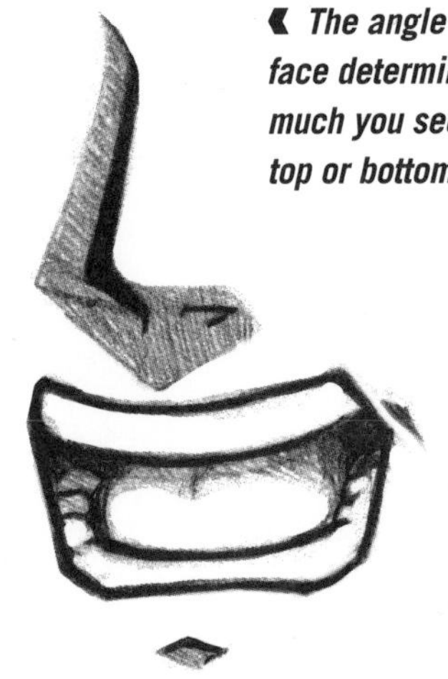

The angle of the face determines how much you see of the top or bottom teeth.

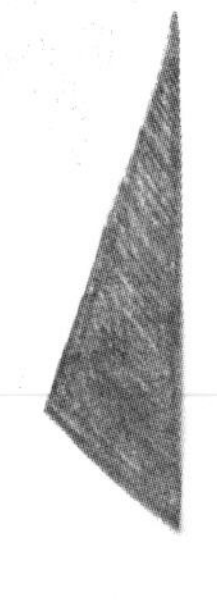

Manga mouths are often quite small unless open, especially in females and children.

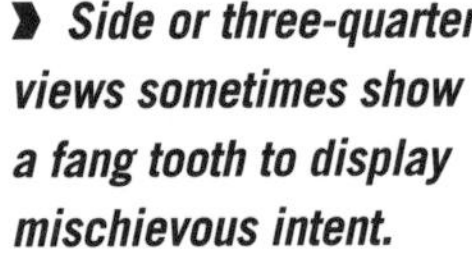

The nose in a profile view can be drawn as a sharp, pointed triangle or a subtle, rounded contour. Mouth lines do not always reach the edge of the profile.

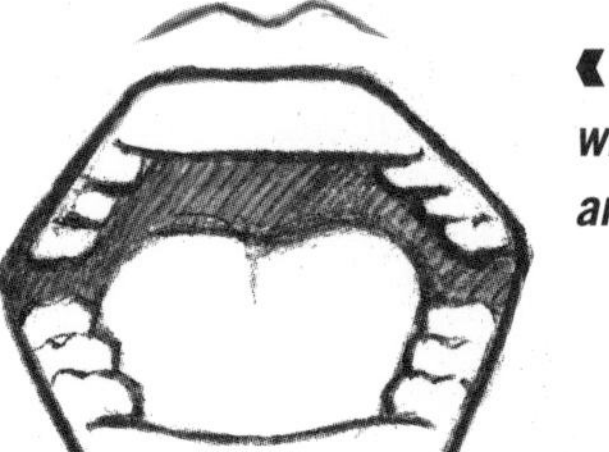

Simplify teeth when drawing an open mouth.

Side or three-quarter views sometimes show a fang tooth to display mischievous intent.

Males tend to have longer, more angular noses.

❮ The mouth may get a little wider with a smile or when open, but the top lip stays in a fixed position. It's the bottom lip that moves down.

❯ If the face is tilted backward so the viewer is looking up at the nose, use short lines rather than large holes for nostrils.

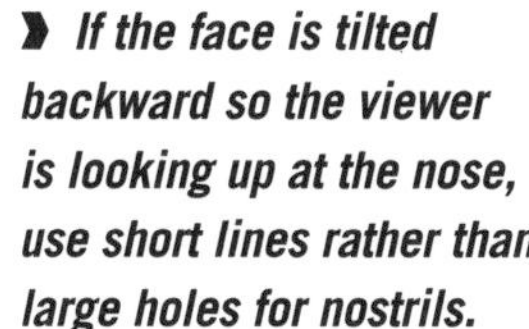

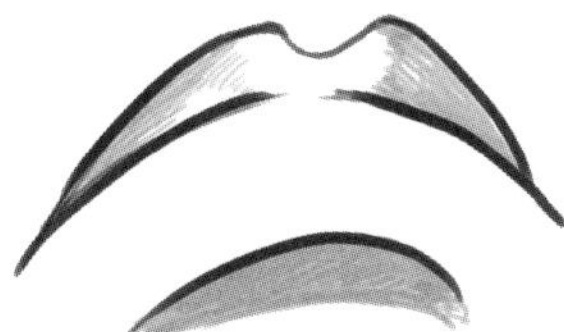

❯ Noses and ears stay the same shape no matter what facial expression is used.

❯ Closed mouths can be drawn as a simple line or with a small gap in the middle.

❮ Full, plump lips are used very occasionally.

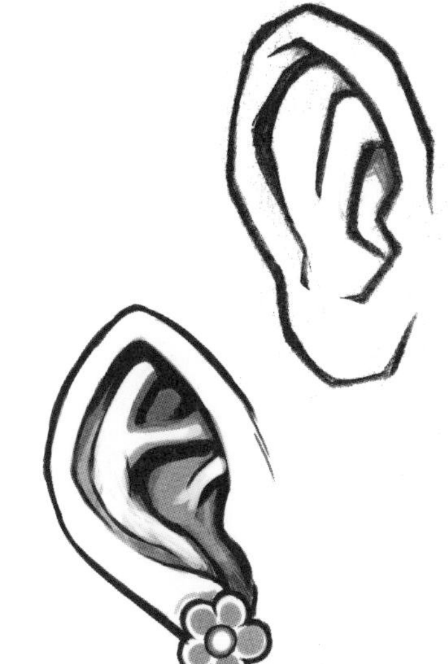

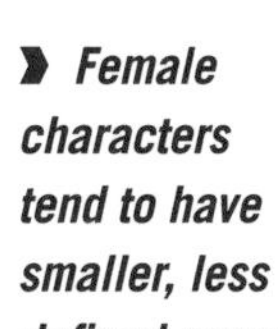

❯ Female characters tend to have smaller, less defined noses.

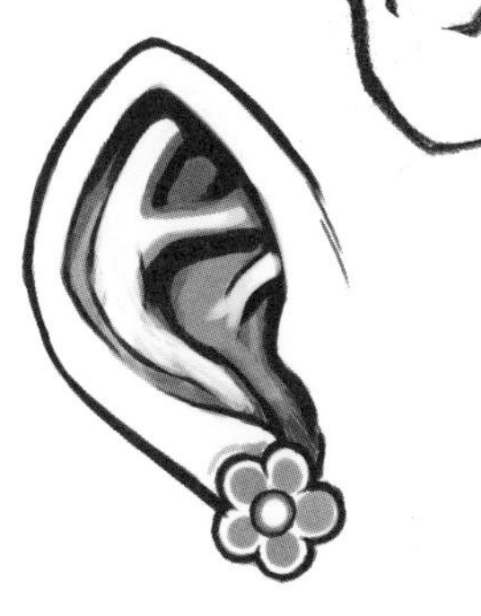

❮ Learn how to draw ears, even though many characters will have them covered with hair.

EXPRESSIONS AND EMOTIONS

By altering facial elements you can create emotion, indicate feelings, or help tell a story. Manga has developed its own unique visual language which conveys a plethora of emotional states. This manga iconography is often expressed with simple, exaggerated features and used to create some comic relief in a story. While the more comical and over-the-top expressions don't appear in all manga, they are seen in many popular stories such as *Full Metal Alchemist, Azumanga Daioh* and *One Piece*. As a result of the ever-increasing popularity of manga, Western animation and comics have recently started to adopt the same Japanese emotional indicators. Here I've drawn a selection of expressions found in manga. I'm sure fans will recognize most of these.

FURIOUS

Adding in some oversized spider-man eyes and a comical monster mouth shows this guy is really angry. Add a popping vein in the form of a simplified cruciform shape to the top side of the head to show extra rage!

INDIFFERENT

These two faces have a generic content expression for when you want to show your character at ease and comfortable. I'll be using these two as a base to illustrate how tweaking just the facial features can indicate a range of emotions.

SHOCKED

When a character is surprised, enlarge the eyes but make the irises and pupils mere dots. Add shadow or vertical lines under or between the eyes to show greater anxiety and disbelief.

EMBARRASSED

The awkward feeling when you've turned up to school or work in just your underwear without realizing it! Use "happy" eyes, invert the eyebrows, and add the all-important oversized sweat drop to make the emotion clear.

FRUSTRATED

This is typically indicated by drawing the eyes as inward-facing Vs. The oversized box mouth shows the character is yelling. This is what happens when you don't save your work on the computer and have a power cut! It can also be used to indicate pain, as if he's just had a car run over his toe!

HAPPY

If your character is pleased, draw the eyes as upward-facing curves. Welcoming, amenable, and good-natured characters will almost constantly show this expression. Don't forget to add an upward curve to the mouth as well. Faint hatching lines or pink or red "blushies" on the cheeks will make him look tipsy.

EXPRESSIONS AND EMOTIONS 2

ROMANTIC

Adding hatching lines or rosy red coloring to the cheeks shows the character has feelings toward someone or is shy about romance. Draw two separate "blushies" or extend the blush across the width of the face, as shown.

LOVING

Love can be expressed using hearts as eyes and placing several hearts above the character's head. The long, open "cat mouth" adds a gasp of excitement.

SIGHING

Invert the eyebrows and draw the eyes as a single curved line to show that they're closed. Add a mushroom-shaped bubble coming from the mouth to show the exhalation of air.

CONFUSED

Confusion can be indicated simply by tilting one eyebrow more than the other. To emphasize the emotion and create a more comedic tone, add round circles for eyes and a question mark at the top of the head.

SLEEPING

Draw the eyes as a single curved line. The mouth is open with a half circle at the bottom to represent sleep dribble. For added clarity, you can include Zs above the head if you like. In manga, an inflated "snot balloon" can show inappropriate sleeping such as during classes or at work.

Evil intent

For those times when your character is being psychotic, mischievous, ominous or scary, darken the top portion of the face with shadow, hatching or a blue tone. Use the same circle eyes as for the confused face, together with an evil grin, to indicate that this is a jokey, exaggerated expression.

Crying

You can illustrate crying with either a single tear shown by a round blob on each outer corner of the eye or, for a "waterfall of tears," add two wavy lines as shown. Invert the eyebrows to add sorrow to the face.

Other things to look out for in manga

- *Lowering the head or hunching the body can show sorrow and dejection.*
- *A blue tone around a character's forehead or eyes can show gloominess or disgust.*
- *Flower backgrounds, cherry blossom or rose petals in the foreground can represent romance or a beautiful moment.*
- *A wavy ghost coming from the mouth can comically represent horror, depression, shame or extreme embarrassment.*
- *Lighting-spark backgrounds can show a character has had a great idea.*
- *Simplified facial features and an absent nose can indicate astonishment.*
- *Falling to the floor, often with one or more extremities twisted above the body, is used humorously to indicate something ironic or unexpected being said or happening.*
- *An exaggerated round swelling the size of an apple indicates injury.*
- *Twitching eyebrows or eyelids can show a character suppressing anger or frustration.*
- *A bleeding nose shows a male character's infatuation with or sexual attraction towards a female. Sometimes male characters' nostrils are enlarged.*
- *Spirals for eyes can show confusion or dizziness.*
- *Drawing "chibi" (child-like) or deformed (big head, small body) versions of the characters indicates humor.*

HAIR

Manga artists use many expressive hairstyles to show different character traits. With female styles, long hair is often very intricate with many flowing, overlapping strands, bangs, and clumps. The trick is to break the hair down into sections for drawing so you don't feel overwhelmed by the task.

It helps to explore hairdressing and fashion magazines and web sites for both conventional and outrageous reference material and practice as many different hairstyles as you can. There are several styles to which you'll keep returning: for example, tapered spikes, especially drawn as bangs or hair in front of the character's face, are favored by many manga artists.

Pigtails and bunches are popular styles for younger female manga characters. A spiky fringe overlapping the eyebrows is often used and fairly straightforward to learn.

Give hair some flow to make it look dynamic and direct it toward one side of the face.

More complex hair styles can take some practice to get right. Start with the largest sections of hair first before adding the smaller, narrow sections.

Hairstyles that flare out don't necessarily need a lot of detail to create an interesting shape.

Short, slicked-back hair can sometimes represent wealthy types.

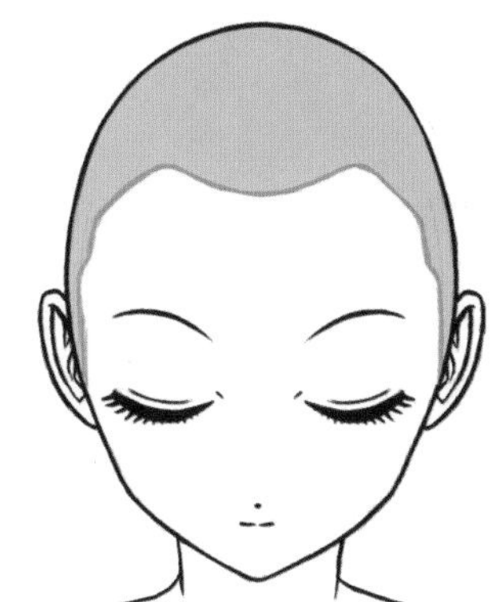

Keep the position of the hairline in mind. Once you've established this, make sure the hair flows out from behind it. Hairlines are more of a subtle "M" shape than a straight horizontal. If the head is tilted downward, as here, the hairline will be lower and if it is tilted upward, the hairline will be higher.

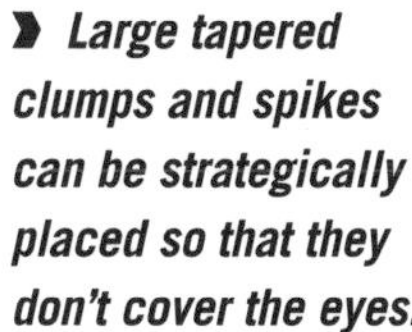

Large tapered clumps and spikes can be strategically placed so that they don't cover the eyes.

Messy or unkempt hairstyles can look fashionable. Or perhaps the character has just got caught in a shower?

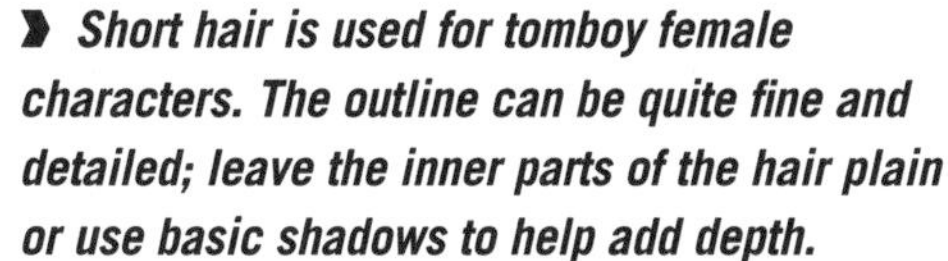

Short hair is used for tomboy female characters. The outline can be quite fine and detailed; leave the inner parts of the hair plain or use basic shadows to help add depth.

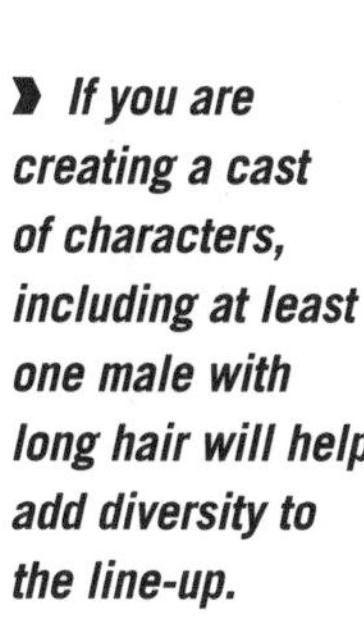

If you are creating a cast of characters, including at least one male with long hair will help add diversity to the line-up.

Gravity-defying hairstyles aren't unusual in manga. Add a floppy fringe at the front with wild spikes at the back.

ADDITIONAL FACE STYLES

Faces are a lot of fun to draw. The step-by-steps below show you how to work up three artworks from different angles.

You can find a wealth of facial expression references on the internet. It's also worth looking through comics and manga to see how artists portray different emotions.

Drawing Hands and Feet

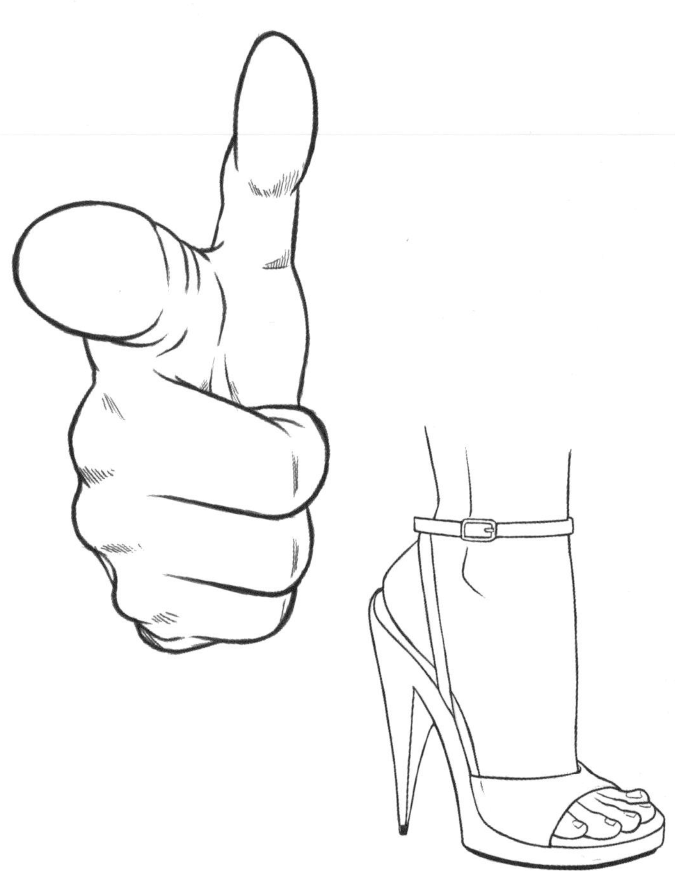

Hands are very important in expressing a character's intentions or simply making an image look more interesting. In Japan it's common to include at least one hand gesture in a portrait shot. The two-finger "V" or "peace" sign is often used to express happiness or make a person look more animated.

Drawing hands and feet may seem daunting at first; each finger or toe must be correctly proportioned and you need to understand how each of the joints articulates. Drawing such small digits can be fiddly work. Beginners sometimes resort to drawing the hands hidden behind the back or in pockets. This can be effective for certain poses, but it will help if you develop the habit of drawing hands and feet sooner rather than later. If you can get them right, it will instantly make your artwork look more competent and appealing.

To start with, draw big. Use a full sheet of paper and try breaking down the hands and feet into manageable parts. Practice drawing interconnected cylinders from different angles to help you understand the many shapes and perspectives that can be generated by showing the fingers in different positions. Practice drawing your own hand from life, or use photos of your hands and feet from different angles.

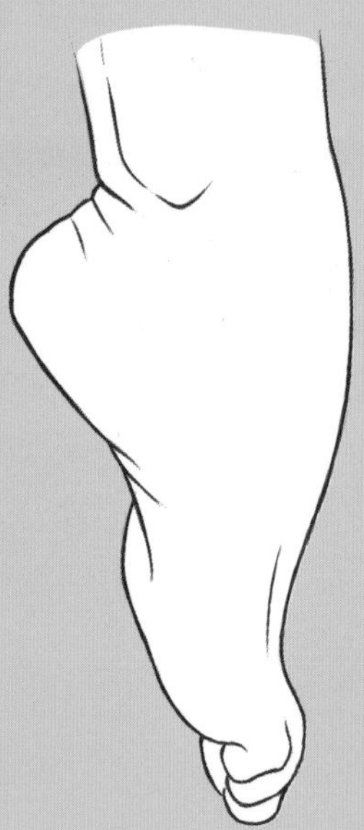

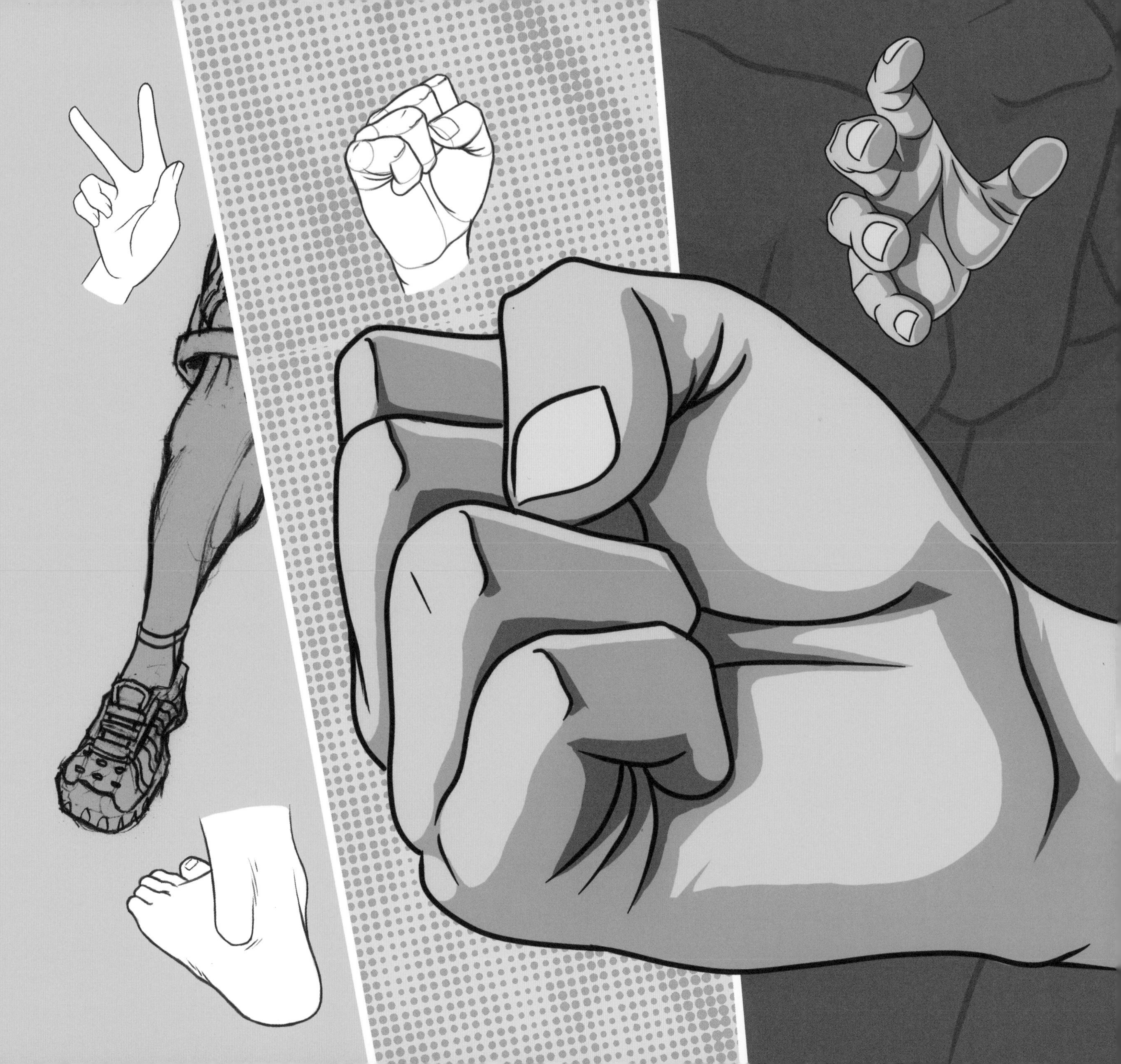

HANDS

Manga hands come in a range of different shapes and sizes, but, unlike faces, they usually have fairly realistic proportions. Drawing manga hands is more an exercise of simplification and knowing where to leave out the details. Whether or not you draw the wrinkles, creases and skin folds you find on a real hand depends on the style you're aiming for. The hand positions and gestures shown here demonstrate some of the angles you might use.

The lines on the palms show where the hands bend.

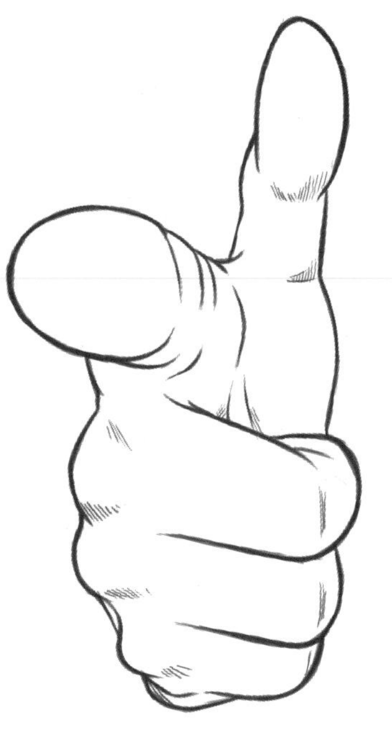

Hands can look more dynamic if the fingers are pointing toward the viewer. The perspective created is called foreshortening.

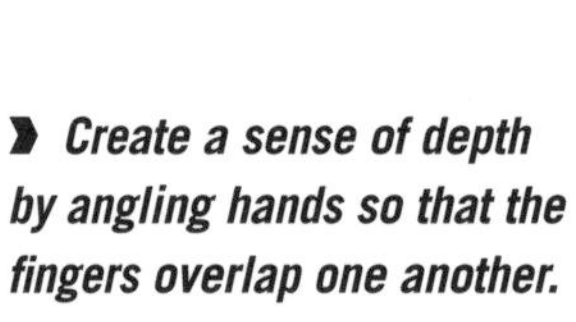

Create a sense of depth by angling hands so that the fingers overlap one another.

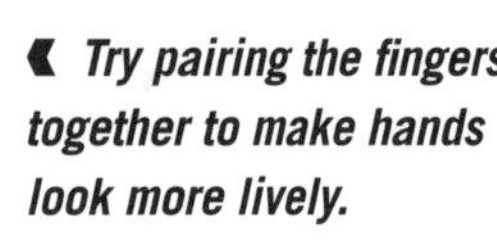

Try pairing the fingers together to make hands look more lively.

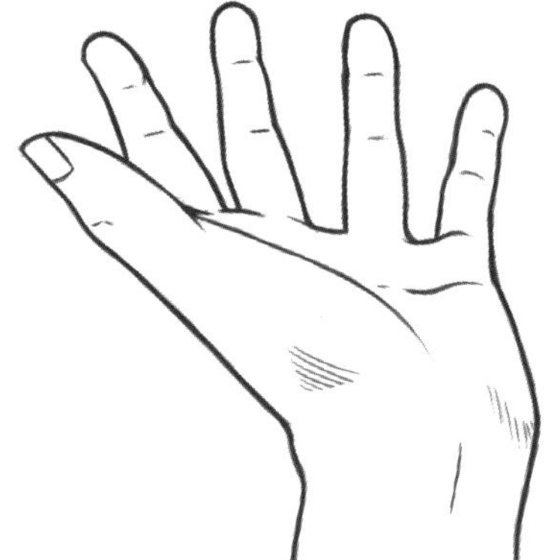

For an expressive emotion, show the fingers fanning out.

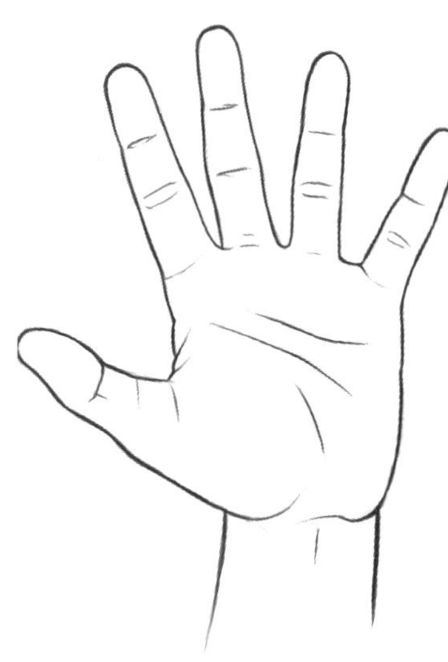

« Don't just add lines and folds for the sake of it—understand where they should be placed by studying photos and considering where the joints are.

» Drawing the nails is not always necessary. Sometimes they can be omitted or you can use a few lines at the fingertips to give the suggestion of a nail.

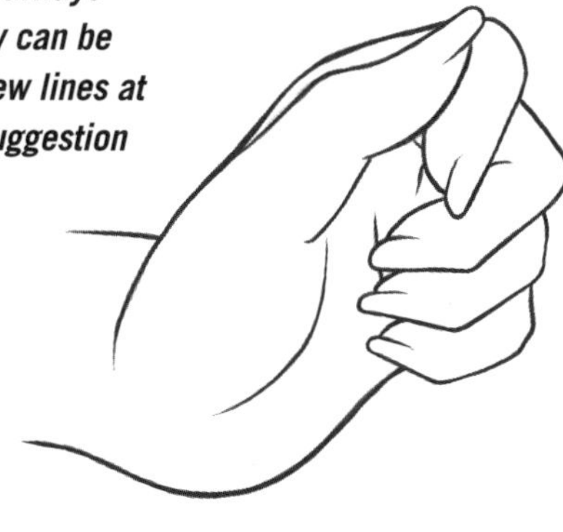

» Women's nails are usually rounded or almond-shaped, while men's are squarer (unless the man is a demon, in which case they are pointed!)

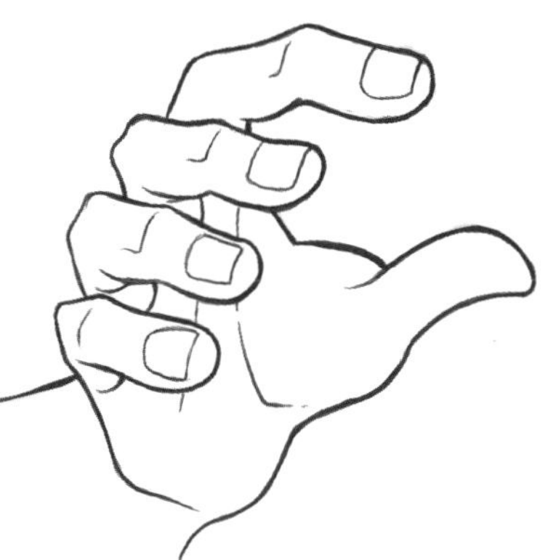

» Female fingers are usually longer and more delicate, while male fingers are thicker, especially in older individuals.

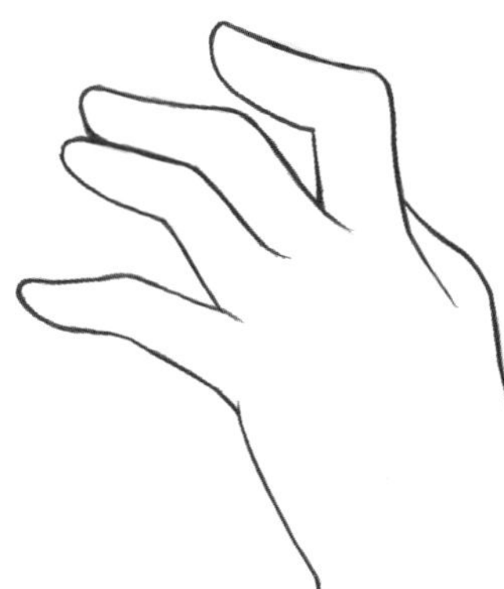

« Some hands are drawn as simple outlines only. It's not necessary to draw fold lines, hatching, fingernails or creases if you are shading or coloring later on.

CONSTRUCTING HANDS

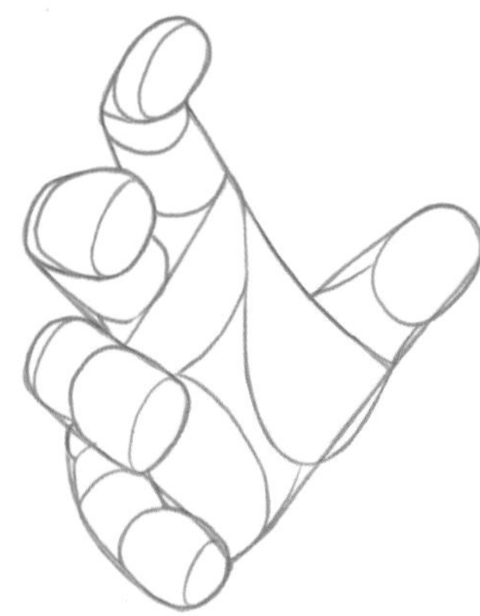

STEP 1

To construct a dynamic open hand, start by drawing in the basic shapes so that you can work out how big the hand will be on the paper. Think of it as a square, with the two bottom fingers overlapping and the index finger extended. The hand should look as though it's coming toward the viewer, making the fingers appear shorter.

STEP 2

Using the initial lines as a base, flesh out the fingers to give a sense of form and volume. Keep it simple and think of it more like a robot hand at this stage, as this will help you to understand angles and where the fingers and hand bend.

STEP 3

Erase the first set of guidelines. Using the blue guidelines, begin to select which lines will be used to make the hand look more realistic, while adding in each fingernail.

STEP 4

Erase the blue guidelines and clean up the sketch. In this example, I've inked the outline to make it look crisp and smooth, then blocked in some color.

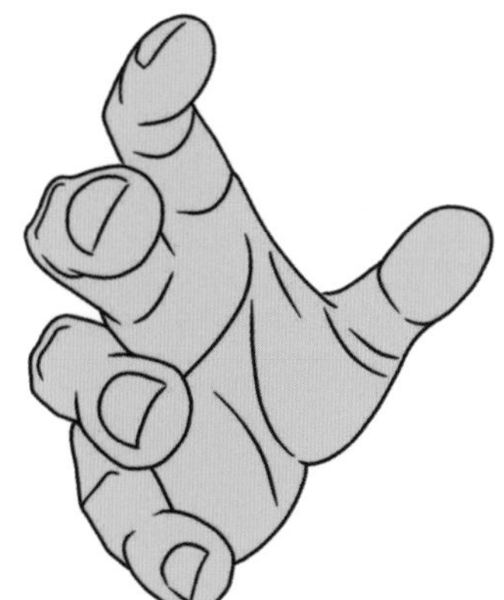

STEP 5

Begin blocking in shadows to create depth. I used a left-hand light source, leaving the tops of the fingers pale and making them darker underneath. The underside could be completely in shadow, but I left a few lighter parts to make the hand look more 3D.

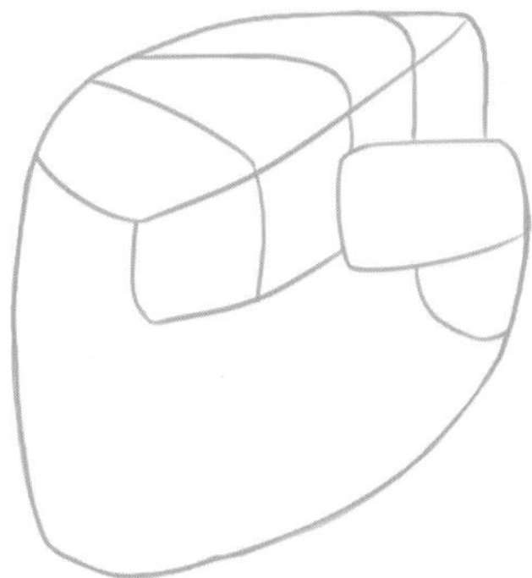

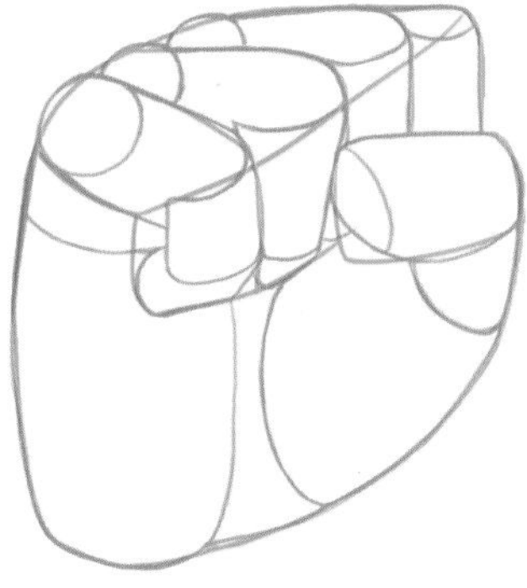

STEP 1

Constructing a fist is like sculpting the fingers out of a cube. Start with a light initial guideline to figure out the shape of the hand and the finger placement. From this angle, each finger will overlap the next, with the thumb overlapping the index and middle fingers.

STEP 2

Refine the guidelines and create more readable, 3D shapes. As with the open hand, think of it as a robot hand to help work out where each part of the hand moves and bends.

STEP 3

Erase the initial guidelines and begin adding details and subtle curves to help make the hand look a little more organic. A realistic hand develops many creases when scrunched up like this, but be selective about where you put the creases to ensure a simplified manga look.

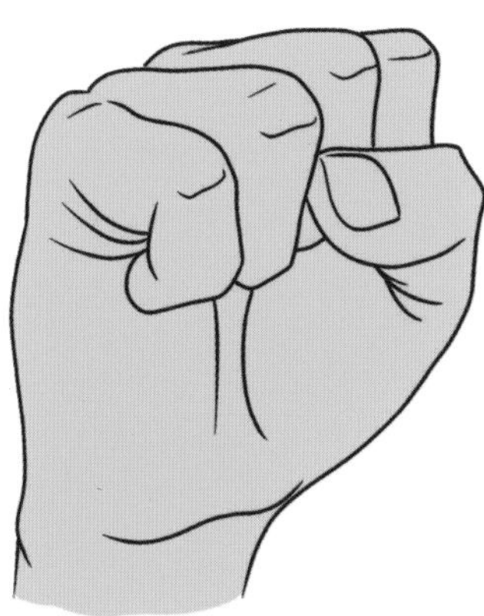

STEP 4

Take out any unnecessary guidelines and ink over the lines to make the drawing look neat and polished. You might consider retracing the image if it gets very crowded and dirty with the initial construction lines. Then add the skin color.

STEP 5

With a top-right light source in mind, add shadow to the left and bottom parts of the hand, with a few darker spots for added depth. This makes it look as though light is hitting just the tops of the fingers and the palm and helps to create a more 3D image.

FEET

Drawing feet in a manga style is much the same as drawing hands. In terms of proportion, the length and width of the feet and the size of the toes will stay true to life. Feet are a little easier to draw than hands since the toes are shorter and generally static if the individual is standing or sitting. The tricky part is understanding the difference between a side and a front view; the side view shows the full length of the foot, which tapers toward the toes; in the front view, conversely, foreshortening makes the foot spread out toward the toes.

Most of the characters you draw will be wearing shoes. These usually follow the natural shape of the foot, apart from high heels, which arch the foot.

In three-quarter views, feet often point diagonally downward unless they are drawn from the rear, in which case they appear to point diagonally upward.

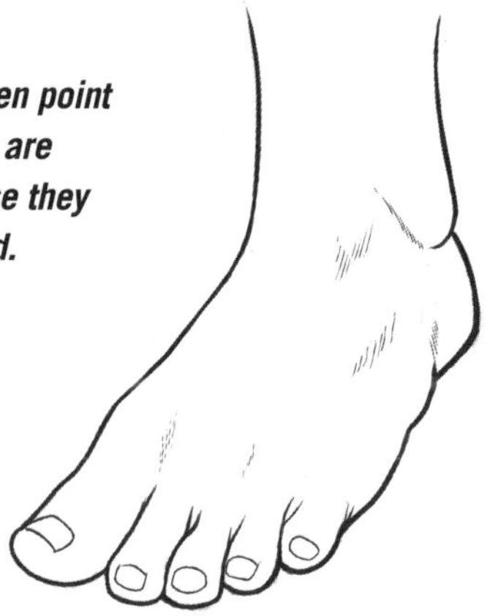

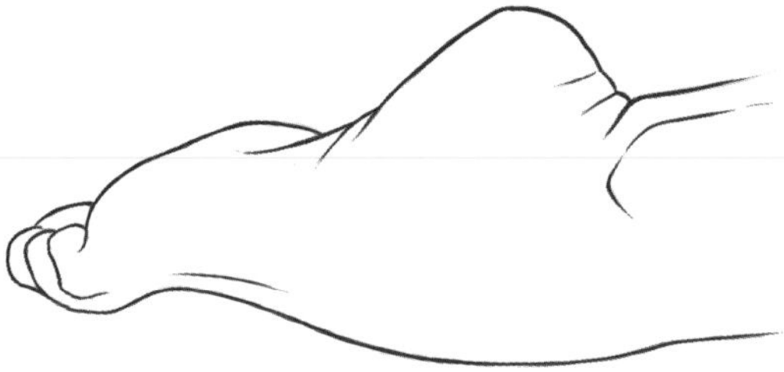

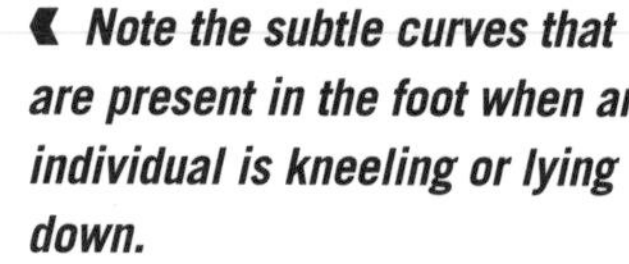

Note the subtle curves that are present in the foot when an individual is kneeling or lying down.

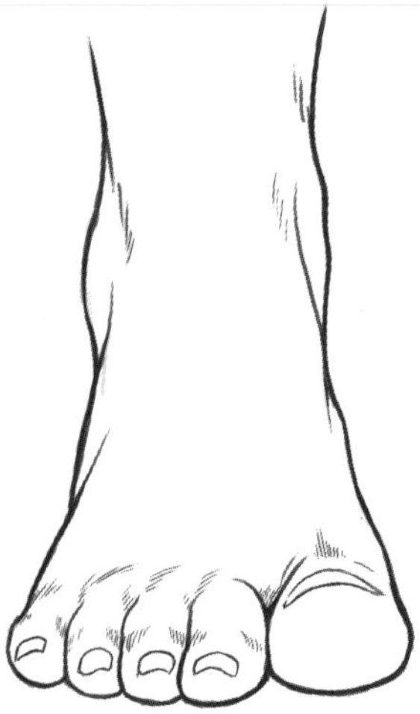

The front view shows more of the top of the foot.

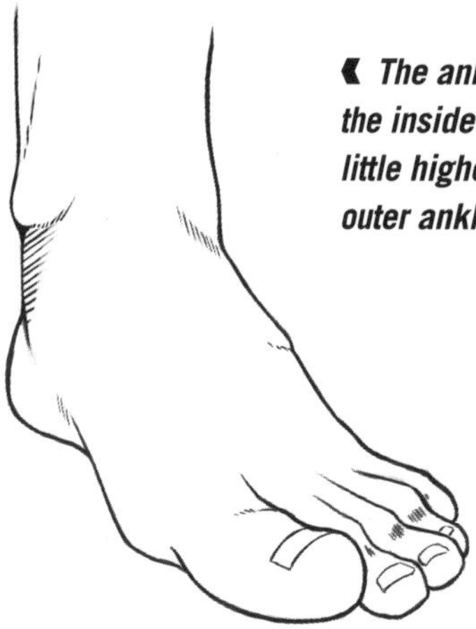

The ankle bone on the inside is always a little higher than the outer ankle bone.

Feet mostly move up and down from the ankle and have only a small range of motion from side to side.

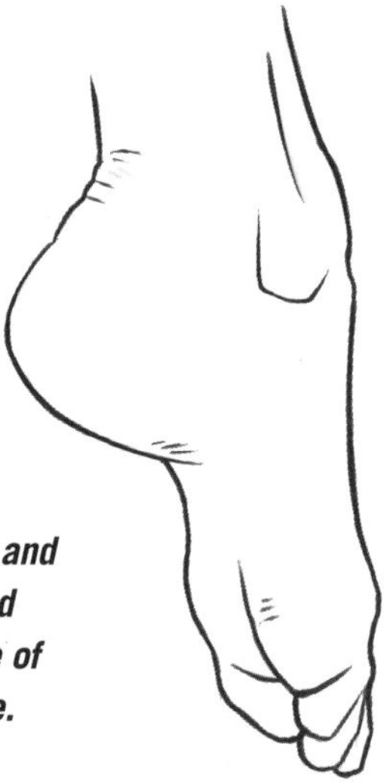

If you're drawing feet quite small, leave out details—you don't need to draw each toenail.

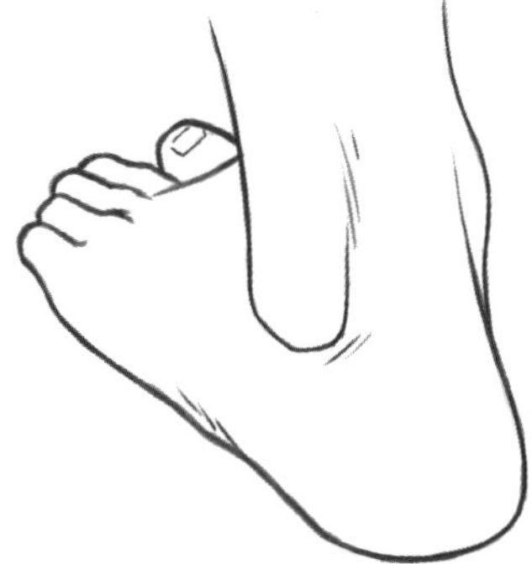

The tops of the feet are generally quite plain unless you want to add a few lines to denote tendons and veins.

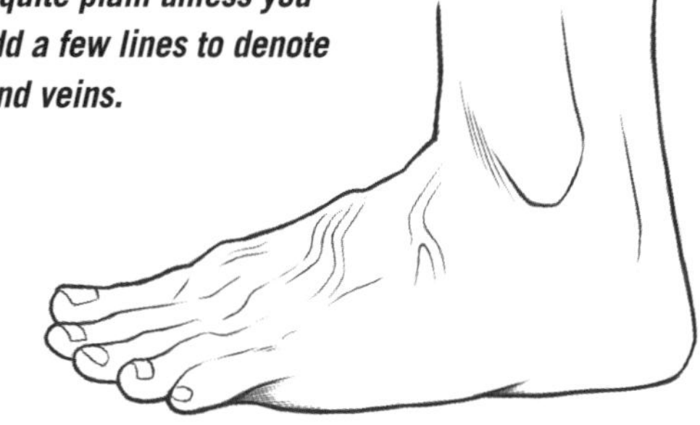

The back of the heel protrudes slightly instead of being a straight vertical line up to the Achilles tendon.

Drawing laces or the underside tread of a shoe can be fiddly and time-consuming, but is worth getting right.

When drawing footwear, always consider the flexibility of material and allow clearance for ankles to bend without obstruction.

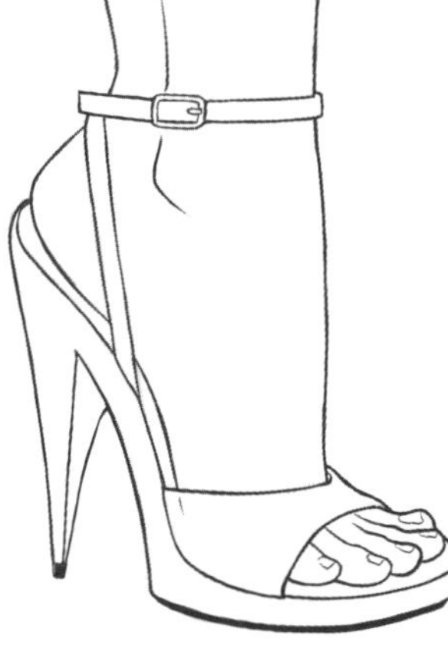

Drawing the underside of the feet or footwear is necessary when you show characters sitting, kicking or running from behind or below.

Very high heels cause the foot to arch; the foot points down and the heel protrudes a little more.

DRAWING FIGURES

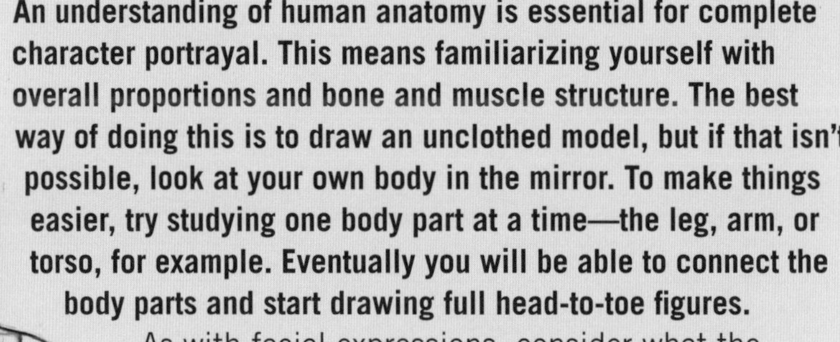

An understanding of human anatomy is essential for complete character portrayal. This means familiarizing yourself with overall proportions and bone and muscle structure. The best way of doing this is to draw an unclothed model, but if that isn't possible, look at your own body in the mirror. To make things easier, try studying one body part at a time—the leg, arm, or torso, for example. Eventually you will be able to connect the body parts and start drawing full head-to-toe figures.

As with facial expressions, consider what the character's pose says about their personality. Open gestures and wide stances suggest a confident, adventurous type, while slumped shoulders and arms tucked in suggest the opposite. Once you feel confident with standing poses, try drawing people sitting, kneeling or in motion to give your work a little more variety.

Start with a front view in a natural standing position, which will help you to learn the lengths of the limbs and body parts. A three-quarter view will make your character look more interesting, but don't neglect the rear view, which is especially important when testing out how clothes look from multiple angles.

When adding clothing, there is always the sneaky option of adding material over parts of the character you find difficult to draw. Toes too fiddly? Hide them in footwear. Can't get the knees right? Cover them up with pants, a skirt or a gown!

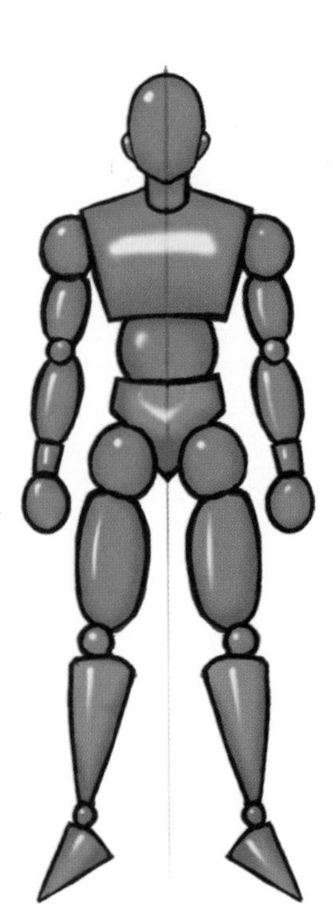

BASIC SHAPES AND PROPORTIONS

The human figure can be constructed using a series of shapes: squares, circles, and triangles, or to make things more 3D, cuboids, cylinders, spheres, and cones. Even if you have only 30 seconds to practice your artwork, draw these shapes—especially cylinders at different angles—to help you later on when you convert these into more complex forms.

THE HEAD COUNT

An average fully grown male is around 7–8 heads tall. So work out the size at which you've drawn your head, multiply its height by 7, then use this measurement to work out where the feet need to be placed. Some manga styles use characters that are 9 heads tall, to exaggerate the length of the legs. A younger character, such as a 10-year-old child, may be 5–6 heads tall. Manga females are typically shorter than males of the same age by 1 or half a head. I've listed average manga proportions opposite. Use these as a guide, while keeping in mind the differences between character types (younger characters are shorter with larger heads, for example). Males have wider chests and narrower hips than females, who usually have slimmer waists.

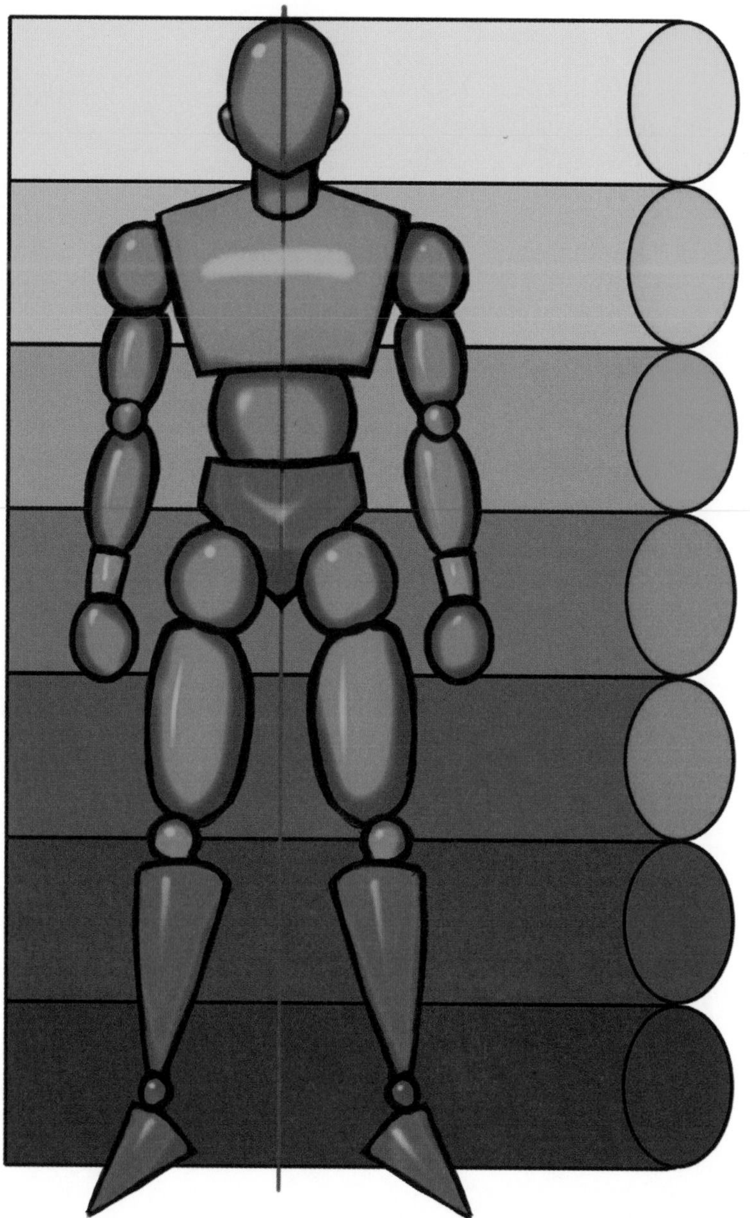

BODY HEIGHT
This is 6–8 heads tall.

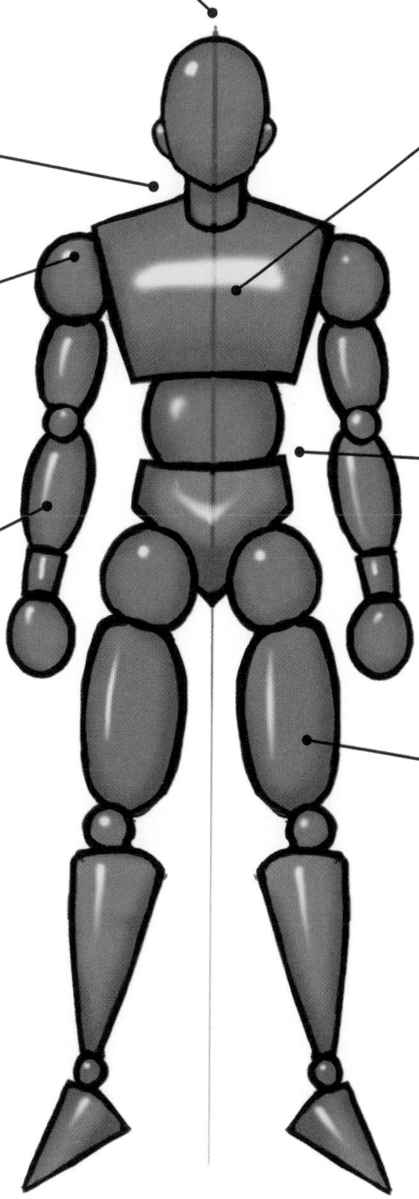

NECK
The neck is between one-third and half the width of the head. This varies a lot depending on the character's build, gender, and age.

CHEST
The distance between the armpits is usually one head-length across, although male chests can be wider. In a female, the nipples are 1 head height below the chin. Breast sizes vary a lot in manga, although they are typically the same width as, if not a little wider than, the width of the chest.

SHOULDERS
At 2 head widths across (or more in this instance) the shoulders are the broadest part of the figure.

WAIST AND HIPS
The waist falls just below elbow height. Its width varies, but it is slightly less than the width of the chest. The slim hips on this figure are the width of the head, though on a less exaggerated form they are 2 head widths across.

ARM AND HAND
The arm is the same length as the top of the knee to the toe. The fingertips end halfway down the thigh. The upper arm is about the same width as the neck and the distance from elbow to armpit is 1 head height. The distance from wrist to elbow is slightly more than 1 head height (the same as the length of the foot). The length of the hand is about three-quarters head height. The elbows fall just below the rib cage.

LEGS
The legs are just over half of the overall height. From the bottom of the kneecap to the crotch is the same length as the bottom of the kneecap to the soles of the feet. The upper leg (thigh) is almost as wide as the head. The knee is 2 head heights above the bottom of the foot. The length of the foot is slightly more than the height of the head.

FEMALE POSE: FRONT VIEW

STEP 1

This drawing of a front-on standing pose shows a young woman in her late teens/early twenties. Start by drawing a stick figure with light pencil marks. This way you can work out the character's proportions. The feminine stance is indicated by the feet, which are placed close together, and the hand on hip.

STEP 2

Flesh out the character using solid shapes—a combination of rounded triangles, ovals, and circles. While real people come in all shapes and sizes, most manga females have exaggerated attributes—skinny waists, large breasts, wide hips, and long legs.

STEP 3

Erase the initial stick figure guidelines. When drawing front-on poses like this, remember to observe symmetry—the shoulders should be of equal width, the left thigh should be the same width as the right thigh, and so on. Sketch a general shape for the hair to determine the volume and length.

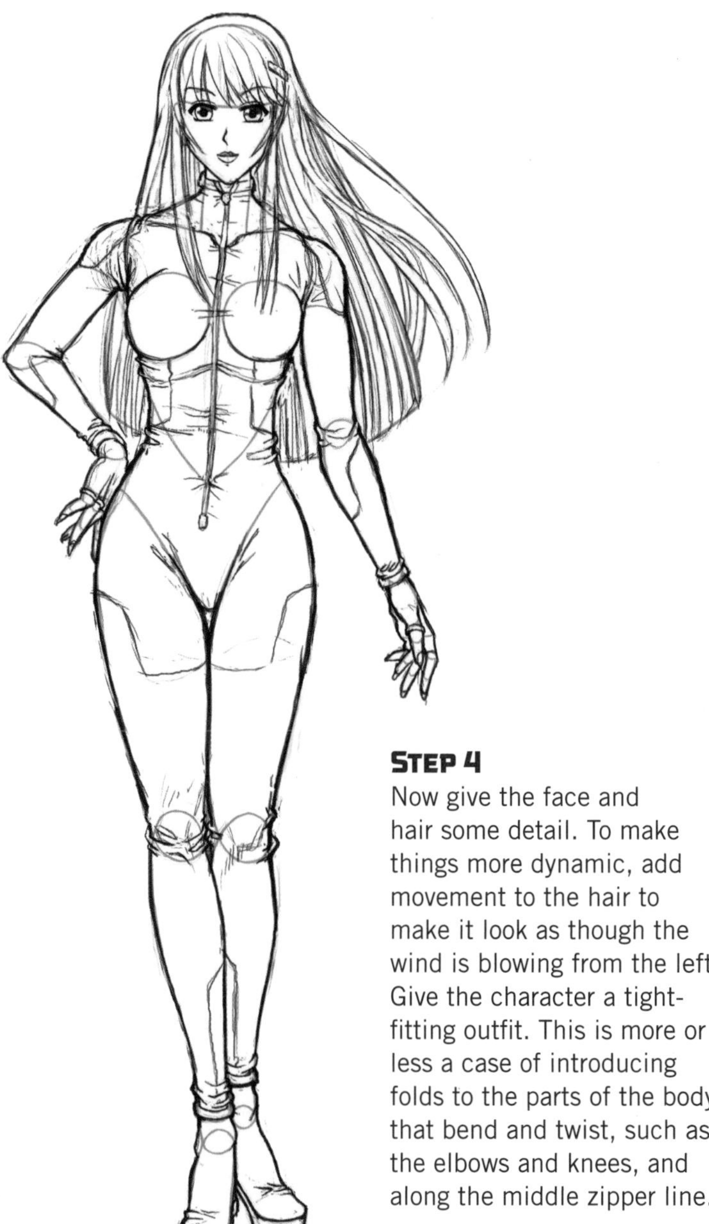

STEP 4

Now give the face and hair some detail. To make things more dynamic, add movement to the hair to make it look as though the wind is blowing from the left. Give the character a tight-fitting outfit. This is more or less a case of introducing folds to the parts of the body that bend and twist, such as the elbows and knees, and along the middle zipper line.

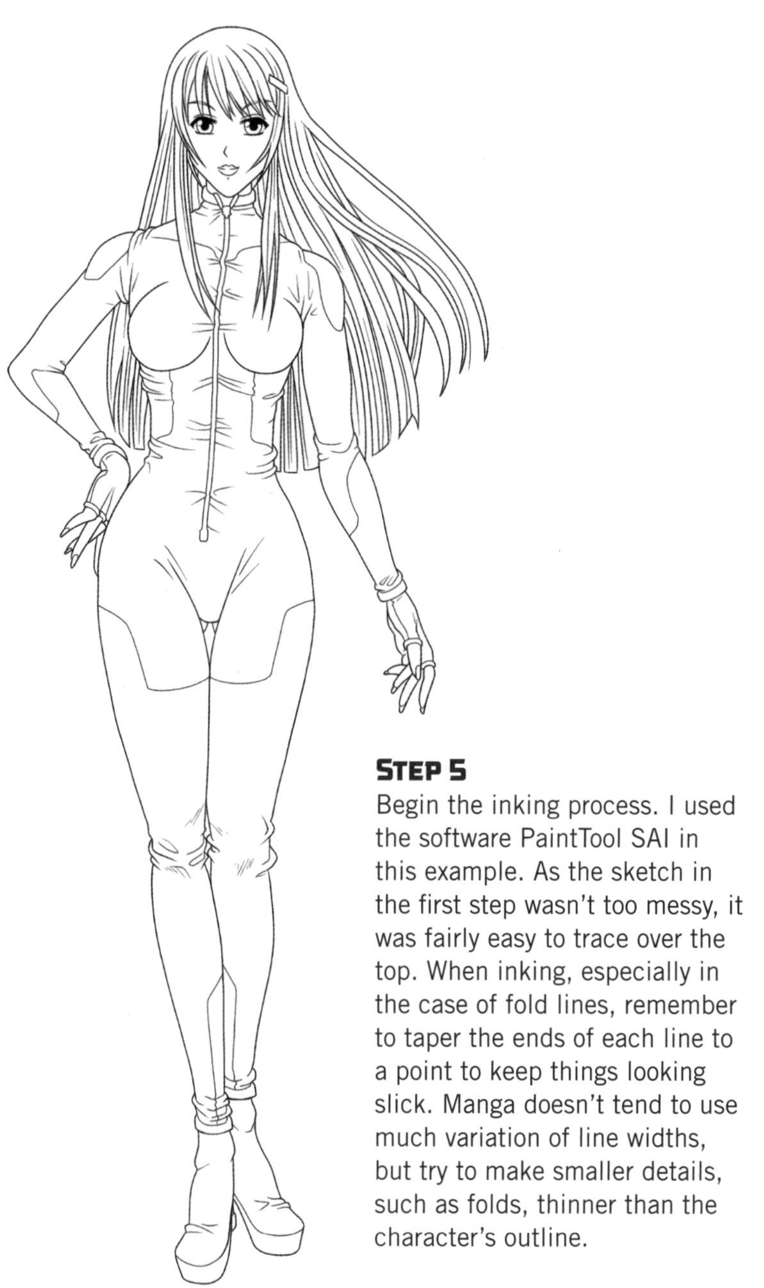

STEP 5

Begin the inking process. I used the software PaintTool SAI in this example. As the sketch in the first step wasn't too messy, it was fairly easy to trace over the top. When inking, especially in the case of fold lines, remember to taper the ends of each line to a point to keep things looking slick. Manga doesn't tend to use much variation of line widths, but try to make smaller details, such as folds, thinner than the character's outline.

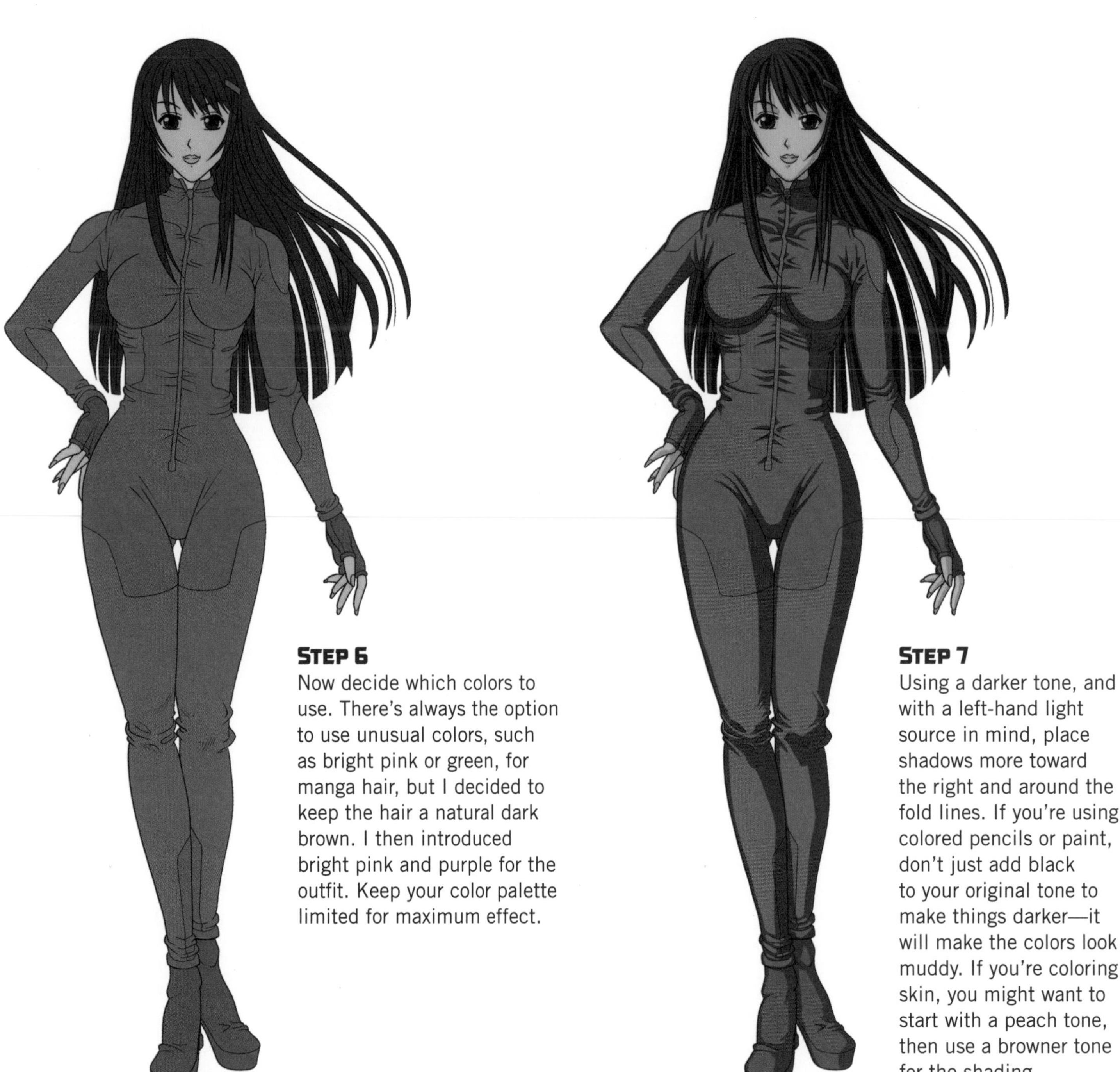

STEP 6

Now decide which colors to use. There's always the option to use unusual colors, such as bright pink or green, for manga hair, but I decided to keep the hair a natural dark brown. I then introduced bright pink and purple for the outfit. Keep your color palette limited for maximum effect.

STEP 7

Using a darker tone, and with a left-hand light source in mind, place shadows more toward the right and around the fold lines. If you're using colored pencils or paint, don't just add black to your original tone to make things darker—it will make the colors look muddy. If you're coloring skin, you might want to start with a peach tone, then use a browner tone for the shading.

Try drawing and inking your own character in the space below.

STEP 8

I decided to go for an airbrushed style by blending in the existing shadows and adding extra shading to make the artwork pop and look more 3D. Add finishing touches, such as light bands, to give the hair some shine.

MALE POSE: THREE QUARTERS VIEW

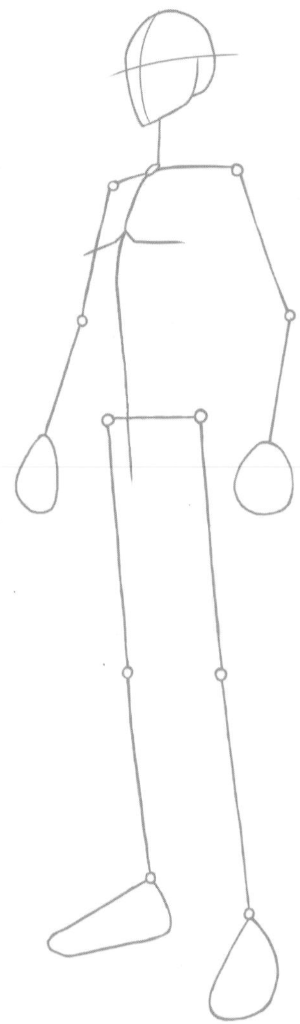

STEP 1
With your character facing to the left at an angle, start with a penciled stick figure to work out the proportions. Three-quarter views involve overlapping, such as an arm behind or in front of the torso.

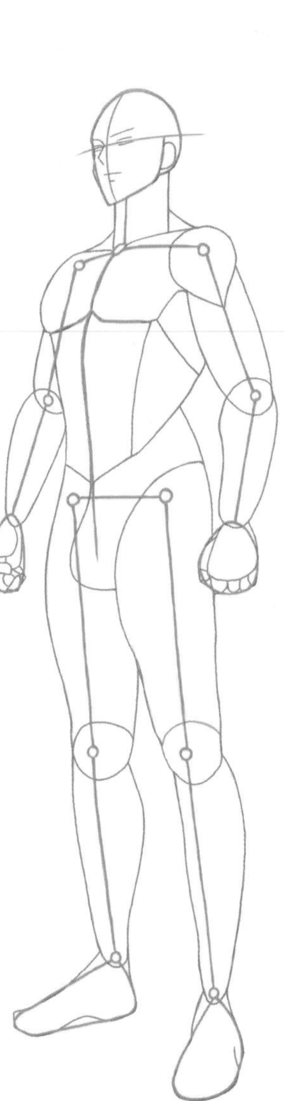

STEP 2
Flesh out the character using solid shapes. I wanted to keep this figure more real by not over-simplifying or exaggerating the body parts.

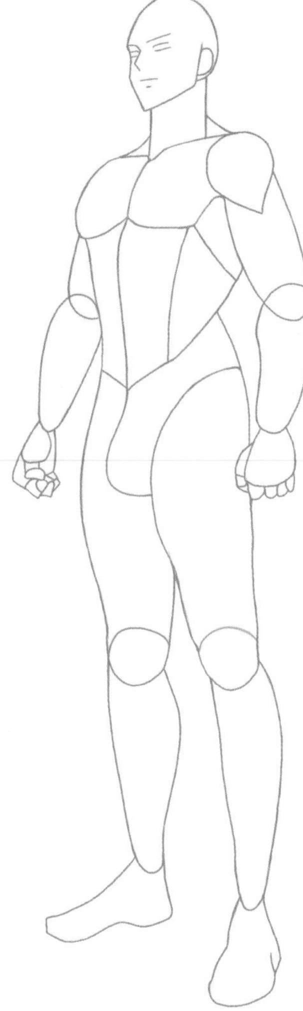

STEP 3
Erase the initial stick figure guidelines. Manga males are often on the lean side, but I wanted this one to have a little more bulk to help illustrate some muscle definition in the next step.

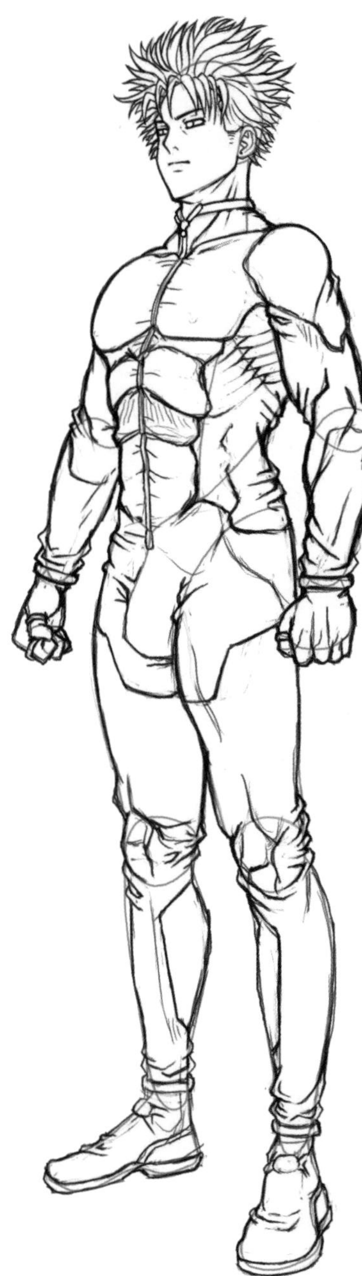

STEP 4

Sketch more details of the character's tight outfit. This will make it easier to understand the underlying anatomy. Creases are placed around the joints and bends. As long as the figure is in proportion up to step 3, adding details such as folds and hair should be fairly straightforward.

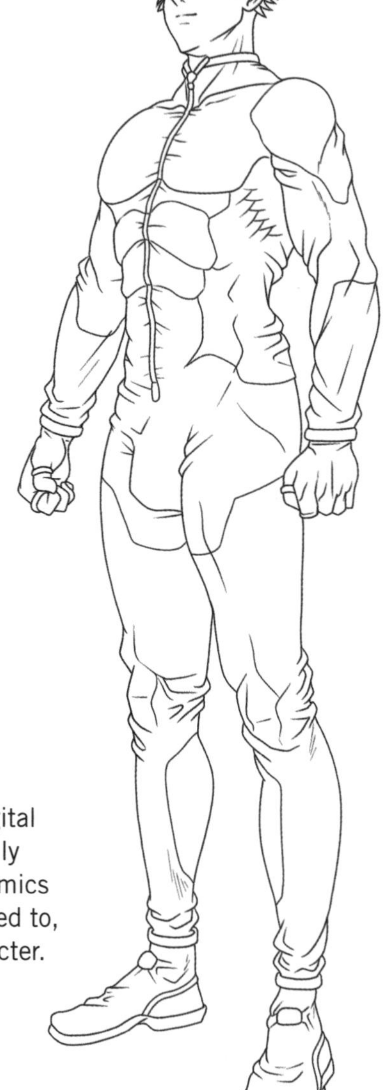

STEP 5

Ink the outlines using a pen or digital software. Manga line work is usually finer than that used in Western comics art. There is less variation compared to, say, a typical Marvel comics character.

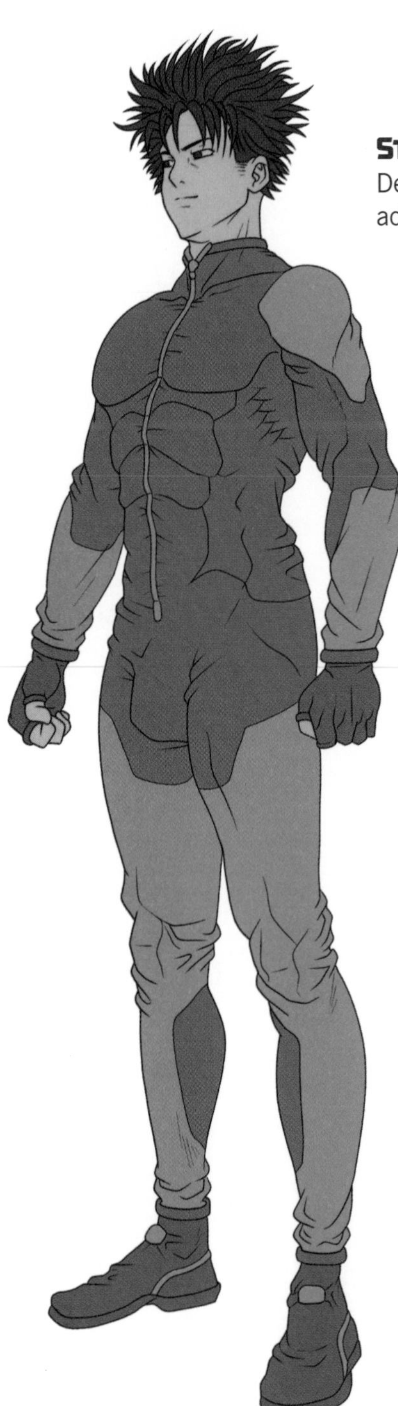

STEP 6
Decide on your colors and add them in.

STEP 7
Using a darker tone, and bearing in mind that this image has a left-hand front light source, place the shadows toward the right and around the fold lines and creases. Think about how shadows contour around the shapes on the body. For example, light doesn't reach the areas under the chin, beneath the armpit or below the knees.

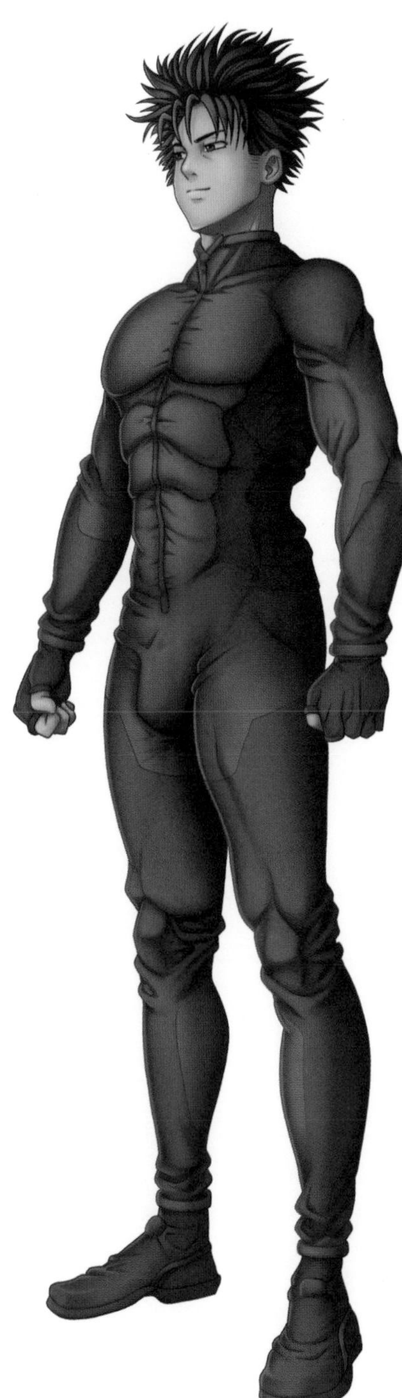

Try drawing and inking your own character in the space below.

STEP 8

Blend the shadows to create a more realistic, 3D form. If you want to achieve a soft, smooth finish, as in this example, use colored pencils, airbrush or digital. Paint or markers can look great, but may be a little more blotchy or textured.

FEMALE POSE: REAR VIEW

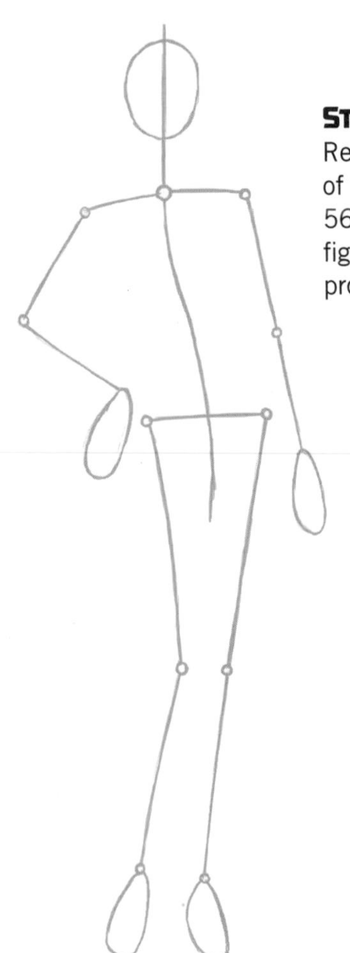

STEP 1
Repeat the build and pose of the character on page 56, starting with a stick figure guide to work out proportions.

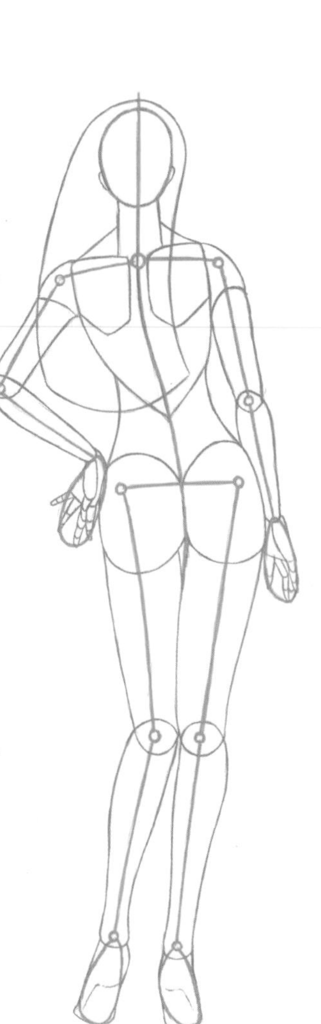

STEP 2
Flesh out the character using solid shapes. The major difference here, compared to the front view, is to map in the shoulderblades and buttocks. Although the hair will cover most of her back, it's worth drawing the whole outline to understand how the character would look underneath and to make sure the proportions are correct.

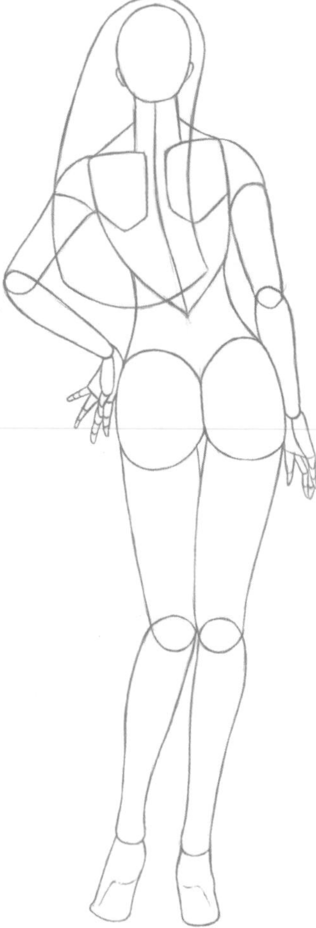

STEP 3
Erase the initial stick figure guidelines. Double check that you're happy with the pose and proportions before adding any further detail.

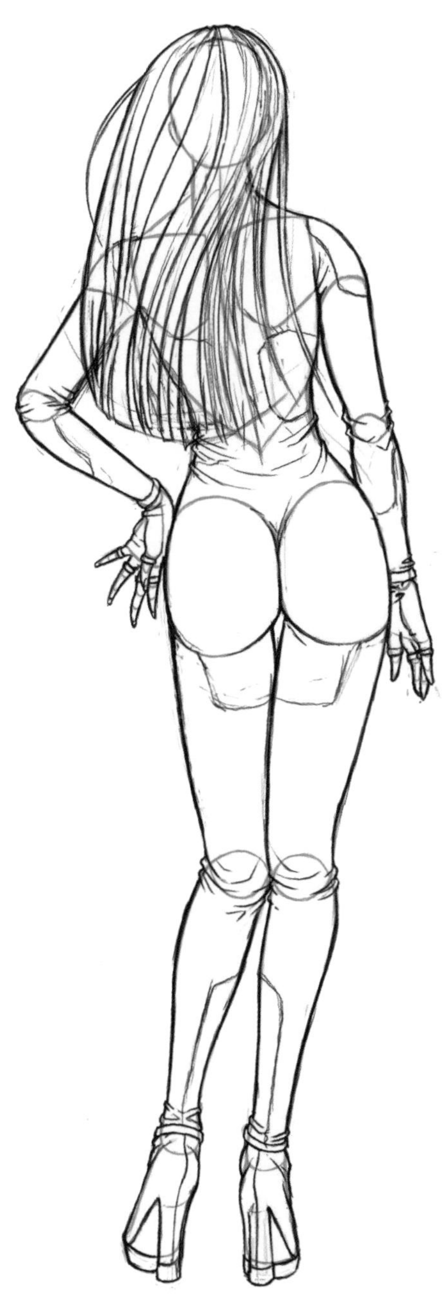

STEP 4

Add details of the figure-hugging suit. Creases and fold lines will be found around the joints and where the figure bends—at the elbows, knees, and lower back. Use curved lines to give a little movement to the hair.

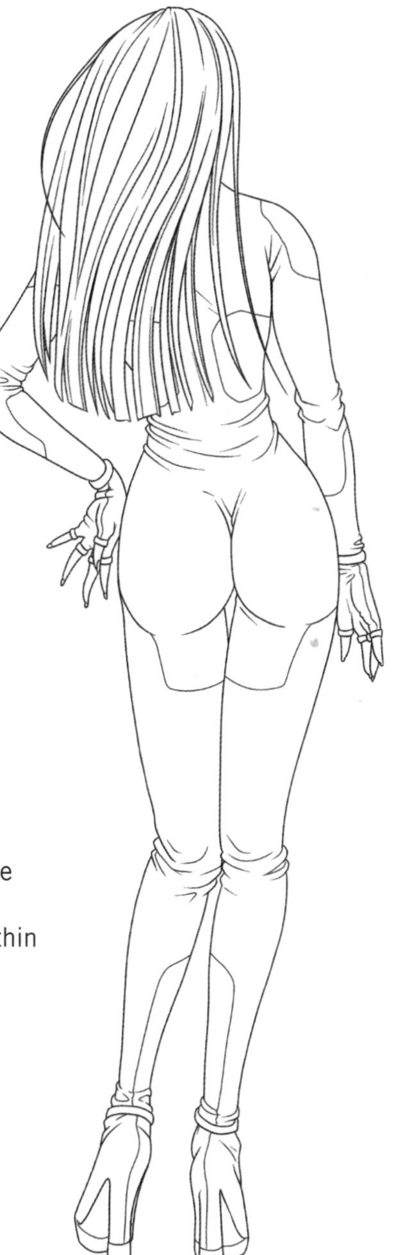

STEP 5

Ink the outlines using your choice of pen or digital software. I used PaintTool SAI to make the lines thin and delicate.

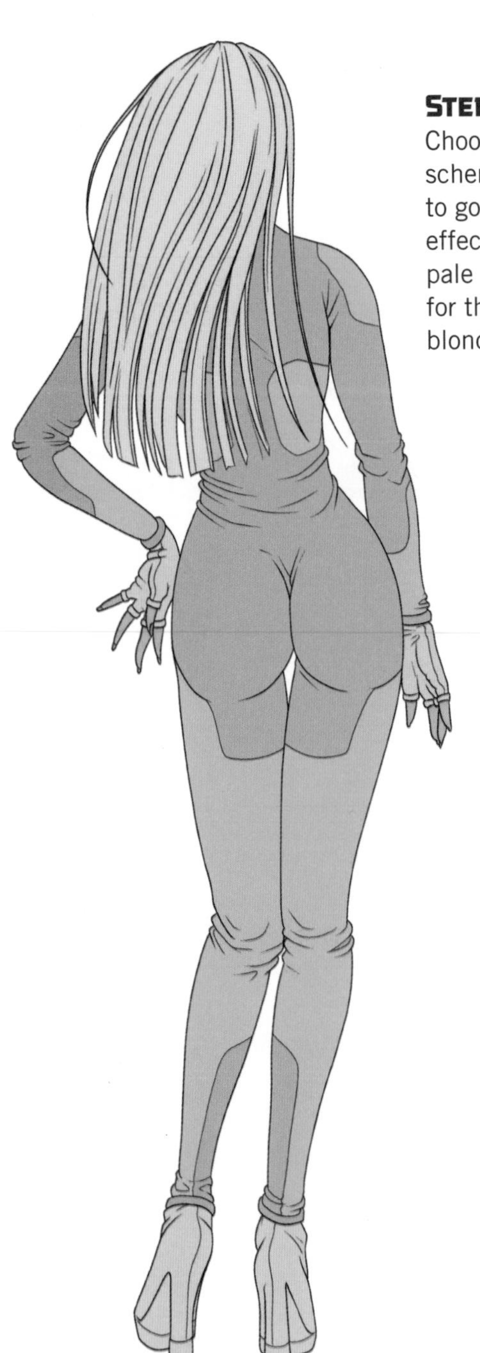

STEP 6
Choose your color scheme. I decided to go for a more girly effect this time, with pale blue and pink for the suit and light blonde for the hair.

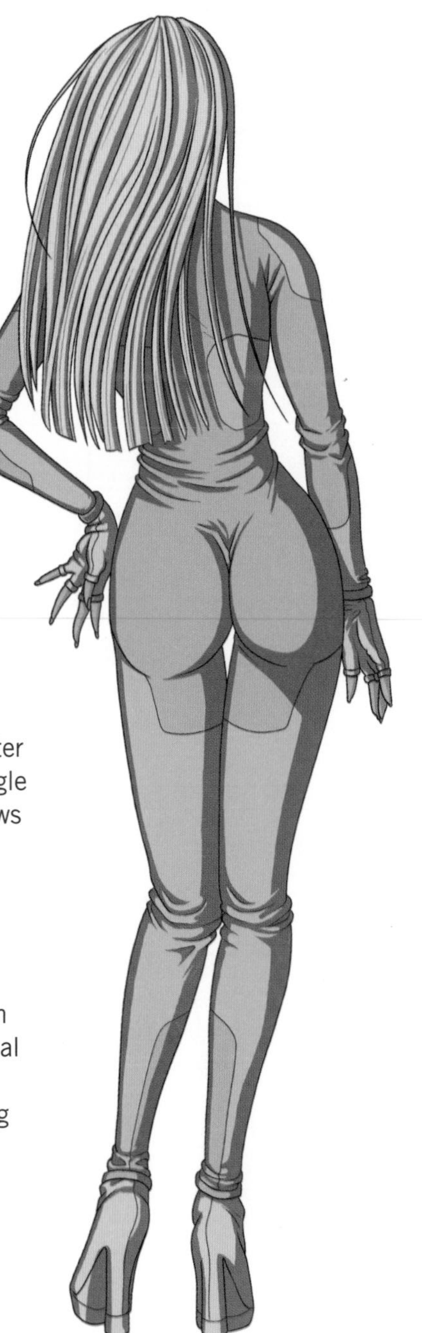

STEP 7
Using a darker tone, and with a light source illuminating the character from a three-quarter angle to the left, place shadows toward the right and around the fold lines. As with previous examples, I've used a two-tone coloring style. For the next stage, I can either build up additional layers of shadow, or begin to render, creating smooth, gradual tonal transitions from light to dark.

Try drawing and inking your own character in the space below.

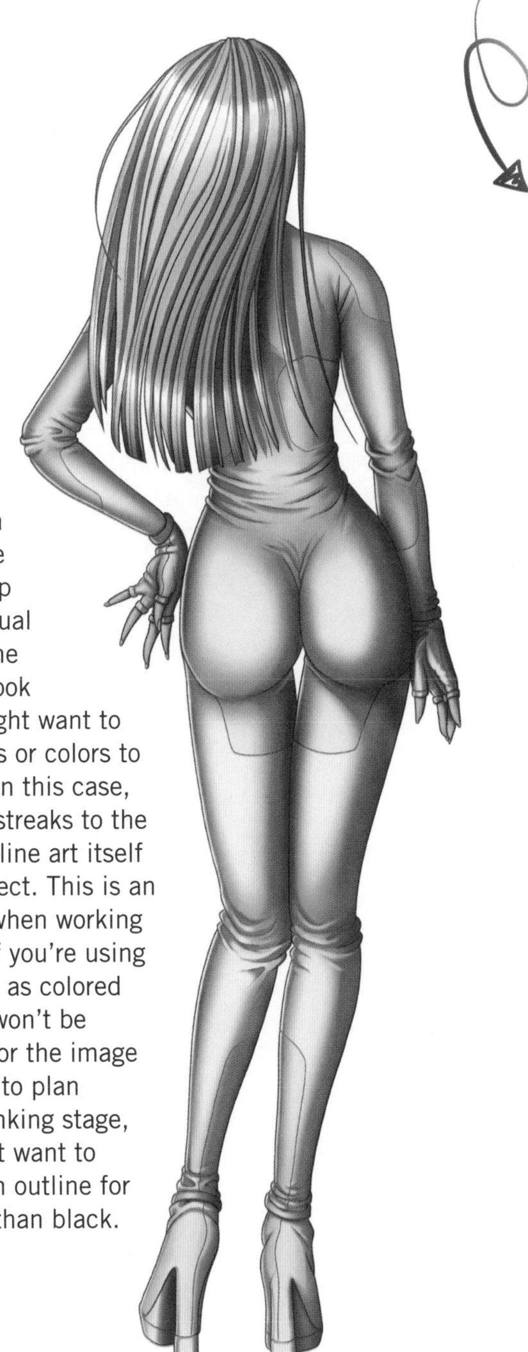

STEP 8

Blend tones together and introduce highlights and an extra layer of shading to give a more 3D image. Keep gradients of color gradual and smooth to make the body, arms, and legs look more rounded. You might want to add additional patterns or colors to the design afterward. In this case, I've added some pink streaks to the hair and colorized the line art itself for a more realistic effect. This is an easy change to make when working on digital layers, but if you're using traditional media such as colored pencil or marker, you won't be able to tweak or re-color the image later on, so remember to plan ahead. At the step 5 inking stage, for example, you might want to consider using a brown outline for the skin areas, rather than black.

Clothing and Accessories

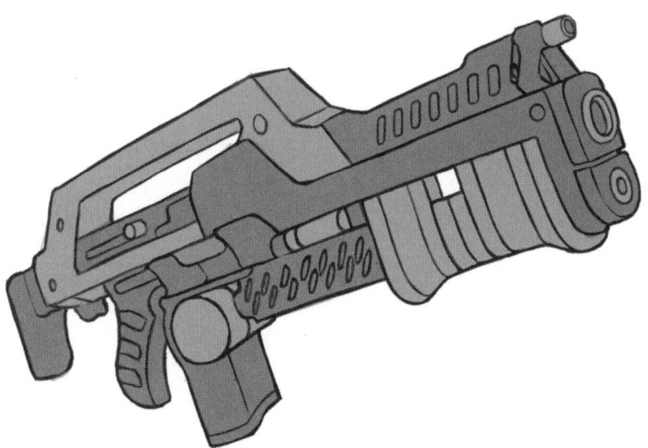

Clothing is another way of showing who your character is. It plays a key role in the manga aesthetic and is often simplified—fabric folds can be drawn as single lines, for example. Yet it is detailed enough to describe form and variations in styling, such as trim, patterns, and seamlines.

Fashion gives us an understanding of how clothes look and fit. Take fashion or styling from history—armor, for example—and compare it with the modern equivalent. Observe how dense material without much give in it is used to cover chests, backs, thighs, and shoulders, while flexible material is used for the joints to accommodate flexing and rotating.

Note how both modern and vintage fashions use pockets, buttons, trims, patterns, and accessories to give garments additional appeal; then feel free to go over the top with exaggerated, impractical coats, hats, and shoes. As long as a character can move around freely, bending and twisting, anything goes. Characters wielding huge weapons or with gravity-defying clothing or accessories aren't unusual in the manga world—so go ahead and experiment! At the other end of the spectrum, practical, modest styling is great for school uniforms, military gear or anything else in a realistic setting.

CLOTHING

This selection of clothing shows different designs along with basic folds. Note that fabric is often pulled downward by gravity. Folds can be indicated either by a simple line, as in these examples, or by shading. See if you can figure out where to place shadows on these. Imagine the light source is coming from the left; shadows will be cast toward the right of the fold. If the light is coming from above, the shadows will be cast underneath the fold. The bigger and more pronounced the fold, the greater the shadow.

❮ Practice the shapes made by wavy, overlapping material and use them for frills, dresses or ruffled trim.

❮ Thick material folds less easily than thinner fabric.

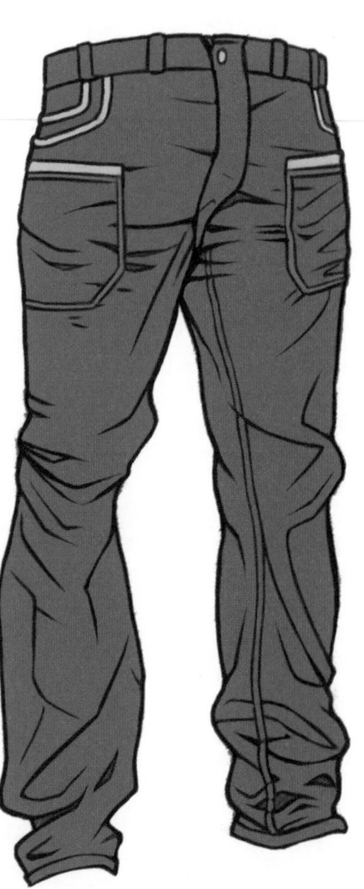

❯ Depending on the style, a pair of jeans can contain a lot of detailed folds. They appear around tight areas, knee joints and other areas that bend, and at the bottom where material gathers.

› Notice how fold lines originate from the elbow or other points of the body that bend.

› Consider utility and appeal—a practical garment can be made attractive with a few decorative elements.

‹ Adding trim or piping to an outfit prevents clothing from looking too minimal.

› Experiment with different materials to see how they fold when draped.

› Add creases to make skin-tight garments more believable.

DRESSING A CHARACTER

Manga art features a number of specific costumes, outfits, and uniforms, so it's worth studying them. They include samurai, ninja, maid, nurse, *miko* (shrine maiden/priestess), schoolwear, suit, cat-girl cosplay, kimono and Lolita fashions. If you're trying to decide how to dress your character, start with an unclothed figure and layer an outfit on top. This helps to ensure that the clothing conforms to the contours of the body, and allows you to check the proportions are correct.

I've included detail to illustrate as many potential fold or stretch lines as possible. You can simplify this if you wish, by drawing in fewer fold lines and concentrating more on the outline shapes.

MALE UNDERWEAR
This consists of briefs that mould to the shape of the body.

GAKURAN
This is middle or high school (age 15–18) boys' school uniform in Japan. Blazers and shirts are often worn as an alternative.

SHINOBI

These ninja characters are often depicted in dark colors to complement their actions, which include espionage, assassination, and combat. To give this custom outfit some individual flair, I've added a red scarf.

CASUAL ATTIRE

Jeans, trainers, and a hoodie—a typical outfit for many young guys.

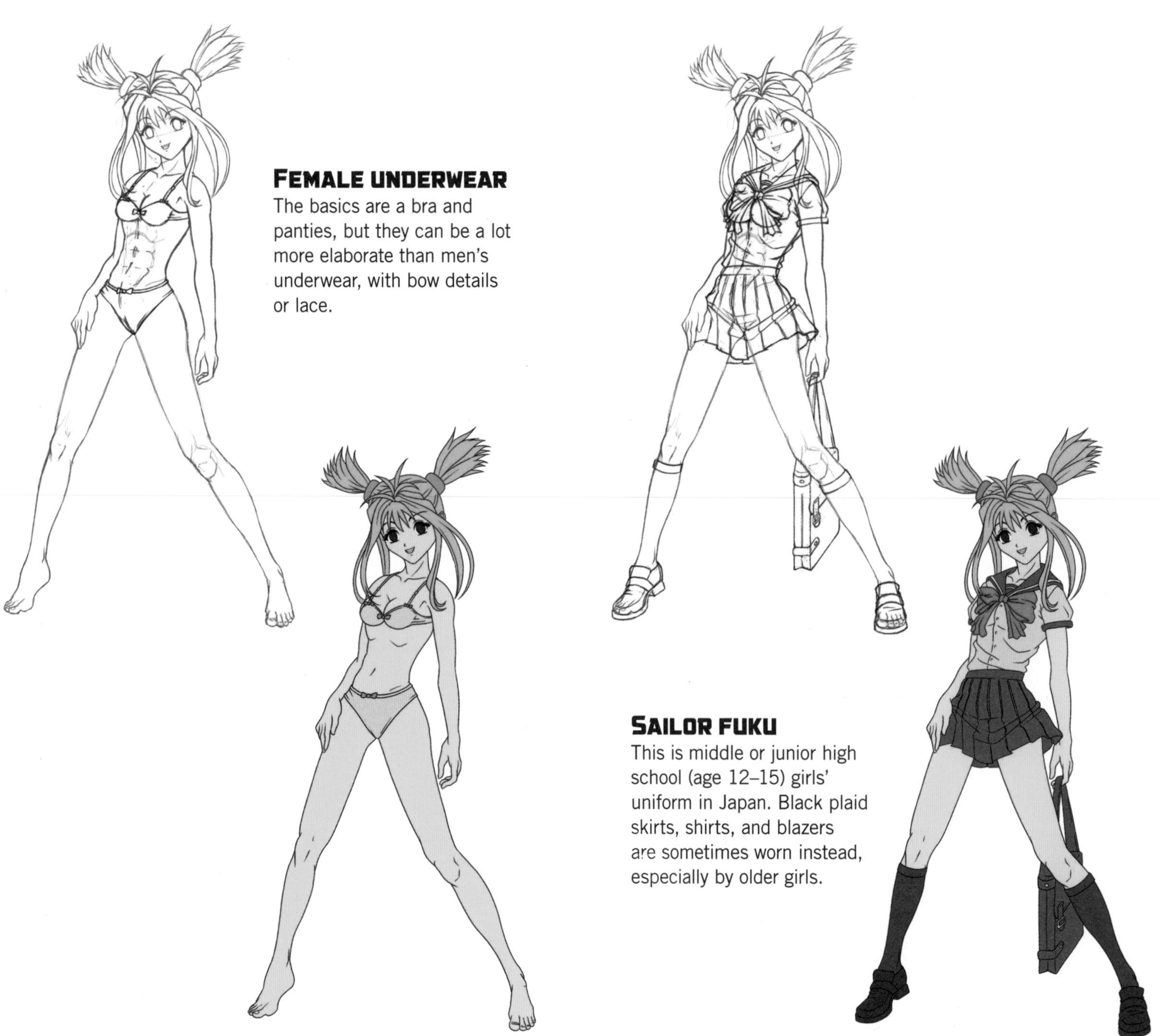

FEMALE UNDERWEAR

The basics are a bra and panties, but they can be a lot more elaborate than men's underwear, with bow details or lace.

SAILOR FUKU

This is middle or junior high school (age 12–15) girls' uniform in Japan. Black plaid skirts, shirts, and blazers are sometimes worn instead, especially by older girls.

KIMONO

A kimono is usually narrower at the bottom than this one, but the wide stance meant I needed to tweak it to allow for an opening at the front. Kimonos come in a huge variety of colors and patterns.

MEIDO

The Japanese maid costume is a popular outfit often worn by anime cosplayers, or by staff working at themed "Maid Cafés" in Japan and other parts of the Far East.

ACCESSORIES

Once you have your character's basic outfit drawn, you can add accessories to complete their style. I've drawn several examples of accessories you might want to give to a character. Others might include backpacks, jewelry such as necklaces and bracelets, watches, mobile devices, food items, and a water bottle.

Big headphones are always a popular addition for manga characters.

Adding a hat is an easy way to give your character a little extra individuality.

Shopping bags add interest and you can decorate them as you like.

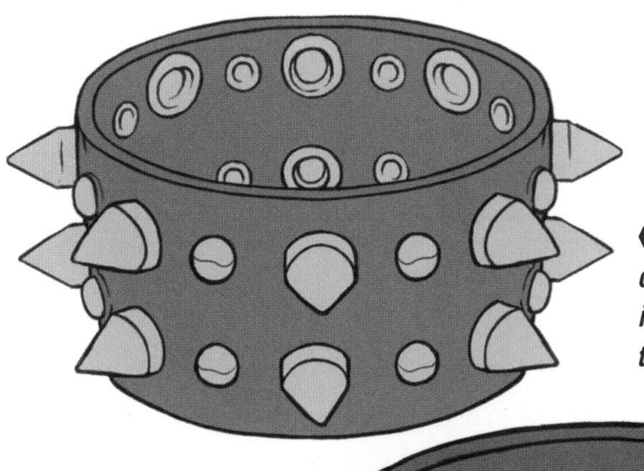

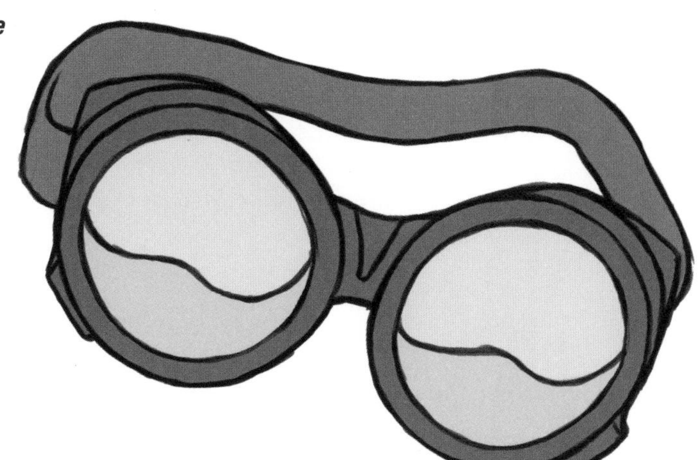

Goggles might sit on the forehead, above the eyes, perhaps half-covered in long manga hair spikes.

The curve of a belt or bracelet can help to illustrate the angle of a torso or limb.

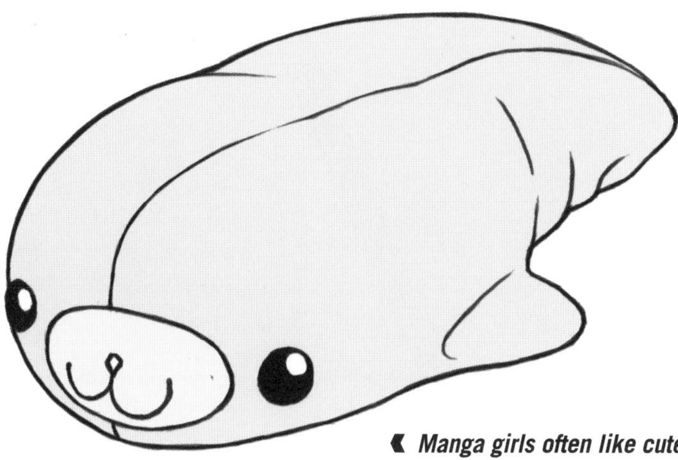

Hats are enormously varied and can say a lot about a character's self-image.

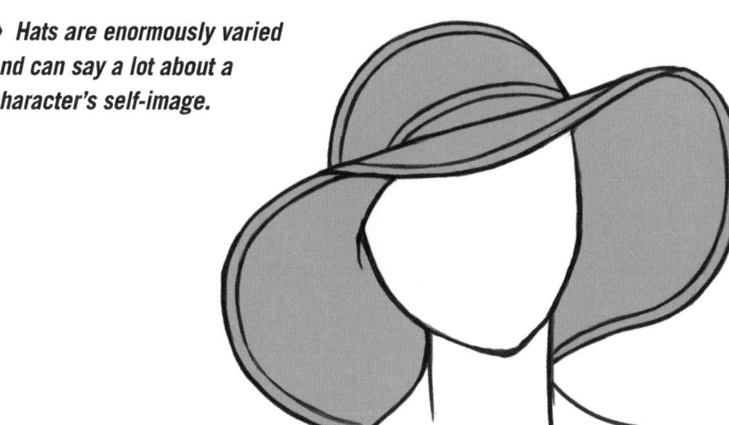

Manga girls often like cute cuddly toys and plushies.

WEAPONS

Manga stories often have conflict as a theme, so it's good to be able to draw a variety of weapons for different characters and settings. Consider functionality—how will the weapons be held, how will they be transported when not in active use, what would a character's weapon of choice be, and why?

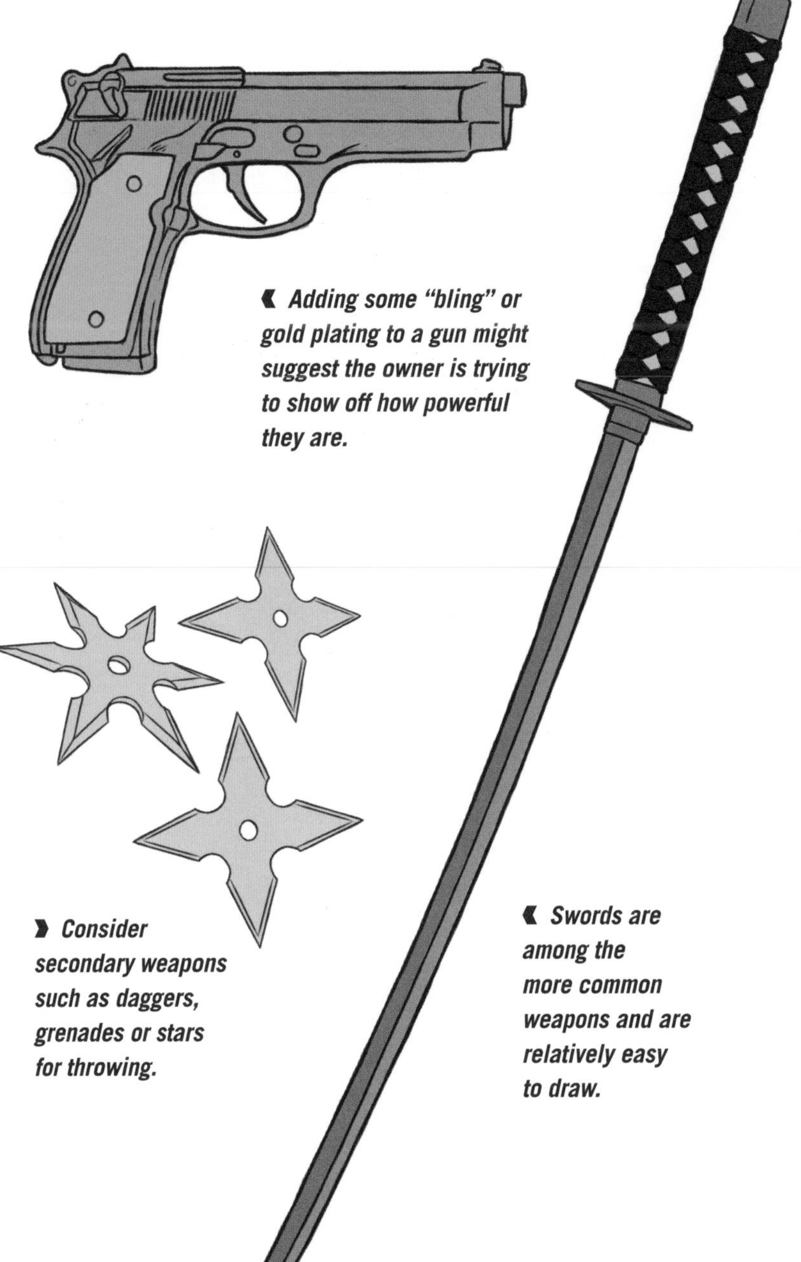

Adding some "bling" or gold plating to a gun might suggest the owner is trying to show off how powerful they are.

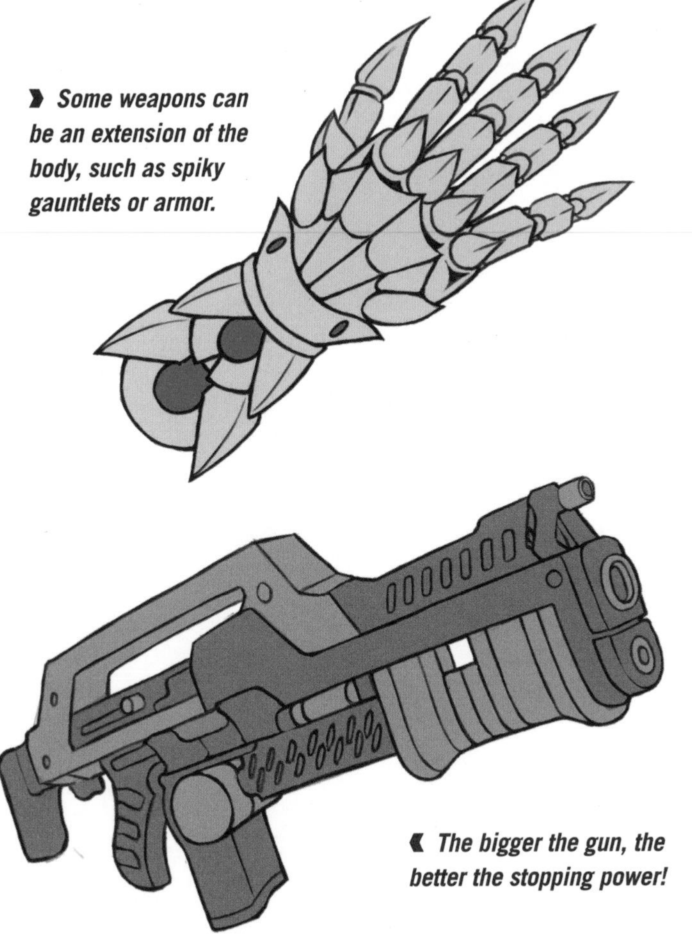

Some weapons can be an extension of the body, such as spiky gauntlets or armor.

Consider secondary weapons such as daggers, grenades or stars for throwing.

Swords are among the more common weapons and are relatively easy to draw.

The bigger the gun, the better the stopping power!

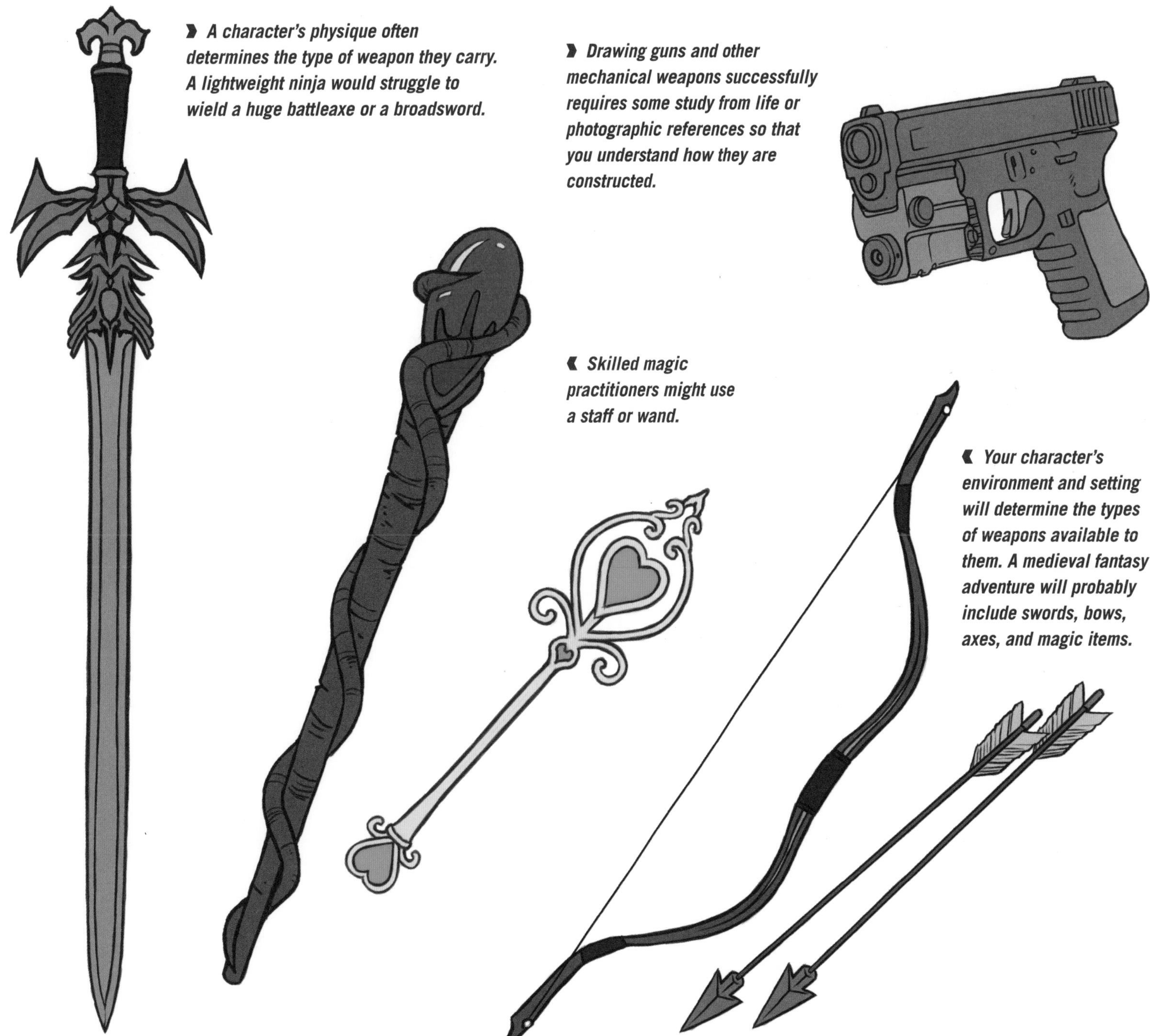

› *A character's physique often determines the type of weapon they carry. A lightweight ninja would struggle to wield a huge battleaxe or a broadsword.*

› *Drawing guns and other mechanical weapons successfully requires some study from life or photographic references so that you understand how they are constructed.*

‹ *Skilled magic practitioners might use a staff or wand.*

‹ *Your character's environment and setting will determine the types of weapons available to them. A medieval fantasy adventure will probably include swords, bows, axes, and magic items.*

ACTION

Once you have acquired some knowledge of basic anatomy and body proportions, the next step is to pose your characters at different angles and performing various tasks to make them look more dynamic and interesting.

From there you can create more complex scenes or even a comic-book page. This will probably be a little tricky at first, but finding some reference images on the internet or taking photos of yourself or friends in a variety of poses will be a big help. When choosing a pose for your character, think about their personality and how they move. For instance, when walking, one character may strut along confidently with their head up high and shoulders back, while another may drop their shoulders, drag their feet and walk along with their head hung low. The mood you show depends on the pose, as well as the facial expression. Try to imagine how you stand or move in different moods and consider how you might apply what you've learnt so far about figure drawing and clothing to the action examples.

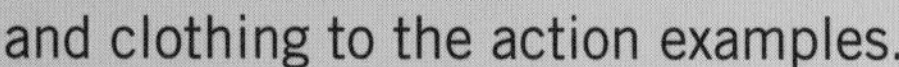

FALLING

STEP 1

Start with a stick figure to work out the proportions. Body parts will be overlapping in this image, which will help create a more dynamic image and a sense of depth.

STEP 3

Before thinking, "Too much detail—I can't do that!" take a deep breath and tackle it one step at a time. First add the clothing. Lightly rough it out before adding the fold detail and refining it. Next move on to the hair, taking time to draw each segment.

STEP 2

Flesh out the character using solid shapes. Loosely draw in a few lines to indicate where the hair will go. The left leg needs to overlap other body parts. I've drawn this see-through to help show what's underneath.

STEP 4

Paint in your chosen colors, adding darker tone around the outer edges of the shapes to create a more 3D look. Most of the colors here use three tones—a base, then two layers of darker color for shading. Manga "speed lines" or "action lines" added to the background help to create an added sense of movement.

RUNNING

STEP 1

Begin with your stick figure as a guide. Running poses and action poses in general often start with one arc line. In this case, there is an arc running from the top of the head down to the foot closest to the floor. This curve helps to illustrate the direction of movement from left to right.

STEP 2

Create the body masses using basic shapes. These are key to making sure your work will look good when it's finished. While the fun part might be adding details such as outfits and accessories, it's important to get the base right and will save time in the long run.

STEP 3

Add the clothing, hair, and sword. The movement of the outfit details and folds is all toward the left, to show that the character is moving toward the right. I've added left-pointing spikes to break the line art, symbolizing motion-blur. A gust of flying leaves also helps to add another layer of movement to the drawing.

STEP 4

Use whatever color combination you think suitable to render the character. Bear in mind that the light source is from the right. This will create shadow towards the left-hand side of the character. Horizontal manga "speed lines" are added as a background element.

SWINGING

STEP 1

This time our stick man will be posed in a Spiderman-like jumping position. As there is a lot of bend in the back, the torso will appear shorter and the right shoulder will obscure the chest and abs. The overlapping body parts will help to add a lot of depth to the image.

STEP 2

This pose starts to take shape as the solid masses are added. As with all these action examples, keep your guidelines light and feel free to be more sketchy than I have been; this step is about getting basic shapes in place so that you can understand the pose.

STEP 3

Add the outfit of your choice—I've gone for a masked Japanese ninja warrior. And, of course, add the rope coming down from the top right to make it look as though he's swinging toward us and to the right.

STEP 4

I experimented with different combinations before making my final decision about colour. You might want to do the same by scanning your line work and printing out a few copies to play around with before committing the color, or by saving an extra copy or two if you are working digitally.

FIGHTING

STEP 1

This artwork has two characters interacting with each other, so is a little more complicated. You need to show the bigger stick man on the right throwing a punch and the smaller stick man on the left putting up his arm to block it.

STEP 2

Bulk out each of the characters in a muscle-bound *Dragon Ball Z* style—they're both warriors, after all. The left character is posed in a typical three-quarters view, while the right character is leaning in, exposing the tops of his shoulders. Keep in mind that the chest and shoulder lines of the two characters are parallel.

STEP 3

I wanted the guy on the left to be dressed in a casual outfit, while his attacker is wearing a judo or karate *gi* (uniform). Remember to add some movement to accessories like the necklace and belt.

STEP 4

To make this drawing more aggressive and intense, I used a strong red background and added inward-pointing manga "action lines" to focus on the point of contact in the middle of the image. To give it a more authentic Japanese manga flavor, *katakana* characters are added to show a "Pow!" sound effect.

ドガバ

COLOR AND TONE

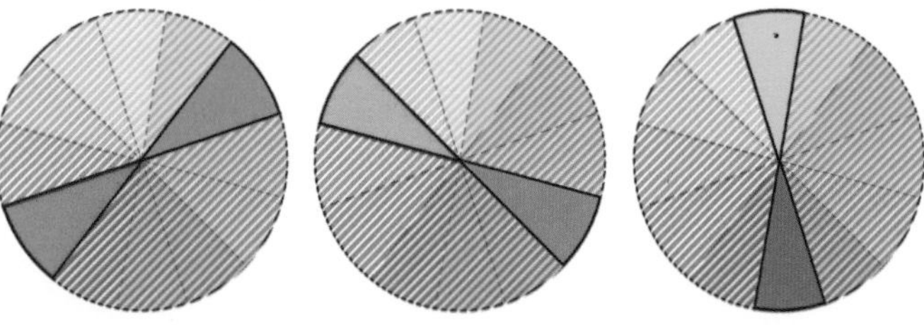

The accurate use of color and tone is vital to the production of believable manga artwork. It takes a lot of practice to render artwork to a professional standard, but you can get a good grounding in the discipline by learning some of the basic rules given in this chapter.

The goal of any artist is to communicate effectively through their work. The most labored image will not necessarily create focus and clarity: there's no need to draw every eyelash, for example, or spend massive amounts of time rendering unimportant elements in an image. Adding a huge variety of tones or details to every surface, such as skin pores, veins on leaves, cracks in brickwork, ants on the floor, and so on may make your artwork too busy, unfocused, and difficult to "read." So you need to decide how much detail to add and how to streamline your color palette.

While the majority of comics produced in Japan tend to focus on line work, often with a monochromatic interior, every manga cover, magazine advert, animation or game intended to grab a viewer's attention will need color. Coloring an image is more than a case of simply staying inside the lines. It's a way of representing a character's emotions, personality, and preferences; it can set the mood of a scene and it's also a way of showing off your unique, individual style.

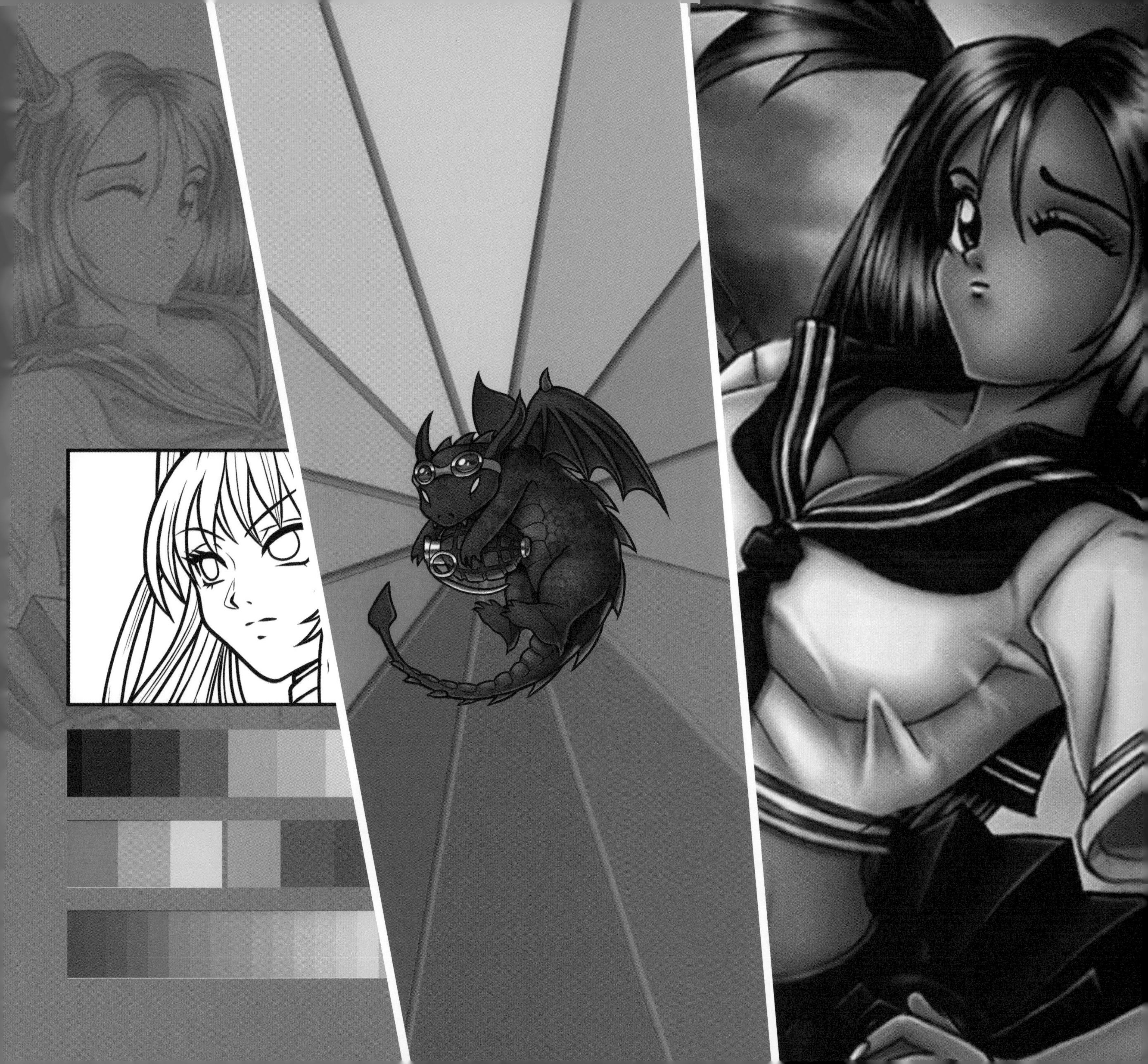

COLOR TERMINOLOGY

People often learn which colors work best together through trial and error. However, there are several rules about what makes a strong image and which color combinations look most effective. Knowing these can quickly help improve your standard of work.

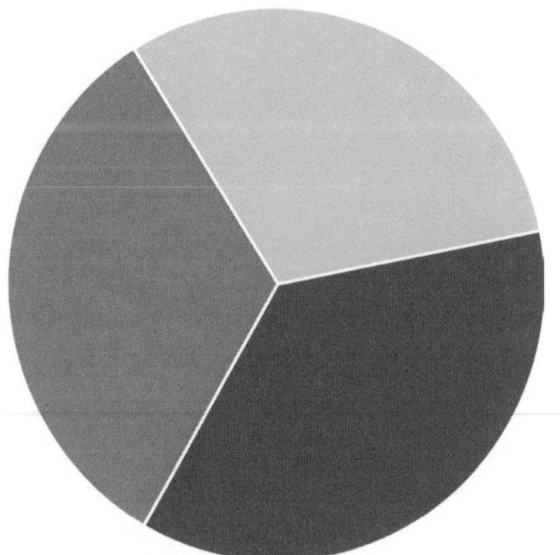

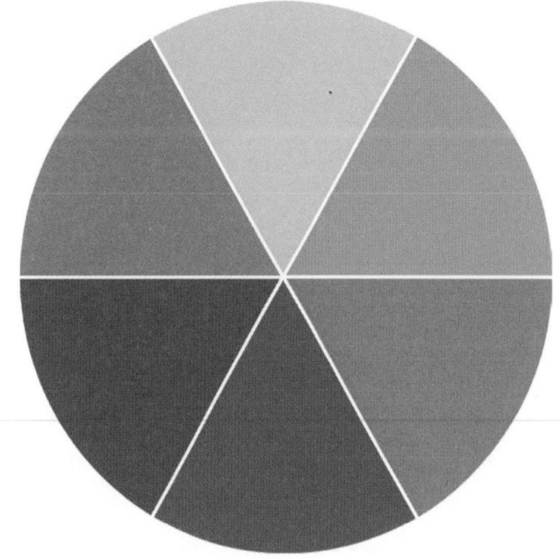

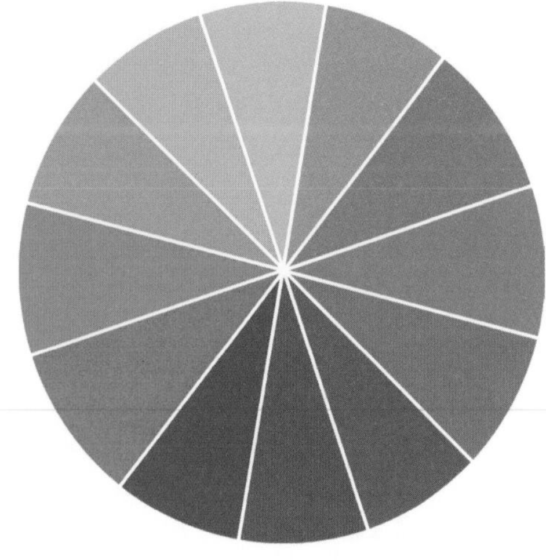

Primary colors

Red, blue, and yellow are known as the primary colors. They cannot be created by mixing any other colors. When two primary colors are mixed together, they can produce every other color (depending on the pairings.) In digital terms, mixing paint is a case of interlacing colored pixels at different percentages.

Secondary colors

The secondary colors are green, purple, and orange. They are created by mixing the primary colors, as follows: yellow + blue = green, blue + red = purple, and red + yellow = orange. The secondary colors can be seen on the color wheel above, between their respective primary colors.

Tertiary colors

The tertiary colors are yellow-orange, red-orange, red-purple, blue-purple, blue-green and yellow-green. They're created by mixing one primary with one secondary color.

Analogous colors

This term describes groups of three colors which all sit next to one another on the color wheel, for example, yellow, lime green, and green.

Value

This refers to the lightness (more white) or darkness (more black) of a hue (another name for a color). A value is often also referred to as a tone.

Warm and cool

Red, yellow, and orange are associated with the heat of sunlight, fire, and lava, while blue, green, and purple are associated with cooler natural phenomena such as ice, night time, and water. Some people prefer cool colors as they feel calmer, while warm colors convey more energy.

Intensity

Also referred to as "saturation," intensity is the brightness or dullness of a tone. Varying the saturation of colors in an image is a good way of drawing the viewer's attention to a certain part of it—the more vibrant and intense the color, the more significance it has. A gray, dull tone can be used on less important parts of an image.

Complementary colors

The opposite hues on the color wheel are described as complementary, for example, red and green or blue and orange. Using such color schemes can be tricky, but provides the most vibrant contrast. For maximum effect, use a dominant main color, such as blue, then use orange for smaller touches or as a secondary light source.

Color palette

This term describes the collection of colors used in your image. You'll need to limit your palette to two or three main colors to avoid it becoming too chaotic.

LIGHT AND SHADE

Shading can be a bit tricky at first, but it's not as difficult as it seems. It's all about figuring out where the light source is coming from, where it will hit an object, and what shape the shadows will take.

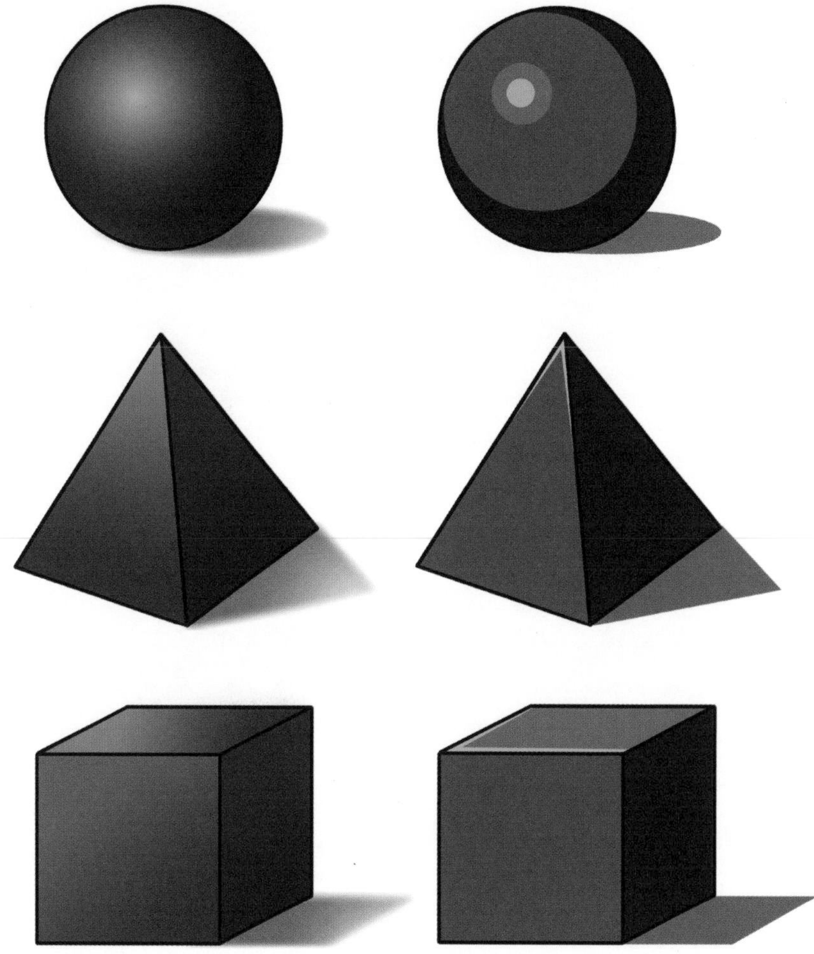

LIGHTING AN OBJECT

Consider the shape of the object from which you are applying a cast shadow. Every shape has its own unique cast. Spheres cast an elliptical shadow, cubes and cylinders cast a rectangular shadow, and pyramids, as you would expect, throw a triangular shadow.

To work out how light hits an object, note how spheres have a gradient shadow—darkening outward from where the light touches the surface. On a cube, light may not reach all the visible sides, resulting in certain planes becoming completely darkened. The top of a pyramid is closer to light from above and is therefore a little lighter than the bottom, though this is only a subtle difference.

CONTRAST

The most effective artworks often make use of maximizing contrast—varying the intensity of certain colors or other elements. The lightest and brightest parts of an image are those you most want to draw the viewer's attention to. With a figure, this might be the eyes or a magical weapon they are holding, for example. If there is to be a setting, the aim is to keep the character as bright as possible, while dulling down the scenery in the background or foreground. The character will then stand out and become a focal point in the image.

Contrast can be created by emphasizing:

- ***Light and dark***
- ***Smooth and rough***
- ***Bright and dull***
- ***Warm and cool***
- ***Blurred and sharp***

RELEVANCE

When you're designing a character's color palette, consider using dark colors such as reds or black for a villain, and lighter shades of blue and white for a hero. Pinks, purples, and pastel tones convey femininity. Pale colors could be used for an unassuming, calm character, while more vibrant colors could be applied to someone more adventurous and extrovert. There may be particular aspects of a character that dictate the color: if, for example, you're designing an Ice Queen, use blue tones and white on her outfit to link in with her cold, frosty theme.

LIGHTING COLORS

Lighting conditions affect the natural colors of objects. It's rare for a sheet of white paper to be pure white, for example. If you take it outside on an overcast day, it'll appear more gray. Indoors, in typical domestic lighting, it'll have a yellow or orange tinge. The color of external lighting may not be something to consider if you're simply putting together a character concept, but it's still a good idea to adjust the hues and tonal variations used for a character or object to make them appear in tune with their environment.

MONOCHROME

Sometimes hues get in the way of understanding the power of values and contrast. Experiment with using just black, white, and gray mid-tones. Many artists practice their lighting knowledge by producing "value studies." These are referenced sketches, drawings, and paintings which help them understand how light works on different shapes, forms, and textures.

In order to create maximum impact, it's important to use a full range of lights and darks. Using more white can be good for showing stronger daytime light or spotlights, while introducing more black can be good for subdued, night-time lighting.

INKING

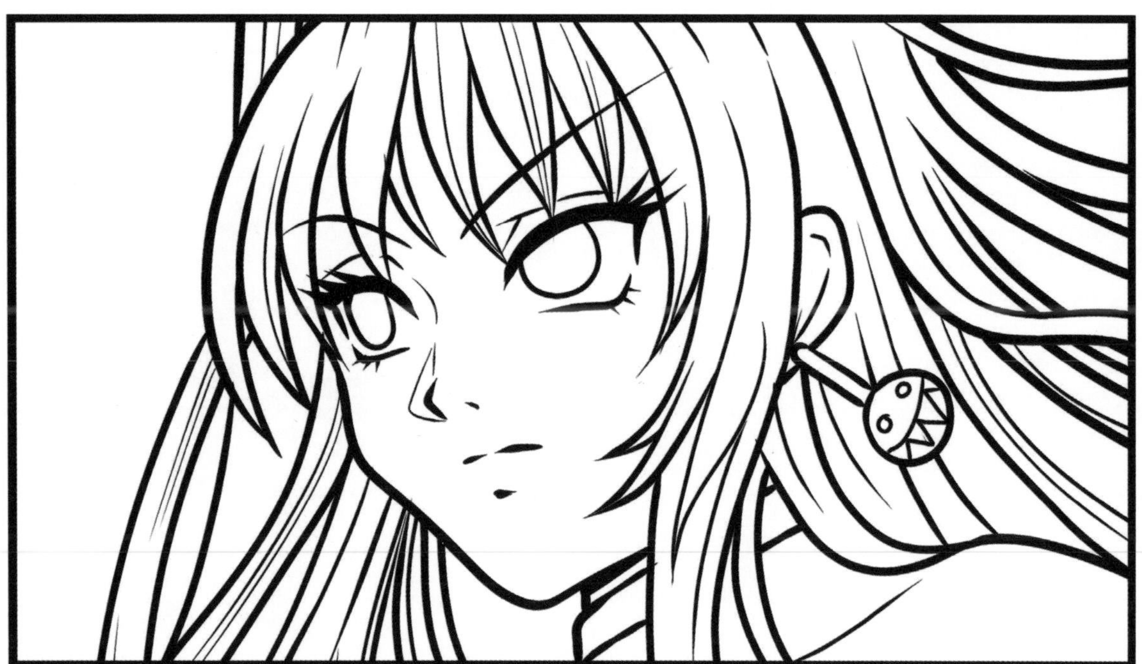

Creating clean black and white art is an important skill that any manga artist needs to master. Most artwork will be drawn with a pencil, then inked on top before being colored or toned. While the pencil works in a similar way to an inking pen, the pen requires much more precision and patience in order to attain smooth, clean lines.

There are two major methods of inking: digitally with the computer, or by hand with pens. Traditional dip pens, or nib pens, use a metal nib mounted on to a handle often made of wood. You simply dip the pen into a pot of ink and draw, pushing harder or varying speeds and angles to produce thicker or finer lines (line weights). Modern-day pens with a continuous ink supply can often rival traditional nibs and brushes in their mark-making; they are a lot easier to control and avoid the risk of ink splattering over a page accidentally.

A mistake that beginners often make is to use only the fingers or wrist during the drawing process. A smooth line needs to be drawn in a continuous arc. Smaller lines may only require moving the fingers slightly, others require pivoting from the wrist, while larger lines need you to lock your fingers and wrist in place while pivoting from the elbow. Using the entire arm increases control and produces straighter, more confident lines.

With a pencil you can take it slow, stroking the lines in gently and building them up to be solid and thicker. However, slowing down too much while inking may result in wobbles and makes it harder to stay on the correct path.

VARYING YOUR LINES

Line weight and thickness are determined by two factors: angle and pressure. For example, using just the tip of a brush pen at a 90-degree angle will create the thinnest line. Decreasing the angle will thicken out the line, as will applying more pressure. This is

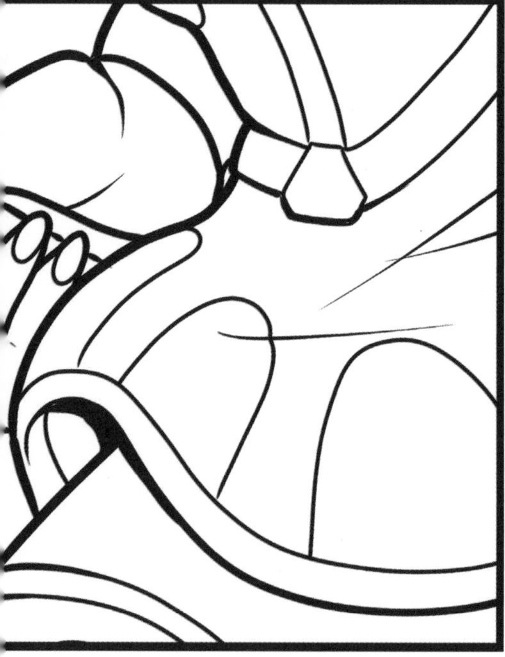

usually true for pencil too, but as the tip becomes dulled fairly fast in a pencil, the point may not be at the exact center. Pencils should be rotated to keep the same thickness and you should avoid over-sharpening them.

As well as arm movement and pressure control, good inking requires planning. Before committing to an inked line, decide where the start and end of the line will be. If it's to be a long, smooth line, rehearse it first and keep the end point in mind while applying the ink. If you are just focused on the tip of your pen it can be easy to go off course, then you have to correct your direction halfway through a line, resulting in a slight kink.

From Sketch to Inking

No matter what type of pen you use, you will need to trace your sketch. Then you can ink the sketch directly, using a soft eraser to rub the pencil lines away once the ink has dried, or you can use a lightbox and trace the picture onto a new piece of paper. This second option might be preferable for the beginner as you don't run the risk of ruining your original sketch. Another alternative is scanning and copying your pencil work, perhaps lightening the line art on the computer before printing it out again to ink.

Once the work is scanned, you can ink it digitally using the computer. I like using PaintTool SAI for that task. Unlike Photoshop, it has a line stabilization feature which helps to prevent wobbles, and it's easy to adjust the pen edge shape and minimum/maximum size of the line while using a pressure-sensitive graphics tablet. However, Photoshop's pen tool does allow you to construct computer-perfect "vector" curves. There are line-smoothing plug-ins and applications available to download and use with most art and design software—Lazy Nezumi is one of these.

DESIGNING THE PAGE

As you continue to hone your technical drawing skills, start to place your characters in their own comic strip or manga story. You'll need to create characters from various angles, draw backgrounds, props, and environments, and maintain consistency so that each panel looks coherent.

Don't waste too much time setting up the story. Ideally, the setup should be so brief that it fits on a few pages or, even better, a few panels.

Try to get to the essence of your story as quickly as possible, and start by illustrating a short story before you launch into an epic series.

Consider writing a script or roughly sketching out the story. It should describe what the scenes for each panel will look like as well as any speech or dialog. The number of panels per page will depend on the scene. Around five is typical, with just one to three panels for more dramatic or action scenes. In general, bigger panels attract more attention than smaller ones, so these should be reserved for important scenes; use the smaller panels to aid the fluency of the story.

HEH
HEH
HEH

PAGE CONSTRUCTION: PLANNING

So you have a story in mind, you know the genre and world it will be set in, and you have an idea about who will play the main roles and how their lives will pan out.

I've decided to draw an encounter between a heroine and a monstrous bad guy. The idea is to create a scene that communicates on multiple levels—I want to show that while it may seem risky for a girl to walk around in monster country, this particular girl is one you don't mess with! The panels or frames need to be read in an obvious, systematic order. Typically, the first panel should set the scene, while the last one should show its outcome.

Before starting on page layouts, it helps if you draw the main cast. You might decide to illustrate the characters from multiple angles or with different facial expressions. Since I'll just be working on a small strip, a single standalone design is sufficient.

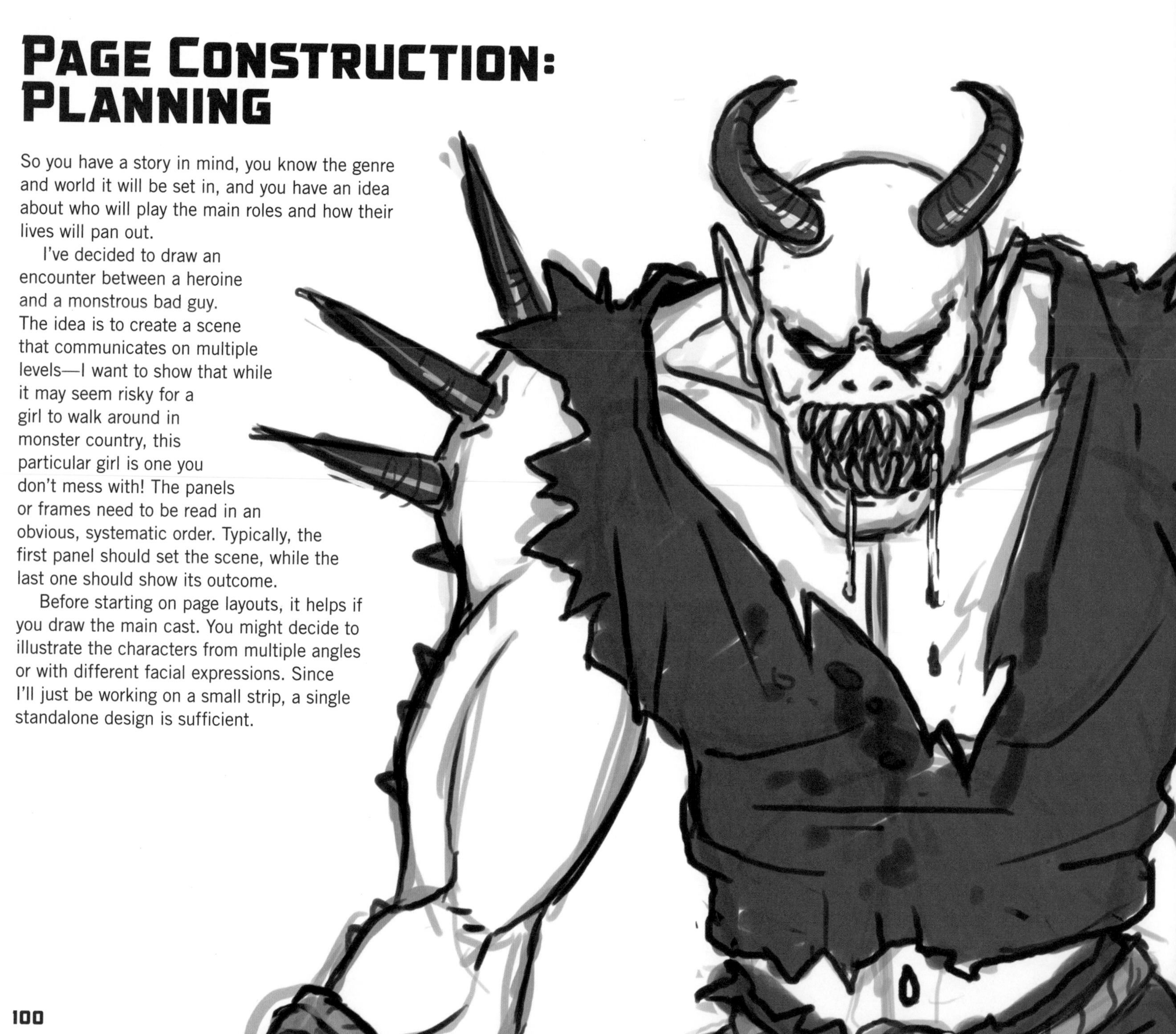

▲ *Thumbnail sketches and/ or a script are an important part of the planning process. Sketch out a rough plan before committing time to a detailed series of drawings. I often try to make panels or character elements overlap, and use different sizes of panel to create a dynamic and interesting layout.*

◀ *If I'm not sure about a certain angle or pose, I might try out some variations before deciding on the best one to use.*

PAGE CONSTRUCTION: PENCIL AND INK

Some artists make neat pencil marks, while others do looser sketches, building up page elements, planning out proportions and layouts, or drawing and redrawing frames. You may wish to retrace your work if it starts becoming untidy or you may simply want to use an eraser to keep the page tidy and to ensure that your audience can read it easily once the line work is refined.

My advice is to make your pencil work as neat as possible in your early projects. Using a pen is a process of finalizing a line or committing new details to enhance your image, so use the pencil stage to try flourishes you've not tested out before.

ADDING INK

The use of a range of line weight, hatching, or feathering to suggest light and shade is perhaps not as widespread in manga as in Western comics. A lot of manga keeps line work super-fine and uses gray tones to add emphasis to certain parts of the image.

In these pages, I haven't shown a light source with the inking. I would ordinarily do this by adding block shadow or hatching where the light doesn't reach, while making the lines thinner the nearer they are to the light source. I have thickened the lines around the outside of the characters and objects closest to the viewer to give more depth and focus. If you don't intend to tone or color your manga pages, this step will definitely give them a more professional look and help make them easier to read.

PAGE CONSTRUCTION: GRAY TONES

Most Japanese manga uses gray or "screen" tones. These are gray shades or textures laid on top of an image; they can be applied fairly quickly to give the artwork an extra sense of depth and detail. Some manga uses these tones quite sparingly, perhaps with a basic flat shade overlay here and there; other manga uses a range of different gradients, patterns, and textures on each page, while etching away highlights from the flat or shaded gray tones to produce a white light source.

Traditionally, screen tones are cut to size with a knife and applied using an adhesive sheet on top of the artwork, but today nearly all manga uses digital techniques to add tone in a fraction of the time.

Here I've used a range of basic tones for my manga pages. This was mainly to add contrast between the characters and the background.

PAGE CONSTRUCTION: COLOR PAGES

You might decide to skip the gray tone and go straight to color for maximum effect. This allows you to concentrate a little more on form and lighting, as with previous examples in the book. Note that I've used lighter tones for the girl to help show she's the heroine, while the bad guy is in dark brown. Red and orange are used on the action line panel backgrounds to help create a sense of danger and drama.

Even though the scene reads pretty well, I decided to add a few speech bubbles and effects to make it clear that the monster isn't simply asking the girl for directions!

NARRATIVE TIPS

Think about pacing. It's fine to have some static pages where characters are conversing, but limit these or try to find ways to make them interesting.

Try to leave as many pages as possible on a cliffhanger. You want to make your reader eager to turn the page to see what happens next. For example, a chance encounter with a monstrous bad guy on page 1 creates tension. How will the girl deal with this? Will she get eaten or injured, or will she have a few tricks up her sleeve? If so, what might they be? Page 2 gives the answer!

RAAAARHHH!!!!
CHIK
HI-YAH!
URGGGHH...

CREATING CHARACTERS

There are endless possibilities for creating characters and it can be fun just to start doodling ideas and seeing where it takes you. Alternatively, you can decide beforehand what type of character you want to create.

You should experiment with as many styles, poses, angles, and personality types as you can. Try to focus on just one element of your concept, such as a weapon or outfit. As your confidence grows, you can tackle both an interesting pose and a complex outfit design, along with some detailed rendering and coloring.

Manga has such a diverse range of genres that it's impossible to demonstrate every type of character you might find, but you are most likely to encounter archetypes such as:

- School students (as featured in *Deathnote*, *GTO*, *Azumanga Daioh*)
- Samurai and ninjas (*Naruto*, *Rouroni Kenshin*, *Bleach*, *Lone Wolf* and *Cub*)
- Maids or nurses (*Hand Maid May*, *Welcome to Pia Carrot*, *Maid Sama*)
- Giant robots (*Macross*, *Gundam*, *Neon Genesis Evangelion*)
- European fantasy (*Berserk*, *Full Metal Alchemist*, *Hellsing*, *Attack on Titan*)
- Monsters (*Pokemon*, *Digimon*, *Yu-gioh*, *Bakugan*)
- Magical girls (*Sailor Moon*, *Cardcaptor Sakura*)
- Fight themes (*Dragon Ball Z*, *Fist of the North Star*, *One Punch Man*, *Street Fighter*)

QUICK SKETCHES

Generating an initial rough or thumbnail drawing is a good way to start as it allows you to plan out a framework for your drawing before committing more time to a final piece. These initial sketches can be messy or reasonably neat, depending on how you like to work. You might just want to use the opportunity to plan out a pose or gesture or work out a detail on the outfit.

Use this opportunity to try out new style ideas. By tweaking the eyes or hair or exaggerating proportions, you can add realistic, cartoon or other comic-book elements and experiment with different ways of representing people.

USING A SKETCHBOOK

Keep a sketchbook or rough paper handy for jotting down ideas or practicing your drawing whenever you have free time—traveling on public transport, waiting for an appointment, chilling in front of the TV, or sitting in a park or coffee shop. Make sure each page is filled with as many concepts and practice sketches as you can fit in.

FINDING IDEAS

When creating characters, there are an infinite amount of ideas to explore. Hyung-Tae Kim, one of my favorite game artists, uses fashion magazines for outfit inspiration, while Masamune Shirow, another favorite of mine, turns to nature and insects for many of his robot and mecha-inspired designs.

While it's great to be inspired by comics, movies, and games, you should avoid simply rehashing someone else's idea. But there's no harm in surrounding yourself with things you think are cool and inspirational. I love checking out the latest sci-fi blockbusters or video games and creating something like that in my own style.

I source character poses from the internet, magazines, photos, and real life. There are sites on the internet that offer 3D character models in hundreds of different poses which can be rotated in different angles. You can use these as a base for your design if you are finding it difficult to draw poses from your imagination. Some artists can construct a figure using a mental library of previously drawn poses, or rely on basic anatomical knowledge. I prefer loosely basing character poses on photos. Here are a few quick concept sketches I created.

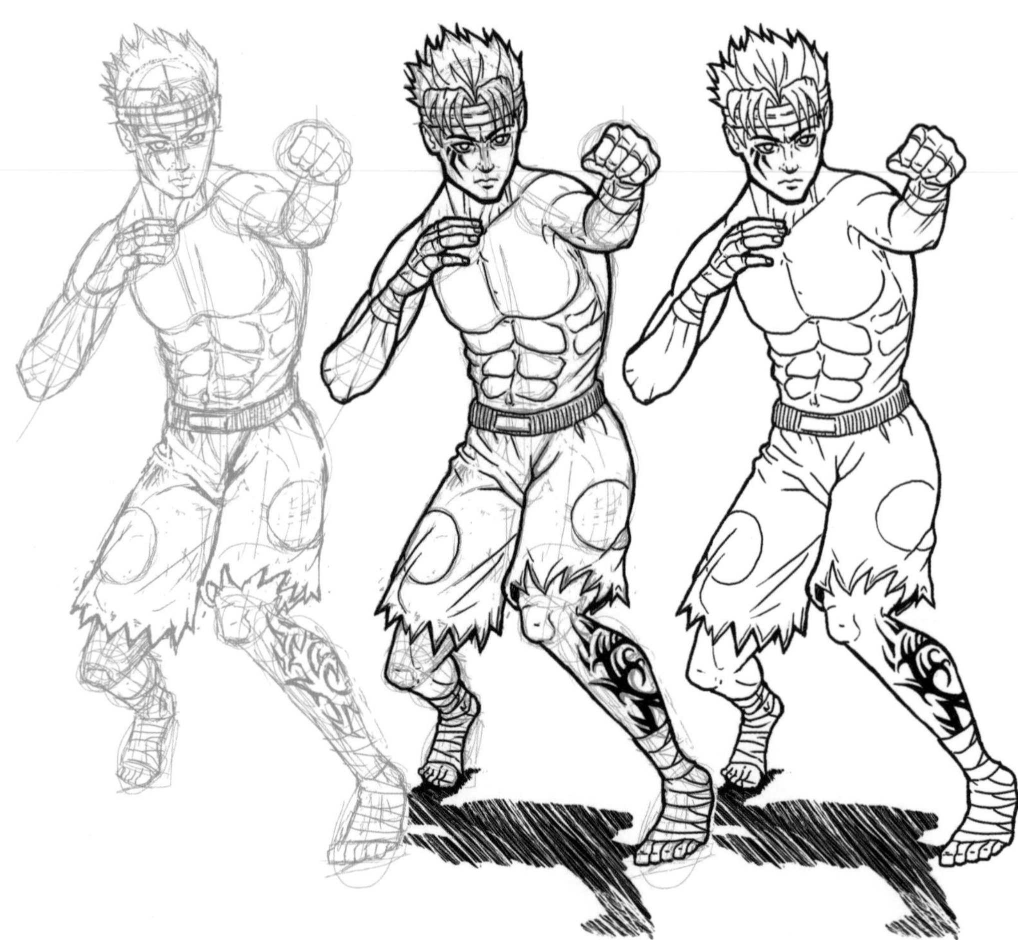

You might find a guy like this in one of the *shonen* martial arts mangas or fighting video games. I usually sketch out art using a light gray or blue, then refine it by using black on a separate layer above. I can then delete the sketchier layer beneath, to leave me with a nice neat drawing minus the initial construction lines.

This cyber-armored girl's pose was based on a simple 3D character model. It's a little more lively than a straightforward standing pose. I filled it in with some gray tones, keeping her armor pretty dark compared to her face.

This gynoid (female robot) character is loosely based on the manga star Astroboy. I wanted to show her in a seductive sitting pose and used foreshortening on her leg to create a dynamic perspective. Sometimes I work straight on the computer, using a black or gray brush like this.

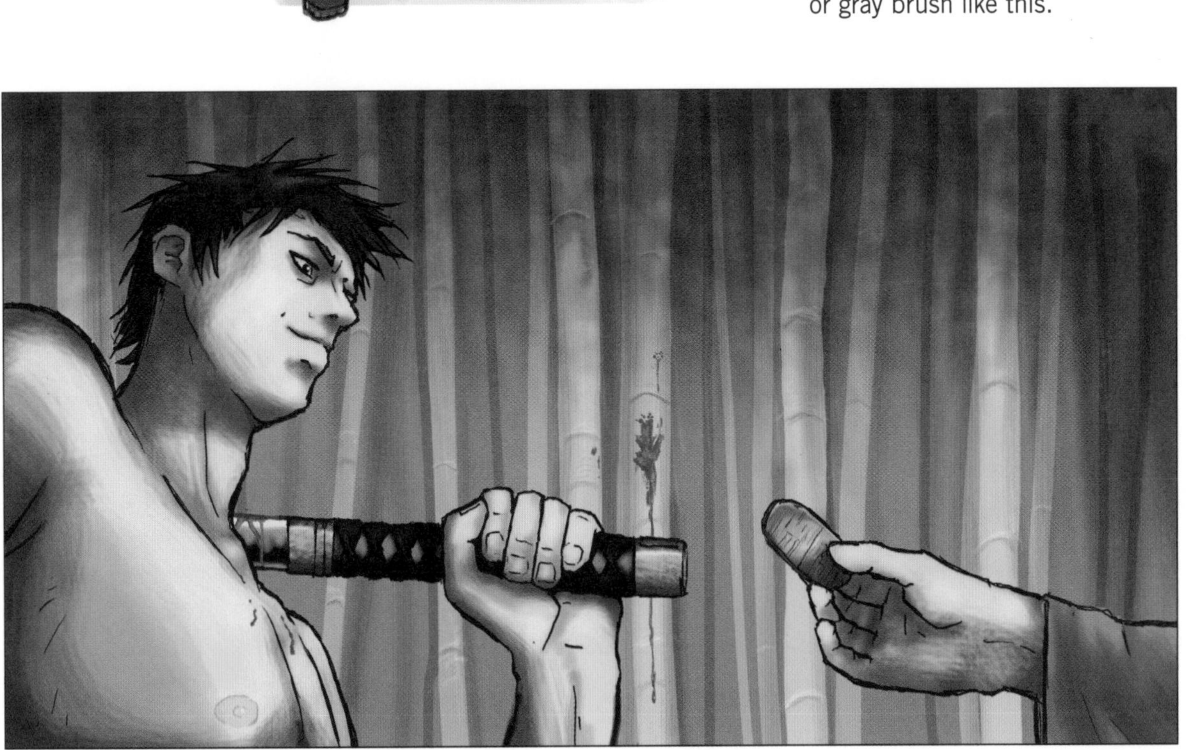

The lone warrior is paid for doing someone else's dirty work. This sketch was given a quick dash of color. I use a tablet sketch like this when I want to experiment with a few basic color tones before moving on to a more polished version.

CHARACTER DESIGN BASICS

When designing a character from scratch, it can be hard to know where to start. I advise thinking of a theme or feature that the character will represent and making it bold and exaggerated. From there on, it's a case of deciding how best to design your character to serve a purpose, compared to doodling generic figures and hoping something evolves from that (although this process can be fun too!)

ICE WIZARD

This character is an intellectual who spends his time researching and educating himself about spells and such. I want him to be physically capable, but he is unlikely to spend all day training and sculpting a heavy weapon-wielding physique. If he's a master rather than an apprentice, he's likely to be older and confident in his abilities, so an upright, shoulders-back, relaxed stance would suit. If he's a goodie, a calm and relaxed demeanor works better than a manic look! Consider what kind of environment and world he'll be based in. Maybe a *Lord of the Rings* type fantasy setting or perhaps something a little more unconventional and modern. If the latter, how would a spell-caster operate in a modern setting?

The setting can determine his personality and outfit style. As he's icy, blue and white clothing is an obvious indicator of his purpose; or you could cover his body in ice-proof material to protect him from being frozen by his own spells. A spell book or potion accessories also suggest his role.

Remember to consider:

- ***Physique and age***
- ***Personality—facial expression and pose***
- ***Outfit and accessories***

Here's a quick colored tablet sketch along the lines described. You can see how I started with a sketchy drawing, which I refined a little more, adding in some basic colors.

DRAWING STYLE

Style is something that develops over the course of an artist's career. It also stems from the many influences the artist has absorbed during his or her life. As far as line work goes, you might like a sketchy look for your characters, or you may prefer neater outlines and smooth shading, as I do.

The way you proportion your characters and the flourishes you add to your image will vary dramatically from artist to artist. This is what determines the style of an image. Manga art can be broken down into hundreds of sub-genres and pseudo-manga styles, but there are always tell-tale signs of its Japanese origins, be they the thin line weights, the shape of the eyes and nose, the hair, the pose or outfit theme. So, if I wanted to draw the Ice Wizard in a more child-friendly "chibi" style, he might look something like the version shown here. Basically it's a case of simplifying his features, enlarging the head and shrinking the body to produce a squished-down version.

MAGICAL GIRL

The magical girl manga sub-genre features school-age kids who typically gain supernatural powers through a magical object or sceptre. To illustrate how outfit and accessories can give a generic figure an identity and purpose, I decided to create a female character and start with a back story to explain her persona. She's Hana (meaning flower in Japanese), a shy, retiring schoolgirl who tries her best but doesn't have many friends. One day she goes for a walk in the woods and discovers a magic sceptre hidden in the undergrowth which transforms her into a super-powered hero! The sceptre makes her confident, outgoing, and energetic, so I've started by drawing a typical manga girl leaping through the air. Next I've styled her clothes on a petal theme and given her a flower-like scepter.

I've assigned her an earth element and, to suggest that she gains her power through nature, I've colored her in greens and browns.

Often the mark of a good character is its silhouette. This should be obvious and easily identifiable. If you are creating a cast of characters, try drawing just silhouettes to start with. When the characters are assembled, make sure each silhouette can be distinguished from the others.

ALTERNATE VIEWS

When designing a character, it's a good idea to consider how it appears from different angles. This example shows the front and back of a figure. Side and three-quarter angles are also useful for helping to get a fuller understanding of how your character works as a whole.

THUMBNAILS

Sketch some small, speedy roughs before attempting a more finalized drawing. These can be used to see how certain poses, features, and elements might look when translated from brain to canvas.

MEDIEVAL WARRIOR

While traditional samurai feature in numerous Japanese stories, many manga and video game fans are equally keen on European-style medieval fantasy warriors such as those featured in *Claymore, Berserk* or *Record of Lodoss War*. The fantasy genre was first introduced to modern audiences by authors such as Tolkien in his *Lord of the Rings* books, which were based on Norse and German mythology. Where fantasy worlds are concerned, you can't go wrong with knights, elves, and magicians! Here I've drawn a female knight, giving her a dynamic crouching pose, a foreshortened sword and wind-blown wavy hair to add movement. Green, brown, and yellow help to communicate her connection with nature, while the gold trim denotes a high rank.

After planning the outfit, I drew some thumbnail sketches to help decide on a pose, then drew over the top of my preferred sketch to refine the design.

JAPANESE NURSE

In the fictional world of manga, oversized instruments or accessories are often used. A syringe, scissors or perhaps a scalpel would fit with someone working in the medical profession; if you were drawing a mechanic they might be holding an oversized wrench or spanner; an artist might hold a super-large pencil or brush. I wanted to give this character a short back-story, which I could then consider when planning further scenes.

Name: Miyu Kitagawa, age 21

Likes: Sushi, marshmallows, cosplay, taking care of patients, and delivering good service

Dislikes: Viruses, diseases, and germs

Bio: She recently started work at a newly opened hospital in Tokyo and shares a small apartment with two friends. She's kind-hearted and always aims to help her patients while putting a smile on their faces. She can be clumsy, though, and tends to knock and spill things and trip over, which causes patients, staff, and visitors to jump out of her way to avoid being stabbed by her syringe! She's cute, but potentially dangerous.

ALTERNATING COLORS

Before coloring your inked line work, consider making copies. This will allow you to experiment with color combinations or shading before committing to a final image. If you're working digitally, try out new color combos after you've finished rendering by changing the hues of different layers.

MANGA MONSTERS

A lot of the monsters featured in *Pokemon* are based on existing animals such as birds, reptiles, and various land-dwelling mammals, so consider using real-life species as a starting point when you are developing a new type of creature. I wanted to create a character that was insect-like, but also aquatic—a waterbug type.

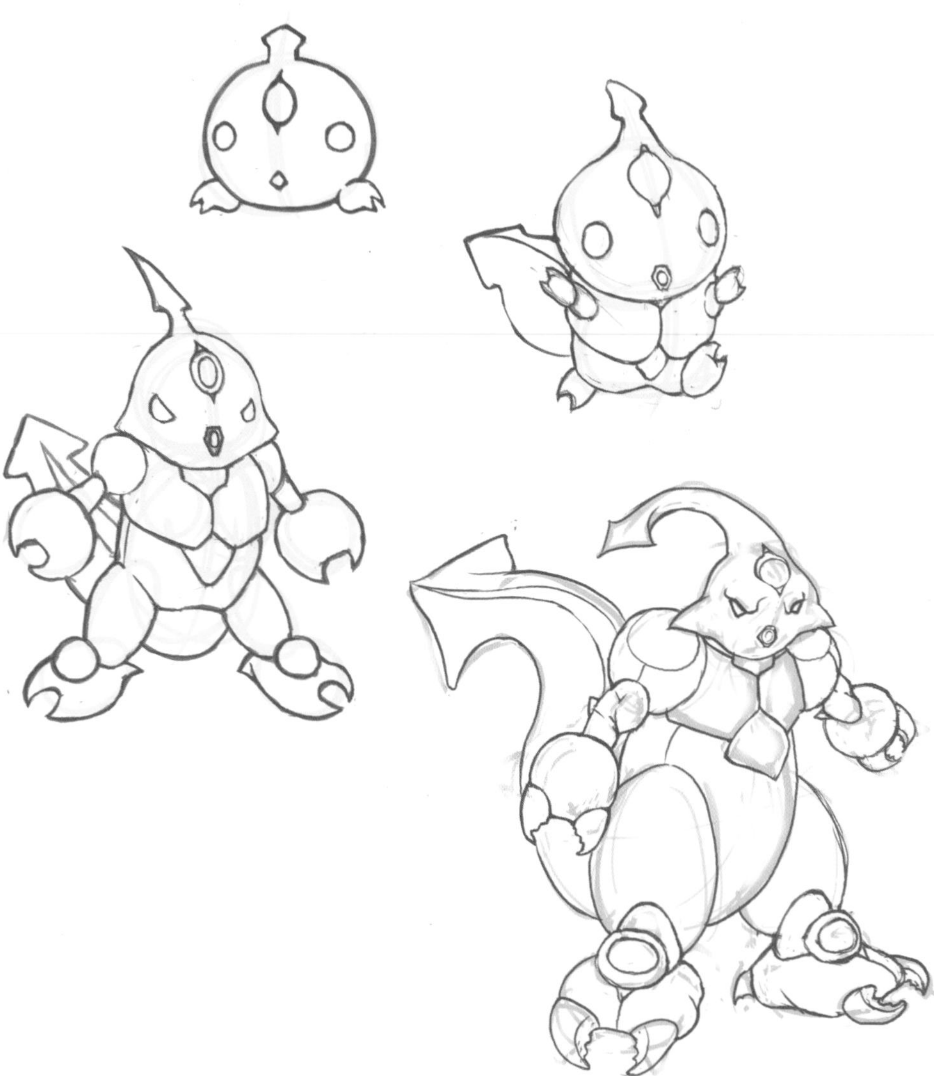

Likes: Water, challenging other creatures, blue-colored things such as blueberries and the sky

Dislikes: Fire and heat, ice and snow, high places, losing fights

Bio: This is a sektar. Sektars live in large lakes and rivers, feeding on small fish and water weeds. They can be over-confident, wanting to battle larger enemies; but sometimes they lose, having bitten off more than they can chew. They are moderately intelligent despite their drive to rush into dangerous situations which can get them into trouble. They lay eggs which hatch and evolve through four incarnations, increasing their power level as they gain battle experience. The more they grow, the stronger and more confident they become.

Special powers:

- Bug Bite—using his powerful pincers to nip at his foes
- Water Blast—spitting a jet of water from his mouth to push enemies aside
- Tail Stomp—hammering his tail on the floor, creating a vibration frequency capable of shocking an opponent's nervous system and freezing them in their tracks

EVOLUTION OF A SEKTAR

Perhaps they have a fifth stage of evolution. What might that look like?

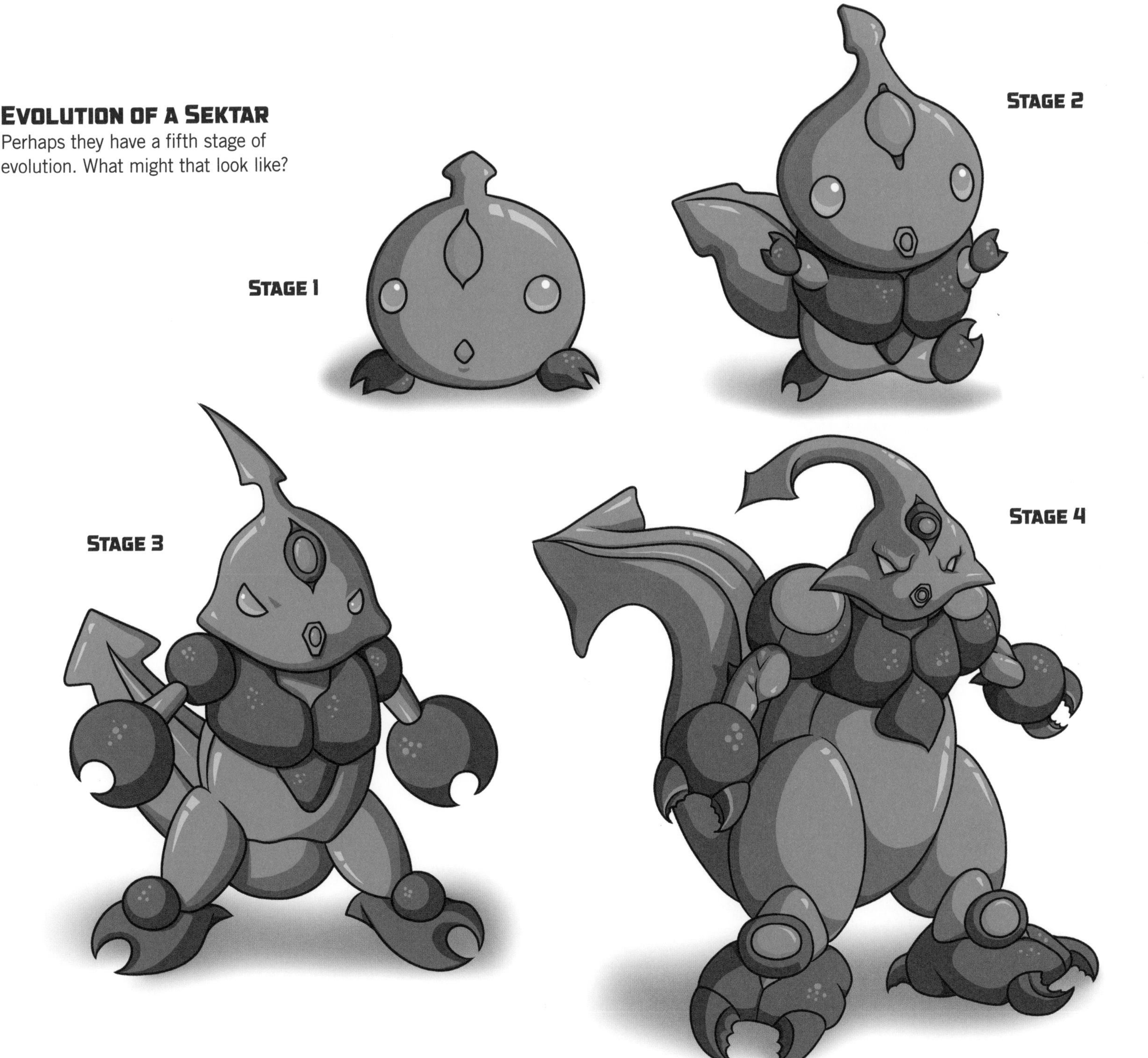

CREATING A MECHA

Manga robots, or mecha, are humanoid-looking or mechanical and tank-like, or somewhere in between. Most of the time they are designed for combat purposes, fighting against armies, aliens, monsters or other mecha. They can be the same size as an average human or they can be giants that tower over cities.

BACK STORY

This is Unit 56A01, otherwise known as Novas Arma, a creation of the military-funded AMP (Assault Mech Project) organization. In 2085 AMP was assigned the task of developing prototype technologies to defend Earth's inhabitants from a race of hostile alien invaders.

While the war between Earth and the aliens raged for a few years, AMP began development and manufacture of their weapons to assist the planet's defense force. However, their production facility was attacked and destroyed by the aliens before Arma was ready for testing. Due to the dire situation of the Earth's defense force, it was decided that Arma be deployed into battle straightaway.

This new mecha proved effective in battle against the aliens, although excessive heat build-up caused it to experience sudden power shortages if in use for more than 30 minutes; this left the unit vulnerable to attack.

With a new wave of alien adversaries on their way, Arma is Earth's only hope for survival. Will AMP be able to build a new production facility to make improvements to Arma's power systems before the aliens arrive?

ARMAMENTS

Novus Arma carries two powerful pulse-beam hand guns so that it can fire at multiple enemies simultaneously without the need for heavy machine guns or rifles; this also makes it fast and maneuverable. It has twin missile cannons mounted to the rear for extra firepower. AG (anti-gravity) boosters attached to the waist enable mid-air combat.

DIGITAL COLOR DRAWING

Traditional pen and ink are rapidly being replaced by, or combined with, graphics software, which allows artists to experiment with color and new techniques without the mess, expense and extra time demanded by conventional methods.

Photoshop is a graphics software application created in the early 1990s and designed for photographers and image editors. Today, artists and designers from all backgrounds, including most of those working in the comic-book, movie, and video-game industry, use Photoshop as a creative tool.

TECHNOLOGY BASICS

The interfaces (layouts) for most software programs are similar to one another. They allow users to select tools and layers and to adjust tool settings with ease. It takes time to learn the basics of any given application. I suggest first exploring the various menus, settings, and tools to see what they do.

Familiarize yourself with the many features of the program before giving yourself a small project to complete—in this case, "draw and color a female face."

Along with your software of choice, it's a good idea to purchase a graphics tablet, which gives you much more accuracy than a mouse. You'll need a scanner, a printer, and a good-quality monitor; a computer to plug it all into helps, of course! Most modern desktop computers and laptops should be able to run the graphics software available. If you work with larger files for print, consider purchasing a high-spec computer with a speedy processor, lots of RAM, and a solid-state hard disk for quick file access.

With digital art, you have unlimited canvases, paints, brushes, and materials at your fingertips. With a little practice, you'll be able to create super-slick artwork again and again.

THE JOYS OF DIGITAL

- ▶Unlimited canvases, paints, brushes, and other materials at your fingertips
- ▶ Minimal cost (after the initial outlay on equipment)
- ▶ The ability to save your work at different stages and go back to edit it
- ▶ The ability to achieve super-flat colors and precise gradients
- ▶ The use of textured overlays means you can instantly change the look of your artwork
- ▶ You can upload and share artwork on the internet
- ▶ You can easily print and reproduce your work
- ▶ The software can help artists with unsteady hands; short-sighted people can zoom in on their work
- ▶ Perfect lines and curves are possible!
- ▶ Resizing, duplicating, or repositioning parts of your artwork is easy
- ▶ You can UNDO at any time!

HARDWARE

If you're starting out in the world of digital art, it's important to know about the hardware you need before delving into the intricacies of Photoshop.

To begin with, all you require is a mid-range computer, monitor, keyboard, and mouse. But if you've got some cash to spend and want to make the most of your digital coloring, it's a good idea to invest in a high-end PC or Apple Mac. Photoshop is a very resource-hungry program and a high-spec system helps to avoid it crashing or slowing down when you're working with large files.

Many industry professionals, especially those involved in graphic design, use Apple Macs, which generally perform better and look nicer than a typical PC set-up. However, PCs with the same internal specifications as Macs are usually a lot cheaper and are what most home users own. My advice is just to use a computer you're familiar with, whichever type that may be. High-end laptop specs can now compete with those of desktop computers.

PHOTOSHOP CC RECOMMENDED COMPUTER SPECIFICATIONS

Windows

- Intel® Core 2 or AMD Athlon® 64 processor; 2GHz or faster processor
- Microsoft Windows 7 with Service Pack 1, Windows 8.1, or Windows 10
- 2GB or more of RAM (8GB recommended)
- 2.6GB or more of available hard disk space for 32-bit installation; 3.1GB or more of available hard disk space for 64-bit installation; additional free space required during installation
- 1024 x 768 display (1280 x 800 recommended) with 16-bit color and 512MB or more of dedicated VRAM; 2GB is recommended
- OpenGL 2.0-capable system

Mac OS

- Multicore Intel processor with 64-bit support
- Mac OS version 10.13 (High Sierra), Mac OS version 10.12 (Sierra), or Mac OS X version 10.11 (El Capitan)
- 2GB or more of RAM (8GB recommended)
- 4GB or more of available hard disk space for installation; additional free space required during installation
- 1024 x 768 display (1280 x 800 recommended) with 16-bit color and 512MB or more of dedicated VRAM; 2GB is recommended
- OpenGL 2.0-capable system

COMPUTER COMPONENT FACTS

Before you go out and buy the best computer you can find or upgrade components on your current one, there are some things you need to consider.

First, not all CPUs (central processing units) are what you might expect—a higher model number doesn't always mean better performance. For example, an Intel Core i5 might perform better than an i7 processor. Whenever I'm about to purchase a new computer system or processor, I like to see how it compares with other computer specs. Checking out CPU benchmark tests on the internet is a good way of determining how well your computer will perform.

It's also desirable to have a big (at least 1TB), fast (at least a 64MB cache) hard drive to store and access all your files. If, like me, you use a solid-state hard drive, this is even better for fast loading times.

For most Photoshop work, a high-end gaming graphics card isn't necessary and won't make your art look better or help Photoshop run significantly faster. When it comes to selecting a graphics processor (GPU), I recommend you research the price of both top- and bottom-end cards and go for something in between, with OpenGL support. A decent GPU should help on those occasions when you're loading, rendering or previewing resource-hungry Photoshop filters such as Blur and Liquify.

RAM

The more RAM you have, the better; this will help you to work on larger file sizes as it will reduce loading and lag time when using tools and processes, and potentially avoid the program crashing or freezing.

Photoshop allows you to customize how it uses RAM and other hardware resources (see page 136).

32- AND 64-BIT PROCESSORS

Older computers may use a 32-bit processor and/or run a 32-bit version of the operating system. On a Windows machine, Photoshop CS6 installs both a 32- and 64-bit version of the software. If you have a 32-bit computer you'll only be able to access up to 3.2GB of RAM on your machine and CPU operations will run approximately 10 per cent slower.

Photoshop version	*Windows version*	*Maximum amount of RAM Photoshop can use*
32-bit	32-bit	1.7GB
32-bit	64-bit	3.2GB
64-bit	64-bit	as much RAM as you can fit on your computer

On a Mac, Photoshop CS6 installs in 64-bit mode only. If you have a 32-bit Mac and OS, you need to install a version of Photoshop earlier than CS6 to run it, and you will then be limited by the amount of computer memory you can access.

Basically, if you are able to run 64-bit, go for it! The only time I switch to 32-bit is to access my TWAIN scanner, as it will only work fully with 32-bit versions of Photoshop. It's important to note that 32-bit plug-ins and filters installed in Photoshop will only work when the 32-bit version of Photoshop runs; similarly, the 64-bit version is needed to run 64-bit plug-ins and filters.

WORKSPACE

I've been using the hardware set-up below for a while now, since switching from a desktop to a laptop computer.

Pink *= monitor*

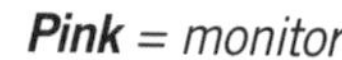

Purple *= laptop/computer/ second monitor*

Red *= wireless keyboard*

Yellow *= graphics tablet*

Green *= padded mouse mat*

Blue *= wireless mouse*

Monitor

Look out for a good-quality high-definition monitor. Flat LCD and LED screens are the norm these days, but prices vary hugely with the top-end displays ten times more expensive than those at the lower end. The screen you use can make all the difference, so don't try to save money by getting a cheap one as colors and tones simply won't look right. I typically work with a dual-view set-up with two monitors, which allows me to use one screen for my main canvas and another screen for Photoshop's tools, palettes and tabs (see pages 136–141).

Printer

If you want to print your work, a decent inkjet photo printer with good-quality photo paper should produce satisfactory results. I have an Epson A3+ printer with six different inks that can be changed individually, instead of replacing a multi-color cartridge. If I need hard copies for clients, for my portfolio or for prints to sell, I tend to go to my local print bureau to get a top-quality result.

Scanner

A flatbed scanner is an essential piece of equipment for any digital artist. I use a Plustek A3 scanner with 1600 x 1600 dots per inch (dpi) scan resolution and 48-bit color depth, which suits my needs perfectly. Regular A4-sized document/ photo scanners are a lot more affordable, but will require you to scan your work in multiple parts before digitally stitching them together (see page 155).

GRAPHIC TABLETS

Once you've become familiar with some basic coloring techniques, try ditching the mouse in place of a graphics tablet (consisting of a pen-like stylus and surface). Not only will it help with precision cursor movements and allow true, freehand CG-ing, it will speed up the coloring process.

TABLET TIPS

Tablet pens often come with a choice of nibs—regular plastic, spring-loaded or fiber. You need to set up your pen according to your own preference. I like a nib that creates a degree of friction on the tablet surface so that the tip doesn't slide about in an uncontrolled way. A plastic nib will last quite a while before it needs replacing, although I prefer the feel of the fiber nib when using a Cintiq.

When setting up your tablet, you can customize your preferences via the Properties menu. I have the tilt sensitivity set to normal and pressure sensitivity at 20% soft, since I don't like to press down on my pen too hard. I leave the double-click distance in the middle. Just experiment until you discover what suits you best.

Tablet buttons can be customized. I set the front button (closest to the nib) as my eraser as this saves time flipping the pen upside down whenever I want to erase. I set the back button to right-click. So far as mapping goes, using the full surface area is fine most of the time, but if I'm working with a dual view set-up with two displays side by side I tend to map just the bottom 50%. This ensures that the mapped area fits in a more proportional ratio with the display surface and the pen cursor travels at the same speed both horizontally and vertically. If mapping is left to the full area, the cursor tends to travel more slowly vertically and faster horizontally.

WHAT SHOULD I BUY?

To start with, you could buy one of the cheaper tablets and see how you like it before investing in a pricier model. Brands such as Aiptek, Genius, and DigiPro have a good range of tablets, but Wacom have built up a solid reputation for tablet technology and most professional digital artists couldn't imagine working without one.

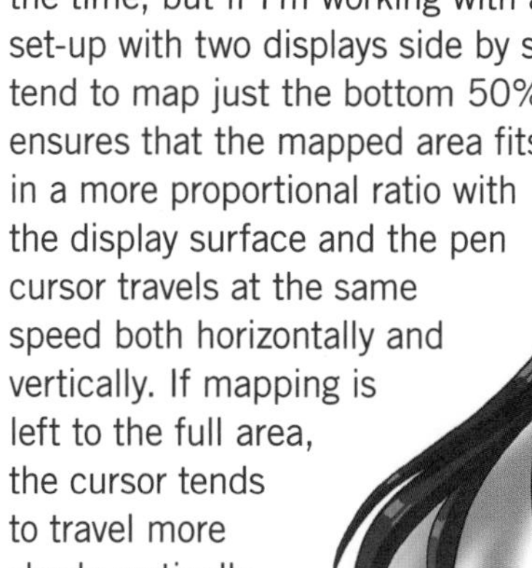

INTRODUCTION TO PHOTOSHOP

When I first started using the computer to color my line art, I didn't appreciate that it would take practice and knowledge to get the results I wanted. I hoped that Photoshop would instantly make me a better artist, but while it can save time compared to drawing and painting with traditional media, it's important to realize that Photoshop can't do the creative work for you.

THE WORKSPACE

Setting up a workspace to suit your own preference helps to familiarize you with Photoshop's layout of tools and palettes. I generally set up my workspace to look like the images on the page here. If using a dual-view set-up with two monitors, I have my main canvas on the left display in front of me, and the tools and tabs on the screen on the right.

If you don't have much experience using Photoshop, spend time familiarizing yourself with the various options in the Menu bar. Once your workspace is set up, you can save it by clicking the Workspace icon near the top right.

SETTING PREFERENCES

Edit / Photoshop –> Preferences –> General [Ctrl+K / Cmd+K]

I leave the majority of settings as they are. In File Handling, I make sure that "Save in Background" and "Automatically Save Recovery Information" are checked and I set the latter to save every five minutes.

In Performance, I set my RAM usage to 90–95%. This allows Photoshop to make use of all that extra RAM on my machine should I need it and still leaves enough to run background system programs. I allow Photoshop to make use of my hard drives as scratch disks—this means that when the computer does not have enough RAM to perform an operation, it will use the disk as virtual memory.

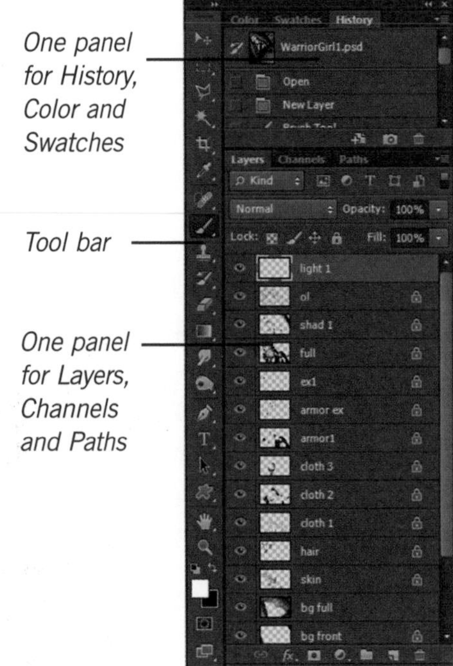

One panel for History, Color and Swatches

Tool bar

One panel for Layers, Channels and Paths

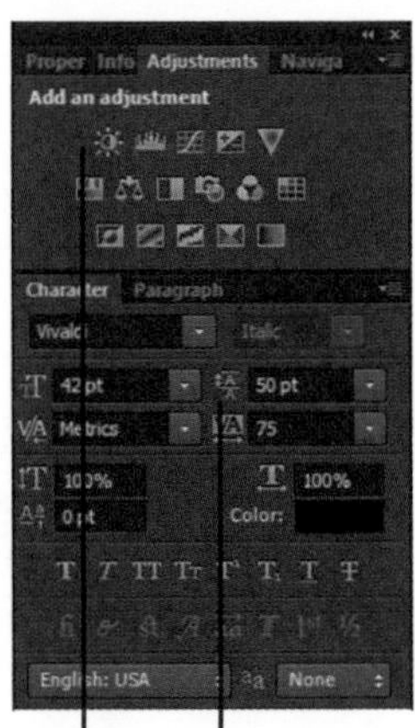

The Adjustments panel is useful, but I prefer using shortcut keys; I usually group this panel with Info and Navigator

Sometimes I have one panel for Character and Paragraph

KEYBOARD SHORTCUTS

Edit –> Keyboard Shortcuts [Alt+Shift+Ctrl+K / Opt+Shift+Cmd+K]

Undo is one of the most useful shortcut keys. By default, Photoshop's Ctrl+Z / Cmd+Z toggles between the Undo and Redo commands. I prefer Ctrl+Z to be set as the shortcut key for Step Backwards so that every time I enter Ctrl+Z, my artwork reverts to its previous state. Ctrl+Y is Step Forwards, since I'm accustomed to using Ctrl+Y to Step Forwards with software such as Dreamweaver and Word.

I also like to swap Ctrl+B to Brightness/Contrast and Ctrl+H to Hue/Saturation, as I use these two adjustment tabs more often.

Next on the Keyboard Shortcuts tab you'll notice a tab for Menus. I find it handy to color-code some of the menus I use most often to make it easier to find them while working. For example, under Image –> Adjustments, I make Brightness/Contrast, Hue/Saturation and Replace Color as red, as I use these most often, and I set Levels, Vibrance and Color Balance as orange. Under Select, I'll set Modify and Expand to red, because I use this a lot.

Once you've set any relevant keyboard shortcuts and Menu settings preferences, you can save these by clicking the relevant icon next to Set at the top.

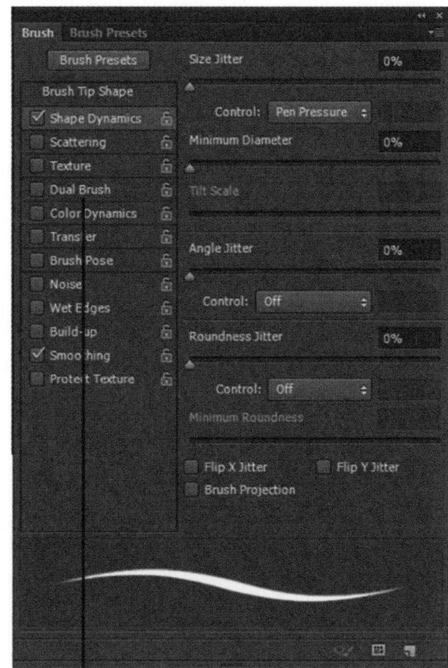

One panel for Brush and Brush Presets (which I keep minimized)

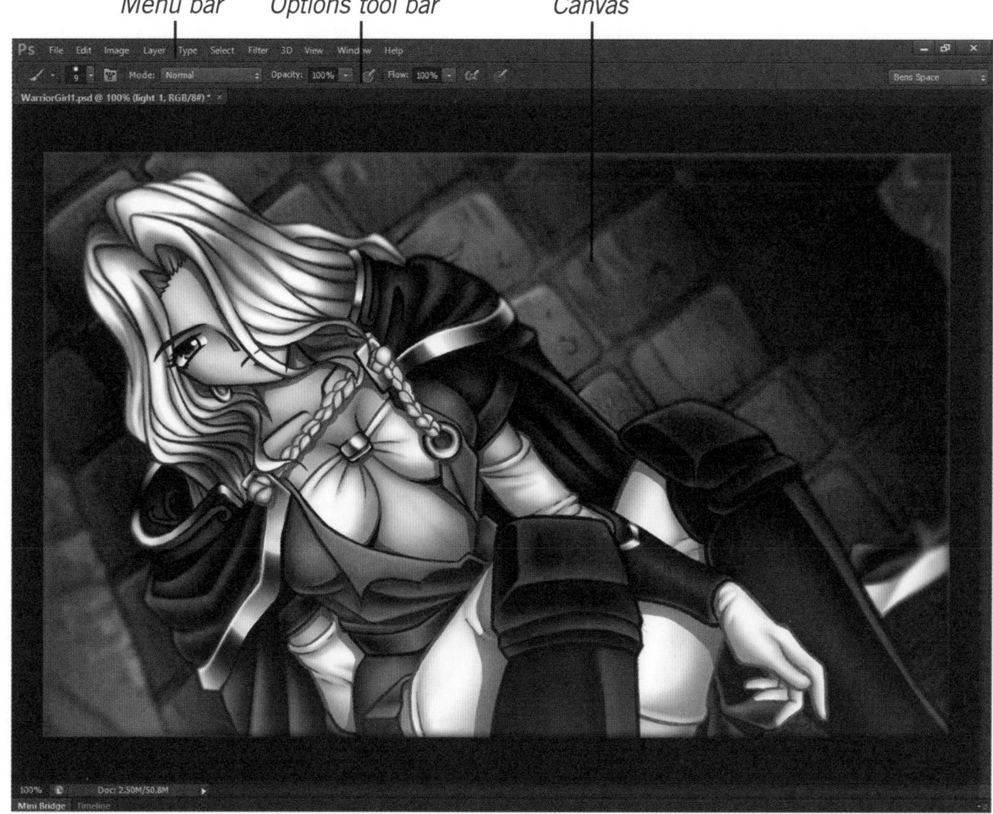

Menu bar
Options tool bar
Canvas

PHOTOSHOP TOOLS

The Tool bar has been consistent in Photoshop and other art and design software for years, so you'll probably be familiar with this type of interface. First, I recommend checking out the Tools overview via the Photoshop Help website (F1). Some of the icons contained in the bar are important, others less so, but the majority can be used for art purposes. To access additional tools, click and hold the cursor on icons with the small triangle in the bottom right-hand corner.

MOVE TOOL (V)

This tool moves selections, layers and painted areas—it's useful if you're copying and pasting parts of an image.

MARQUEE TOOLS (M)

These can be used to select parts of an image or create square borders on completed artwork by filling in the selections. The Elliptical Marquee tool is good for drawing circles—hold down Shift while creating the circle selection to make a perfect circle. To create an outline from your selection, go to Edit -> Stroke (or right-click the selection Stroke) and choose the line width. The color of the line will be the same as the primary color selection, unless you change it.

LASSO TOOLS (L)

As selection tools, Lasso and Polygon Lasso are used a lot for "cuts" and "cel-style" solid tones. The Magnetic Lasso is rarely used for digital art. If you don't have a graphics tablet, you'll spend more time using the Polygon tool, since the Freehand tool can be tricky to use with a mouse. This is one of the three possible tools/methods I choose for laying my initial base tones—after making a selection, I fill it with color. I often amend my selections: if you've made a mistake, instead of starting a new selection, hold down Shift to add extra selections to your initial one—this is a very handy trick to learn. Use the Alt/Opt keys to take away part of a selection. You'll notice the minus and plus symbols next to the cursor as you hold down the keys.

MAGIC WAND TOOL (W)

Don't be fooled by the name, it won't do your art for you! Instead, it creates selections which fill similarly colored areas. I mostly use it when I'm working from clean, inked lines to lay flat base tones. With the wand selected, click the area within your drawing, then go to Select -> Modify -> Expand and select a pixel expansion value. Expanding the selection will avoid a filled flat tone looking scummy round the edges. At the resolution I work at, I'll usually expand an extra 4–8 pixels and make sure my selection doesn't go over the lines. Very thin lines may not work with this method and you may need to add with the other selection tools; that is, by holding Shift and using a Lasso to get at areas the wand can't reach.

CROP TOOL (C)

Use this to trim your finished art, or if your scanned art needs clipping back. You can also use it to expand your canvas.

EYEDROPPER TOOL (I)

I use this tool every time I color to pick tones from my artwork. With the Brush tool selected, hold Alt/Opt so that the brush changes to the Eyedropper (this avoids having to toggle between the Eyedropper and the Brush tool). Other tools in the Eyedropper tab, such as the 3D Material Eyedropper or 123 Count, aren't necessary. However, I do sometimes use the Note tool, which allows me to write reminders of how I want certain elements to look—then I attach the notes to my image file.

HEALING TOOL (J)

Use the Healing tool to repair or retouch images. It is also great for photo-editing and can also be used to fix patterns in texture overlays.

BRUSH TOOL (B)

This is the most frequently visited tool in the bar, used for laying down initial flat tones or rendering those tones. The Brush tool is used in conjunction with the Brush tab to simulate painting with a paintbrush. By adjusting brush settings such as Opacity and Flow, you can make Photoshop simulate an airbrush effect—something I like to use to color my artwork. Brushes can be adjusted to hard for more solid tones or soft for airbrush shading. To keep lines as smooth as possible, set the brush spacing to 1% on the Brush tab. Pencil, Color Replacement and Mixer Brushes aren't necessary for this kind of art.

CLONE STAMP TOOL (S)

This paints with a sampled part of an image. I never use this, nor do I use the Pattern Stamp tool, which paints with a pattern defined from your image, another image, or a preset pattern.

HISTORY BRUSH TOOL (Y)

I seldom use this tool. It makes a copy of the image as it was in a previous state, then uses the content of this copy to paint with.

ERASER TOOL (E)

This tool effectively works like a brush and I turn to it a lot. A good tip is to use it on a locked layer tone so that the secondary color selection is used instead of an area being deleted. It saves time swapping and picking a second color with a brush because I have my tablet pen button (not end) set to eraser.

GRADIENT TOOLS (G)

Don't rely on these instead of an airbrush. I use a Gradient fill for part of a background or color overlay. It's good for filling areas quickly. I use it instead of the Paint Bucket fill tool, which can leave an unwanted thin outline of pixels around certain objects or selections.

BLUR TOOL (R)

You may want to use this occasionally to help blend out unwanted pixels.

SHARPEN TOOL (R)

(The same icon as Blur.) This sharpens the soft edges of an image. I have hardly ever needed it and have never found it particularly effective compared with Sharpen Filters.

SMUDGE TOOL (R)

(The same icon as Blur.) While it's handy for putting a shine on hair or fabric, this tool takes a lot of RAM. If you have set a big Smudge brush size, and you smudge an area for a long time, it may take several minutes before the smudge is fully applied to a high resolution image. Use it sparingly.

DODGE TOOL (O)

I've seen people achieve excellent results with this tool, which lightens a tone progressively the more times you click, but it gives less control than Brushes. If you want to experiment with it, I recommend using it on 50% pressure or less and applying it to mid-tones.

BURN TOOL (O)

(The same icon as Dodge.) The opposite to Dodge, the Burn tool darkens a tone the more you click it. While these can be fun tools to experiment with, using too much Dodge or Burn can often leave artwork looking muddy or over-saturated.

SPONGE TOOL (O)

(The same icon as Dodge.) This alters the amount of "pigment" or saturation on a shaded tone.

PEN TOOLS (P)

Similar to the Polygon Lasso (dot-to-dot style selection), but you have a lot more control over it. Pen tools are often used for digital inking. The Pen allows you to control nodes and curves to create perfect lines. Using the Pen tool takes practice and experience to fully understand how to make the most of it.

TYPE TOOL (T)

For adding text, this tool is usually just employed at post-production stage, for details on a character or building or on top of speech bubbles.

PATH SELECTION TOOLS (A)

You will only use these if you want to move paths created using the Pen tool.

SHAPE TOOLS (U)

These are great to use when working on web sites and graphics, but I don't find them so handy for character art. The most important is the Line tool, which draws straight lines. To create a tapered straight line, click the Arrowheads setting icon on the tool options bar at the top and set the width to 100% and length at around 1000%. Tapered straight lines are great for manga-style action and speed lines. Hold down Shift for vertical or horizontal lines.

HAND TOOL (H)

For moving the canvas—the regular Hand tool works in the same way as holding the spacebar on the keyboard. I tend to use the scroller on my mouse to move up and down an image or I just use the scroll bars on the right and bottom of the window.

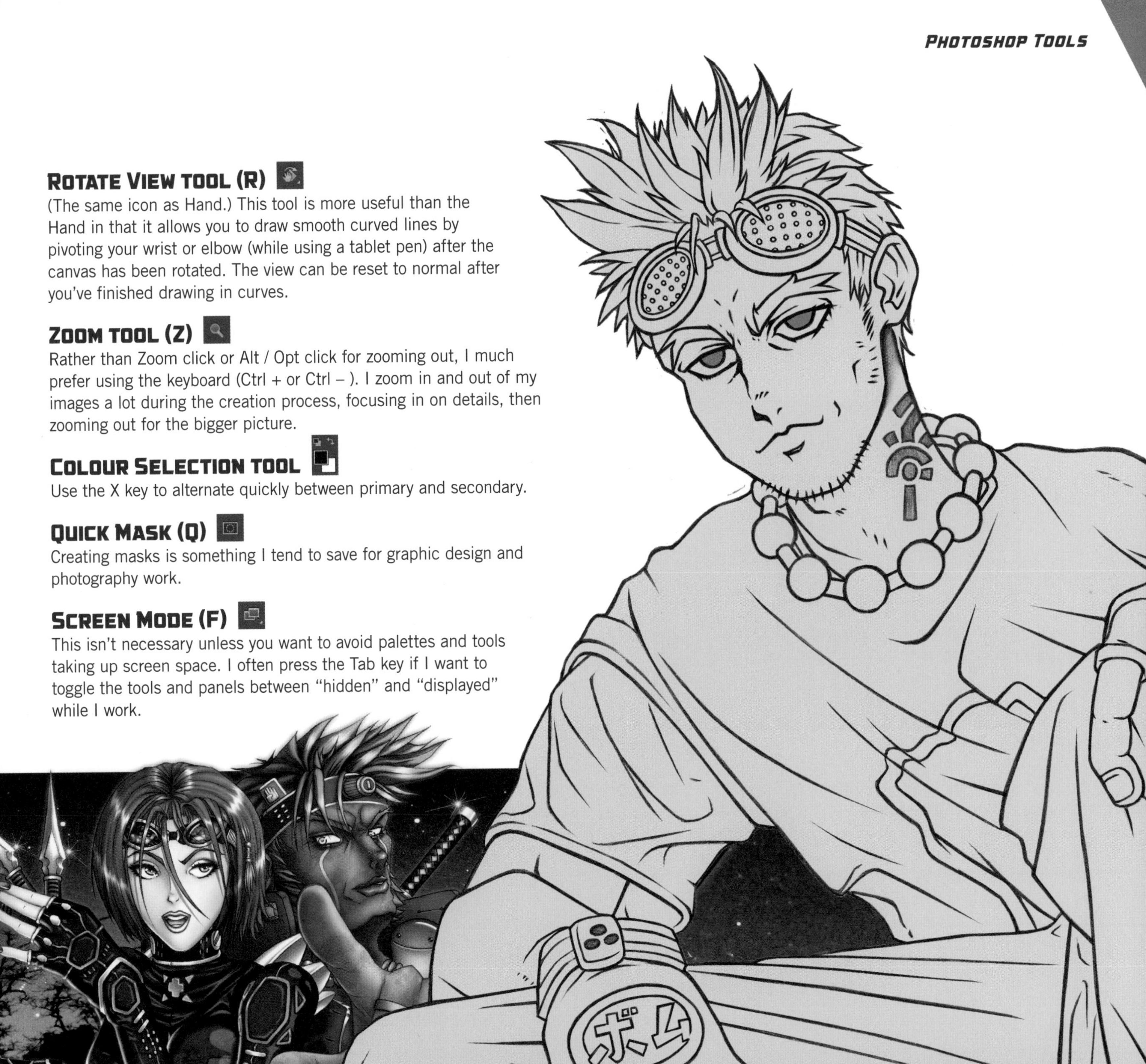

ROTATE VIEW TOOL (R)

(The same icon as Hand.) This tool is more useful than the Hand in that it allows you to draw smooth curved lines by pivoting your wrist or elbow (while using a tablet pen) after the canvas has been rotated. The view can be reset to normal after you've finished drawing in curves.

ZOOM TOOL (Z)

Rather than Zoom click or Alt / Opt click for zooming out, I much prefer using the keyboard (Ctrl + or Ctrl –). I zoom in and out of my images a lot during the creation process, focusing in on details, then zooming out for the bigger picture.

COLOUR SELECTION TOOL

Use the X key to alternate quickly between primary and secondary.

QUICK MASK (Q)

Creating masks is something I tend to save for graphic design and photography work.

SCREEN MODE (F)

This isn't necessary unless you want to avoid palettes and tools taking up screen space. I often press the Tab key if I want to toggle the tools and panels between "hidden" and "displayed" while I work.

WHAT ARE LAYERS?

Layers work like sheets of acetate or clear plastic. The lines you paint on one layer won't affect another layer in the Layers panel. If you paint on a layer above you'll cover up the layer underneath, but you won't paint over it.

Go to the Photoshop Help site (F1) and read the extensive information on layers while experimenting on your own. Layers are a very important part of the digital process and you need to know how to use them and how they work.

By putting different colors on different layers you can shade each one without adding, for example, unwanted hair color on a girl's face or skin tone on a guy's jacket. Each layer can then be edited individually at any time.

Shown here is the Layers panel for the Purple Princess (an original character created for a web-based project). It has three layers—Border and Pattern at the top, Character in the middle and Background at the bottom. If I wanted to draw on to the artwork, I would first need to select the relevant layer.

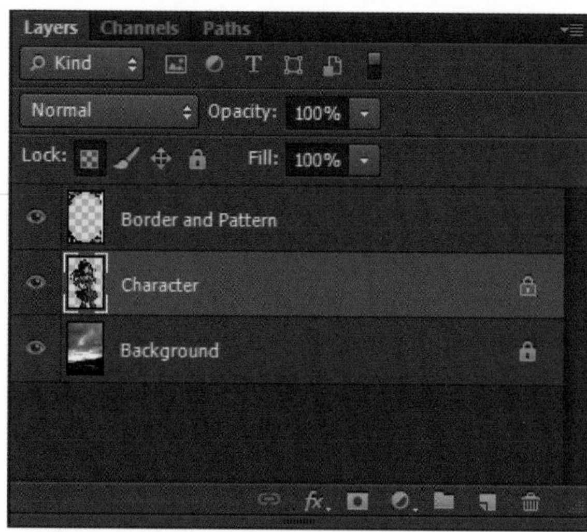

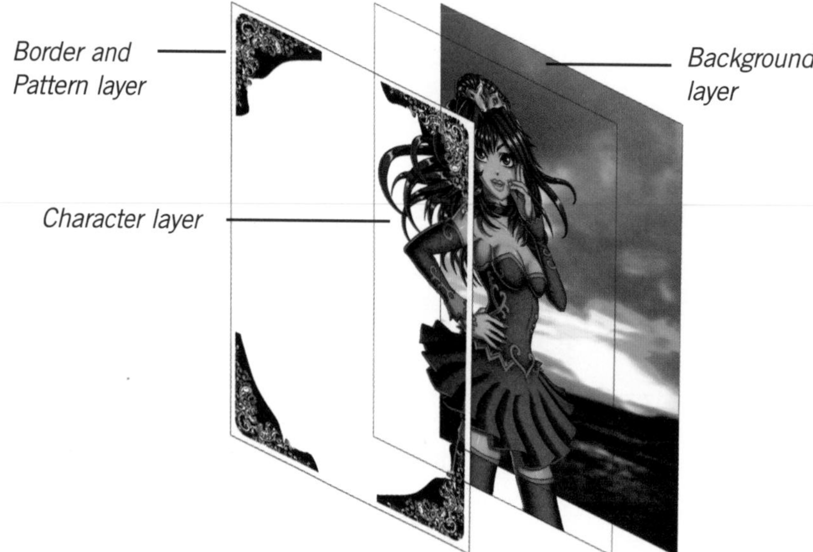

You can see that the Character layer is currently selected, as it's highlighted in blue. I have applied a transparent pixel lock to this layer, indicated by the clear padlock icon on the right of the layer title. This means I can only paint on to or edit pixels that are visible and not transparent; it effectively creates a mask, so I can't paint onto an area outside the character margins. The knowledge that you can't paint outside the lines or selected tones makes layers really helpful. Notice that on the Background layer I have added a Lock All icon, indicated by the solid padlock icon next to the layer title. This means I won't accidentally paint onto or edit this layer. Once you start creating art in Photoshop, it's possible to build up a stack of layers and it's not uncommon to start painting on the wrong layer by mistake. To lock a layer, click one of the four lock icons next to the word "Lock" on the Layers panel. I often find that "Lock Transparent Pixels" and "Lock All" are the only lock types I need.

Here I could draw straight onto the Border and Pattern layer if I wanted to, as it's not locked. All I need to do is click that layer, then begin drawing on the canvas space.

You can reorder layers by dragging and dropping them into a new position within the Layers panel stack. Note that when you import a new image or open a canvas in Photoshop, it will be shown as a less editable layer, named Background. To convert it to a regular, fully editable layer, double-click the title and rename it.

I often use dozens of layers per artwork; in the long run, it can be a lot quicker to name them than to go through them all trying to find the "purple cloth material" one, for example. You can rename layers at any time by double-clicking the layer's title.

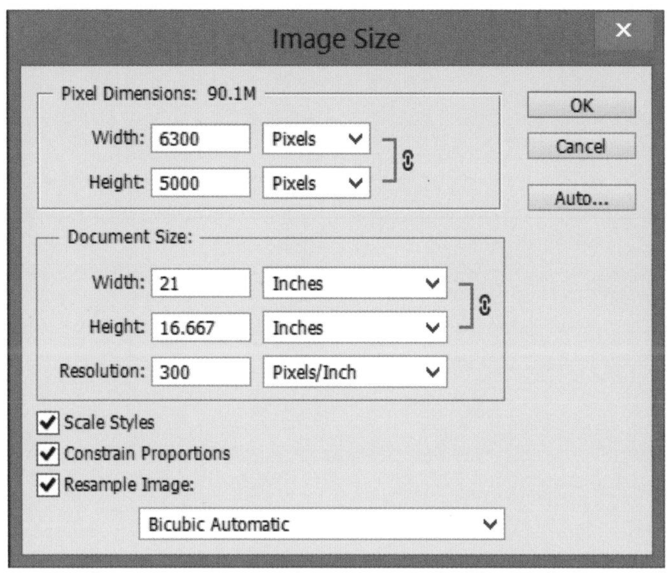

SAVING IMAGES

New artwork needs to be saved as a file to prevent it from being lost once Photoshop is closed. Whether you're scanning work or creating a new image, you need to work on a high-resolution file with high dpi (dots per inch) or high ppi (pixels per inch). Then you'll want to make sure the end quality of the image stays as sharp as possible, whether it is printed or uploaded to the internet.

For a good-quality print, 300 dpi is the standard requirement, while 72 dpi is adequate for web use. However, I recommend always working on images with at least a 300 dpi resolution, since it's easy to scale down artwork but impossible to up-scale without a degree of quality loss.

Check out your image size specifications by clicking Image -> Image Size [Alt+ Crl+I / Opt+Cmd+I]. Note that Pixel Dimensions corresponds with Document Size, so if I were to change my pixel width from 6300 to 63, my print size would result in a width change of 21in (53.34cm) to 0.21in (0.5334cm). Clicking OK would shrink the image and, although the dpi would remain a constant 300 dpi in a square inch, the image would now only be a little over a fifth of a square inch, if printed.

If I wanted to print my image at double the width, 42in (106.68cm), I could upscale my pixel dimensions by doubling those values. Photoshop would then increase its file size to accommodate the extra pixels. If I didn't want to increase the file size of my image prior to printing, I could lower the dpi to 150 after unchecking the Resample Image box. Either way would result in a lower-quality print, so the larger the image size and resolutions you can handle, the less chance there is of reducing the image quality if you want to print at a large size. However, large files mean you'll need a large hard disk to house them and a computer with enough RAM to process and edit them, or you will risk computer and software crashes. If you know your image will never need to be printed large-scale or will only be used for the web, then it makes sense to work on smaller files to suit your needs.

FORMATS

A saved Photoshop file is called a PSD and has a .psd file extension. It's a raw, uncompressed file format which holds all the information for different layers and Photoshop-related data. If you can handle files that are of large pixel dimensions and/or sizes above 2GB, you'll need to save your work as a PSB file.

If you do manage to create a 2GB+ file, it will probably be too large to attach to emails or upload to the web. After I finish creating an artwork I save it as a PSD; I then save a second web-size version for sending to clients by email or sharing on the internet.

To do this, resize the image to smaller pixel dimensions, for example from 6300 x 5000 to 1000 x 794. Then go through the familiar File –> Save as [Ctrl+Shift+S / Cmd+Shift+S] routine. Name your file and select Format, then choose JPEG. The image will be flattened and processed as a compressed, web-ready image. An image quality of 9 or 10 is usually sufficient to make it look acceptable on the web without generating a big file size. Image quality lower than this can show signs of compression.

When saving specifically for the web, check out File –> Save for Web [Ctrl+Shift+Alt+S / Cmd+Shift+Opt+S]. This allows you more control over how your web-ready file will look once it has been compressed as a JPEG, or you can use a smaller color palette by saving as a GIF or PNG file.

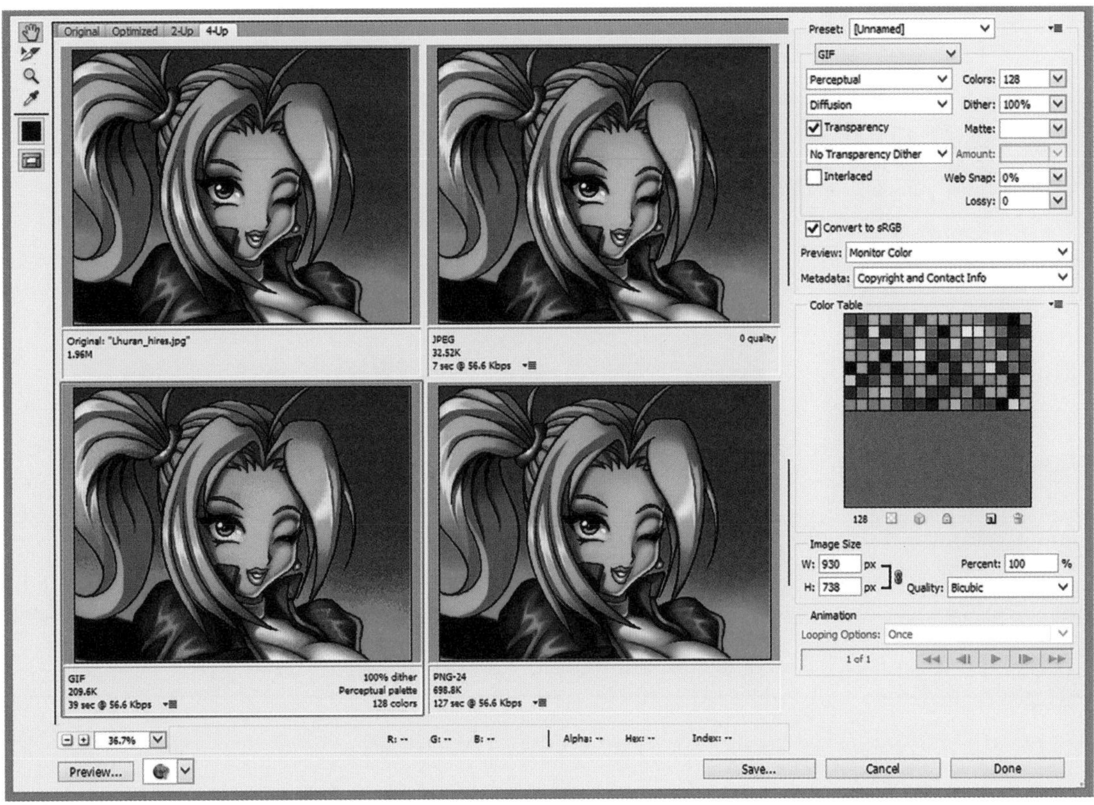

Scanning, Adding Color, and Cel Shading

You'd like to combine your traditional pencil or ink work with Photoshop? No problem! This chapter delivers comprehensive instructions on how to scan your character drawings and clean them up digitally.

If you like working with a lot of black-and-white drawings or manga pages, digitizing these works and optimizing their quality is an important step to learn. This chapter also describes the method for sketching in Photoshop and shows how to add color and work in a cel style.

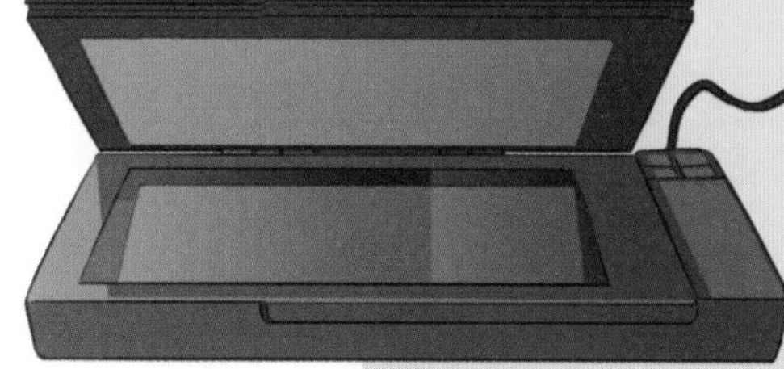

FACE SKETCH

The following step-by-step shows how to use Photoshop to sketch a character face. I usually do numerous face sketches when trying out new drawing styles. This one is the kind of generic, tough-looking guy you might find in *shonen* (boys') or *seinen* (mature guys') manga.

STEP 1

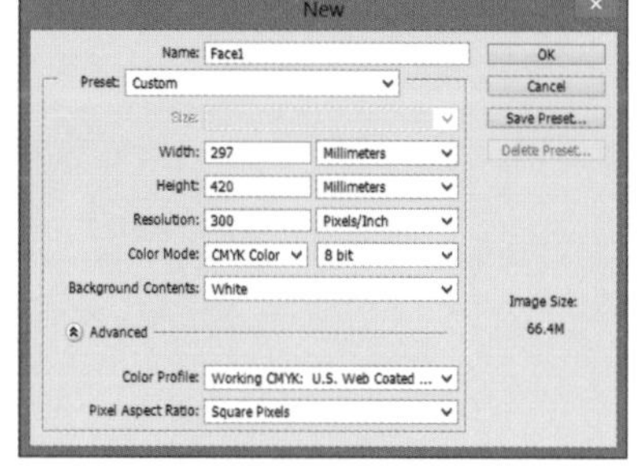

With Photoshop open, start by clicking File –> New. You'll be presented with a box allowing you to customize your canvas. Start by writing the name of the file. In this case I've named it "Face1." This will be used as the file name once it is saved. I number every new file I create with a 1 in case I want to save separate second or third versions. Click the box where it says "Custom" and choose International Paper and Size: A3. Select a 300 dpi resolution and set color mode to CMYK, as this image is going to need good-quality printing.

I sometimes work in 16-bit color mode, as opposed to 8-bit. Other than increasing file size, what does this mean? 8-bit color uses a tonal range of more than 16 million colors, while 16-bit uses trillions! On its own, it doesn't make a difference since our eyes can't see that many colors, but with 16-bit you can sustain the image quality when tweaking contrast levels on the artwork.

Next, set Background Contents to white (or transparent) and click OK.

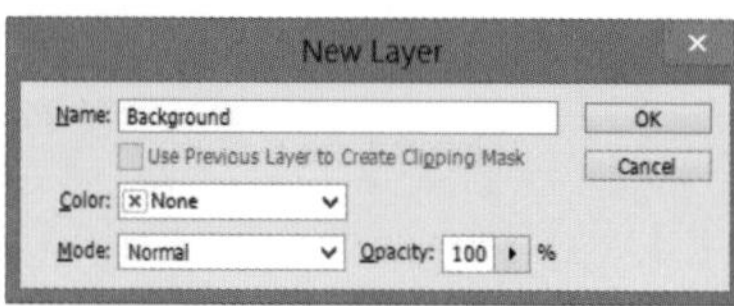

STEP 2

If the Background Contents are set to white, double-click the layer named "Background" and rename "Layer 0" in the dialogue box as "Background." This will "unflatten" the layer, converting it to an unlocked, usable state.

If the Background Contents are set to transparent, fill the background layer with white. This makes sketching easier to see than on the transparent gray checkerboard background. To do this, select the Paint Bucket tool, make sure white is selected as the primary color and click on the canvas to fill. Apply "Lock All" to the background layer to make it uneditable.

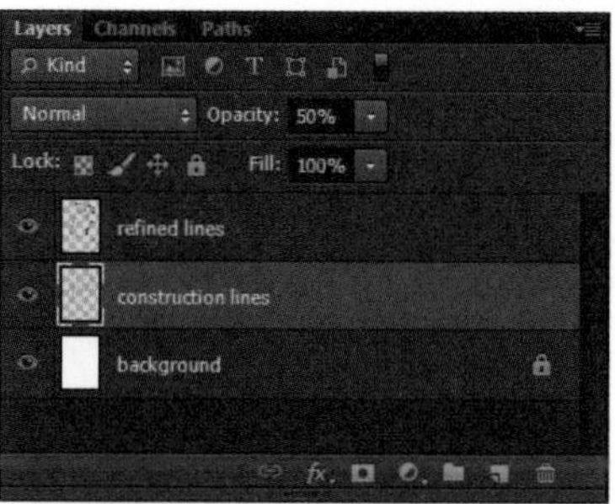

STEP 3

Create a layer named "Construction lines." This will be the base for creating a face. Using the Brush tool, select a 9-pixel round brush with 100% hardness and 1% spacing, then check the shape dynamics box, which will be controlled using the tablet's pen pressure. On the brush options bar at the top, set the flow percentage to 6%. Alternatively, the flow can be kept at 100% and brush opacity can be reduced to around 35%. This will create a pencil-like brush which you can use to darken the lines by going over them a second or third time. At this stage it's a good idea to set up the Eraser –> Select Eraser Tool. Choose a 19-pixel, hard, round brush. I usually keep the flow and opacity at 100% for the eraser, but lowering either of these values can work too.

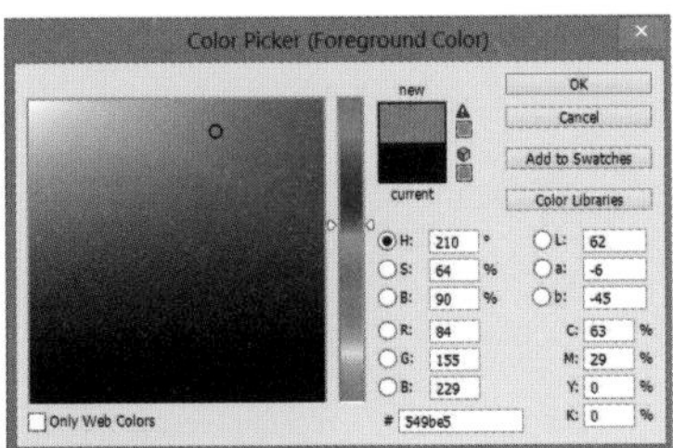

STEP 4

Make sure the "Construction lines" layer and the Brush tool are selected. Then click the primary/ foreground color on the tool bar to bring up the Color Picker screen. Select a blue tone and click OK. Alternatively, select a blue from the Swatches menu panel.

STEP 5

Now you're ready to start making marks. Lay down the usual facial construction lines to work out proportions.

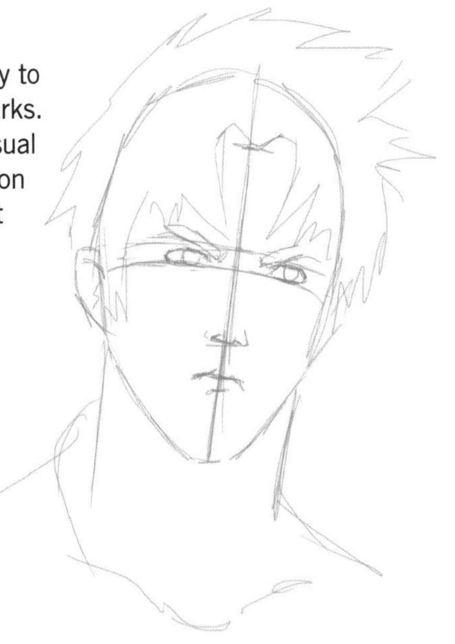

STEP 6

Then try to give the face a little more form and detail. Any stray lines can be removed with the eraser, by clicking the tablet pen button.

STEP 7

Once you have finished with the blue, it's easier to refine the drawing by sketching over the top in black. To make the blue lines even less visible, simply adjust the layer's opacity to something like 50%. Next, add another layer, name it "Refined lined," then select a black for the foreground color and set the flow a little higher, to 12%, before you start. Remember this is just a sketch, so don't spend too long retracing over the top and refining. You can zoom in to the image with Ctrl + / Cmd + or zoom out with Ctrl – / Cmd – to improve accuracy when adding details.

SCANNING

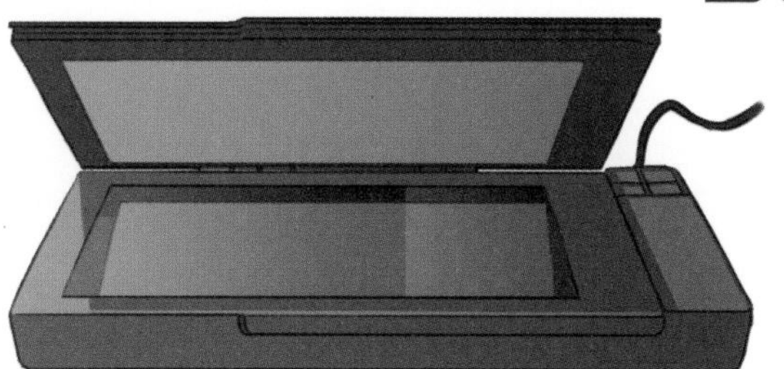

It's important to be able to transfer traditional artwork into a digital format on the computer without losing any of the original quality. It's good to know how to enhance your images to make them look cleaner and sharper than your original artwork, especially if you intend to color them.

STEP 1

Place your artwork on the scanner and open up the 32-bit version of Photoshop to allow use of the TWAIN scanning interface. The 64-bit version can also be used, but it only supports scanning technology and interfaces such as WIA and ImageKit. A 64-bit Photoshop TWAIN plug-in is available via the Adobe web site.

Go to File –> Import –> (your scanner name). A scanning menu or window appears. From here you should be able to perform a "prescan," or scan preview. Once the prescan process is complete, the preview display on the left indicates how the scanner will translate the drawing or artwork once it is in Photoshop.

There are several things you can do next to get better scan results. First, set the scan resolution option to 300 dpi, which should always be the minimum when scanning artwork. This produces a high-resolution scan that will be easier to color and work on later; you can always downsize your image if you intend to publish it on the web or email it to friends. If you intend to scan a rough sketch, perhaps to put it on the web or to email, 72 dpi is fine. Also, if your computer has a low amount of RAM, try scanning at lower resolutions to avoid Photoshop crashing.

STEP 2

Use the cursor to draw a selection box around the image (see dotted lines on the image opposite). As this will ensure that you scan only the information inside the box, it will save on time. If you're scanning a sketch in pencil or black ink, confirm that the output type or Color Mode is set to Grayscale and not B/W (black and white), Color or RGB /CMYK (color). With B/W, the scanned lines will be jagged and pixelated; and the color options will pick up unnecessary colors when all you want is the gray/black line art.

You can adjust various Image Settings, which might include Auto Tone, Unsharp Mask, Grain Correction, Contrast, and Exposure. Try out several options to see how your artwork looks. At this stage, I like to get a slightly higher-contrast scan to make my pencil art look clean, dark, and defined, although there will be opportunities later on to readjust contrast settings.

If you're scanning from a sketchbook, make sure the scanner lid is firmly pressed down so that all the details are picked up. In order to apply an even pressure, try leaving a heavy weight on top while the scan is underway; if you hold down the lid with an unsteady hand, the scanned lines may be crooked. Finally, click "Scan" to scan the image into Photoshop.

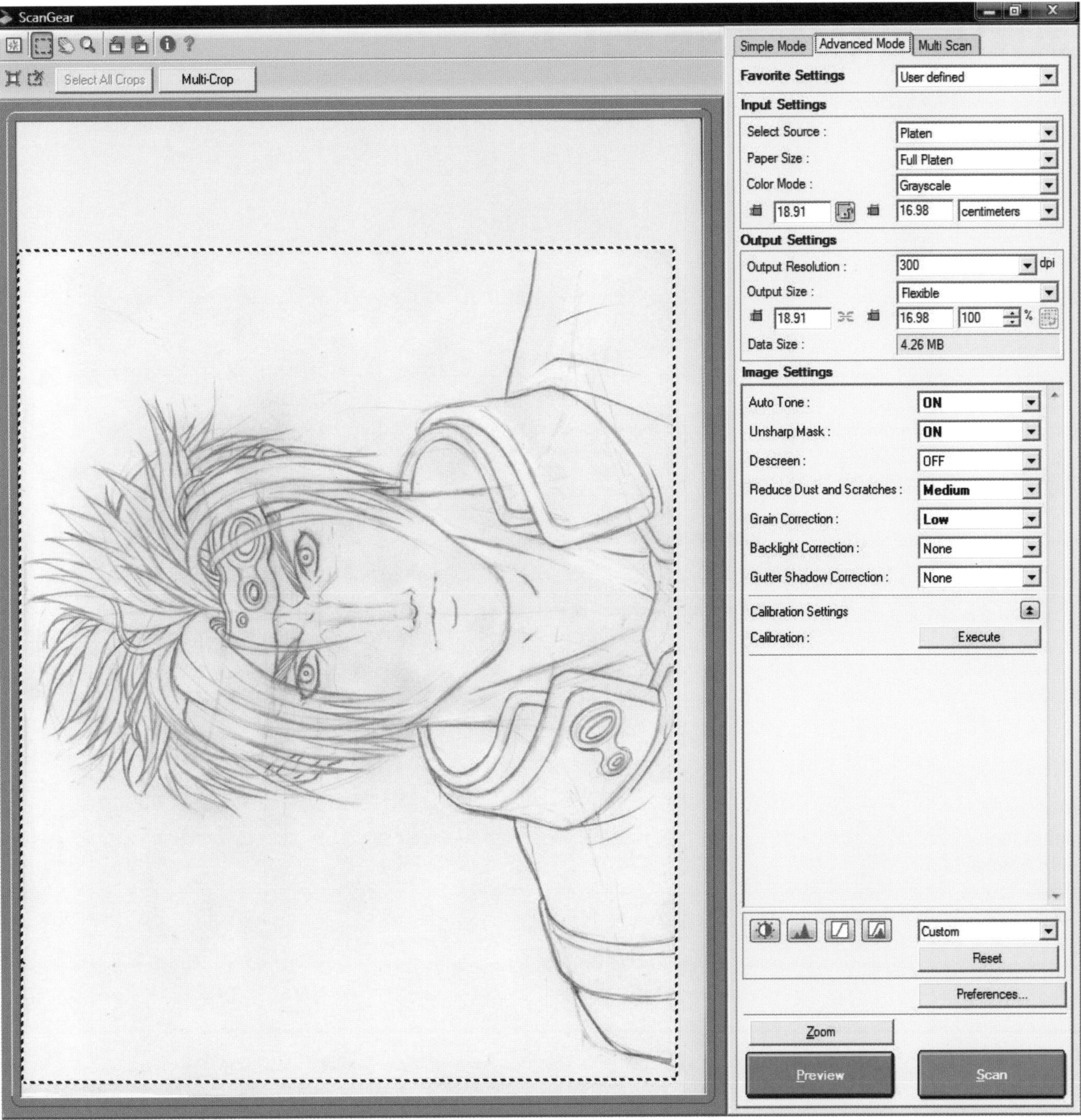
ScanGear
Select All Crops
Multi-Crop
Simple Mode
Advanced Mode
Multi Scan
Favorite Settings
User defined
Input Settings
Select Source :
Platen
Paper Size :
Full Platen
Color Mode :
Grayscale
18.91
16.98
centimeters
Output Settings
Output Resolution :
300
dpi
Output Size :
Flexible
18.91
16.98
100
%
Data Size :
4.26 MB
Image Settings
Auto Tone :
ON
Unsharp Mask :
ON
Descreen :
OFF
Reduce Dust and Scratches :
Medium
Grain Correction :
Low
Backlight Correction :
None
Gutter Shadow Correction :
None
Calibration Settings
Calibration :
Execute
Custom
Reset
Preferences...
Zoom
Preview
Scan

CLEANING UP THE SCAN

After scanning your artwork into Photoshop, you'll need to make adjustments to improve the scan before you start working on the image.

STEP 1

First, adjust the levels: Image –> Adjust –> Levels [Ctrl+L / Cmd+L]. Spend a little time tweaking the tonal range until the lines look nice and dark. For this image I selected Input Levels 129 for the dark tones, 0.74 for mid-tones, and 246 for light tones. If you don't need to perform a full clean up on your artwork at this point, just increase the light tone value until the lightest areas become pure white; this way you'll end up with a clean black-and-white sketch.

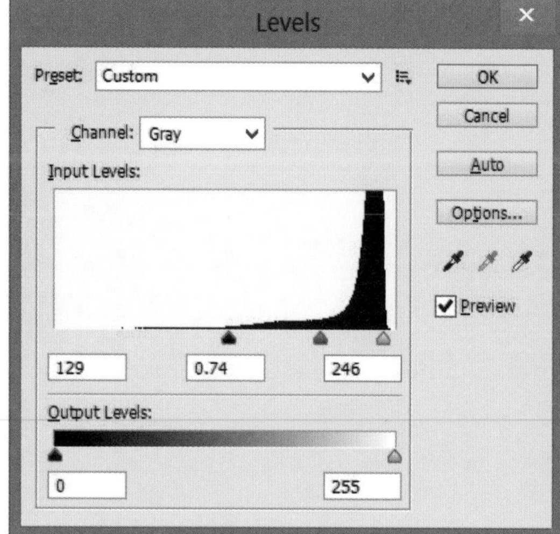

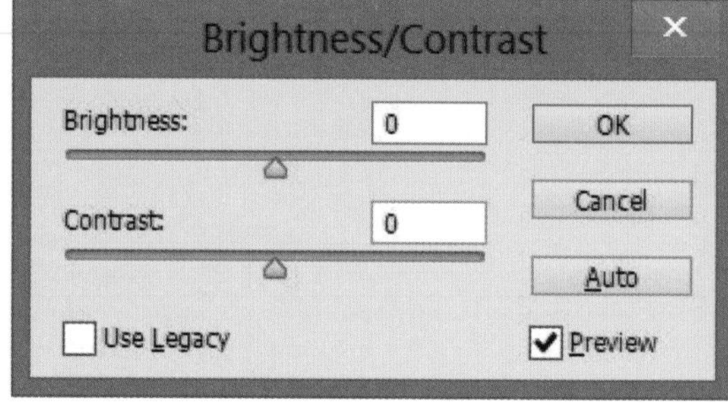

Instead of using Levels, you might want to try Brightness and Contrast: Image –> Adjust –> Brightness. I have assigned the shortcut key Ctrl+B / Cmd+B for the Brightness and Contrast menu, since I use this type of adjustment a lot.

It's important to prepare the image in the correct way, whether or not you want to color it later.

STEP 2

A scanned image doesn't always appear completely straight, so you might need to adjust and rotate the canvas. I advise making it slightly bigger around the edges by 100 pixels or so. Then go to Image -> Rotate canvas -> Arbitrary and rotate it CW (clockwise) or CCW (counter-clockwise) from 0.5 degrees to 5 degrees, or however much you need to get the image lined up perfectly. Next, crop the image, using the Crop tool.

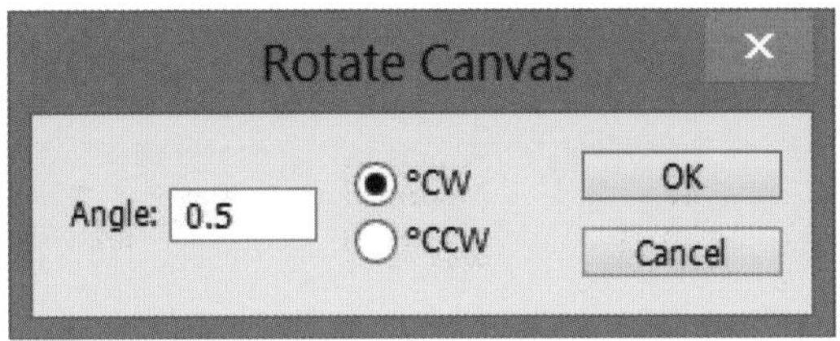

STEP 3

If certain parts of the scan are lighter than others, you can darken them by using the Burn or Airbrush tool set on Color Burn at 10% pressure. This is a subtle change, but it helps to make all your pencil lines look more consistent.

There will probably be a few smudges on the image. To remove these, use the Pencil or Paintbrush tool and color white over the affected areas. To clean up small nooks and crannies, try using the Polygon Lasso tool, then simply fill in the selection that needs to be cleaned with white, or just click Delete, ensuring that white is your secondary color.

STEP 4

If done properly, fully cleaning up the image can take some time. The best way is to zoom in on the image, then use the Polygon Lasso tool to go round each line on the picture to neaten it up.

You can make additional selections by holding the Shift key (the cursor icon will change to a + sign). To subtract from part of your existing selection, hold the Alt / Opt key.

BEFORE

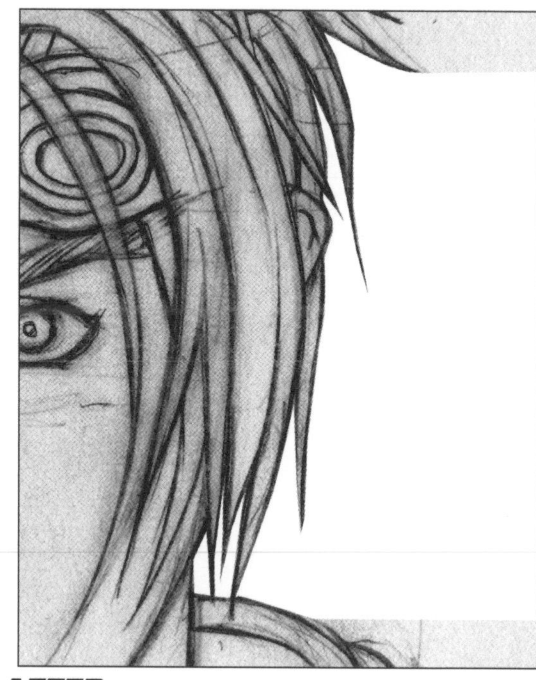

AFTER

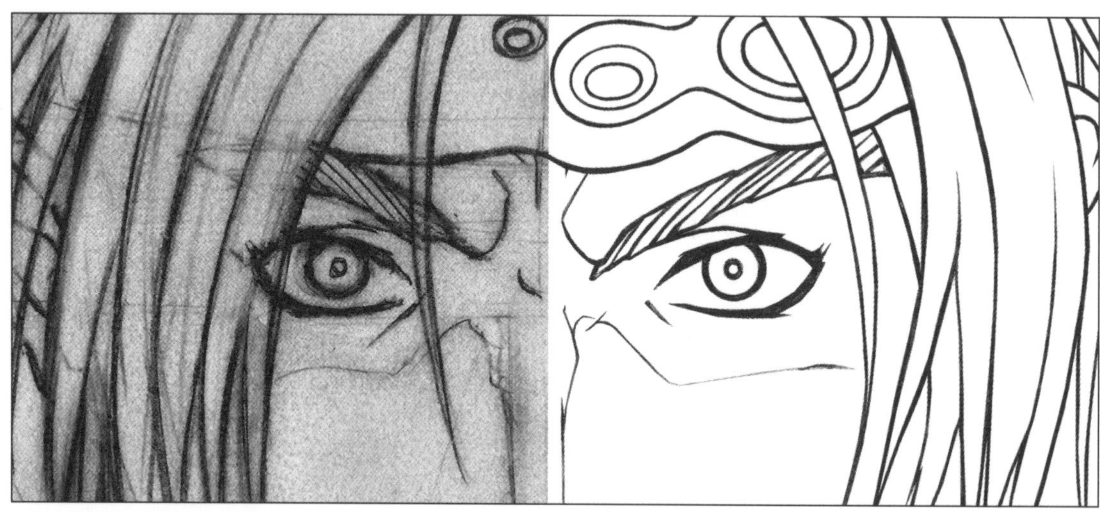

STEP 5

If you want to save your image as it is and put it on the web without coloring in the line work, then adjust the image size: Image –> Image size (Cmd+Alt+I). You'll possibly want no more than a pixel width of 800 pixels, but it depends on whether or not your image has a lot of detail. Look at artwork sites and see what sizes are used there. Once your artwork is resized, you can save it as a jpeg.

STEP 6

If your original artwork is larger than the size of your scanner surface, you will need to scan it in sections and join them up in Photoshop. For example, if you have scanned an A3-sized picture in two sections with your A4 scanner, first adjust the canvas size (Image –> Canvas size) of the scan #1 to a little over double and make sure you have white selected as the secondary color.

Go back to scan #2, select the layer "Background" in the Layers panel and copy or drag this layer on top of scan #1. Use the Drag tool to move scan #2 so that it fits next to scan #1. A good tip for adjusting the scan #2 position is to zoom in at 100% and get the lines flush with scan #1.

If the lines simply refuse to join up properly, try rotating scan #2: Edit –> Transform –> Rotate [Ctrl+T / Cmd+T]. After it is lined up nicely, flatten the image (Layer –> Flatten Image).

PREPARING TO CG

Here I describe two popular methods of coloring your scanned artwork.

Method 1

STEP 1

When working with a new canvas, you'll notice a single locked layer, named "Background," in the Layers palette. To make this editable, double-click "Background" to bring up the New Layer dialog box. Rename the layer "Line Art" and click OK. Alternatively, to unlock the "Background" layer and make it editable without renaming it, hold Alt / Opt and double-click the layer.

STEP 2

Go to the Channels panel and click the circular channel selection icon at the bottom. The image lines should be filled with dotted selection lines.

Next press the delete key—this will get rid of all white areas. You will have a grey checkered background which shows that the image is now transparent.

The checkered colors can be changed in the Photoshop preference settings: Edit –> Preferences –> Transparency & Gamut [Ctrl+K/Cmd+K]. I generally use light gray and dark gray squares, so if there is any unwanted white on my layer it's easy to spot.

STEP 3

As Step 2 has taken some of the black from the line art, it needs to be reapplied. Deselect the channel selection, then move back to the Layers panel and check the Lock Transparent Pixels box. Use the Pencil tool with a large brush size (5,000 pixels is the max) and cover the whole picture to restore black to the outlines. I find it easier to use a black to transparent gradient fill. If this gradient starts from outside the canvas area it can cover the entire canvas in one hit. Now the black line work is a layer on its own, similar to the outline of a typical animation cel.

Layers tab: channels method

STEP 4

Adjust the image mode from Grayscale to Color: Image -> Mode -> RGB. Create a new layer underneath the line art layer called "BG" or "Background," fill this layer with a white solid fill and check the "Lock All" box.

STEP 5

Create a new layer above Background white and beneath Line Art, and call it "Skin." The image on the left shows how the Brush tool can be used to add color without affecting the Line Art layer.

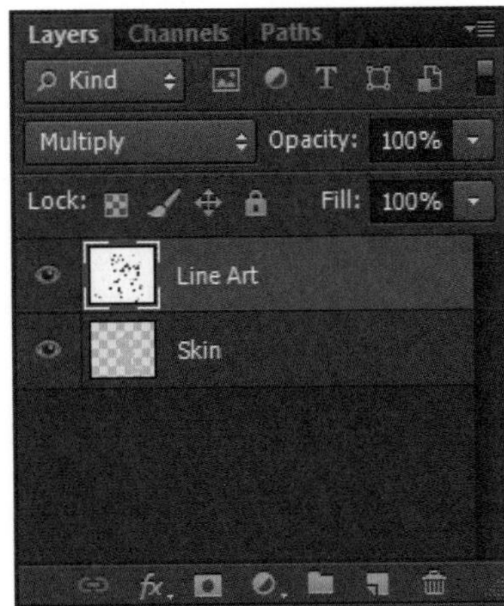

Layers tab: multiply method

Method 2

STEP 1

In the Layers panel, make the Background layer editable and rename it "Line Art." Adjust the image mode from Grayscale to Color: Image -> Mode -> RGB.

STEP 2

With the Line Art layer selected, go to the Layer Blending Mode drop-down menu and select Multiply. This will allow all white areas to be viewed as transparent. Create a layer underneath the Line Art layer called "Skin." Start to paint the skin—you'll see the color is visible beneath the Line Art layer.

LAYING FLATS

The next step is to add colors to all parts of the picture. I often work on a different layer for each color or tone. However, I do sometimes use the same layer for different colors; for example, eye and mouth colors are placed on one layer named "Eyes Mouth." Having fewer layers means that file sizes are smaller so Photoshop uses up less of your computer's RAM; it also makes your workflow more manageable. The disadvantage is that if different colors are placed on the same layer you won't be able to adjust the eye color without it affecting the mouth color, for example, unless you use the Wand or Lasso tools to isolate a particular area.

Instead of using multiple layers for color, and CGing to minimize file size and reduce computer processing, some people use Channels and /or selections on a single layer.

The process of laying your initial colors down is called "flatting" or "laying flats." There are three ways to do this:

- Select the Brush tool and manually paint areas of color onto layers
- Use the Polygon Lasso to select areas, then flood-fill these selections using the Paint Bucket tool
- Provided the line work is suitable, use the Magic Wand tool, then flood-fill the selections

USING THE BRUSH TOOL TO LAY FLATS

Following on from Step 5 on page 157, continue using the Brush tool to apply a skin tone to the Skin layer until all areas are filled. There's no need to confine brush marks to within the skin areas—don't worry about messy overlapping tone at this point.

USING THE POLYGON LASSO

To create a selection, start by clicking somewhere along the edge of the line art, then release your mouse button. This adds an anchor point. Move the cursor and click again to add a second point further along the line art, then release your mouse button. This draws a straight line between the two points. Continue this process to create a shape area and end the selection by clicking on your original anchor point. Use the Paint Bucket tool to fill the area within the dotted line with the primary color selected.

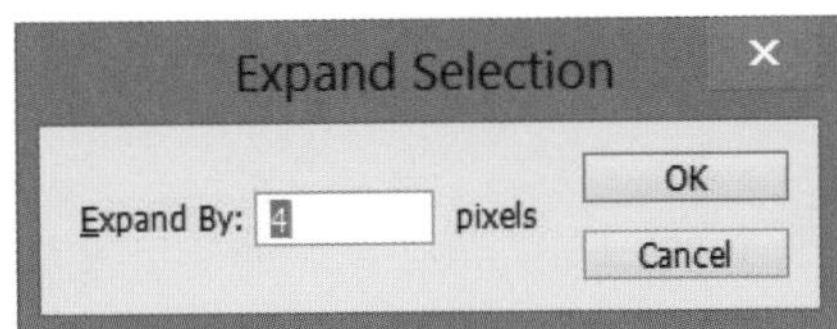

USING THE MAGIC WAND TO LAY FLATS

If you prefer sticking with the Brush method to add the remaining color flats, that's fine. However, as the line art in this exercise is clean, digitally inked and without gaps between areas, using the Magic Wand is the most efficient way of laying flats. Sometimes the Polygon Lasso Brush is also required to fill gaps the Magic Wand can't reach.

STEP 1

With the Magic Wand tool selected and the Line Art layer highlighted in the Layers panel, click on the image in the open white space where you want to make a selection—in this case, the hair area. Hold Shift and click to select additional portions of hair. Note the "marching ants" that denote where the selection area is. Go to Select –> Modify –> Expand. Expand the selection by 4 pixels. This will enlarge the selection so that once a color is added to the layer underneath, the fill goes all the way to the edge and slightly beyond. If you don't do this you'll be left with pixelated areas where the flat tone doesn't quite meet the line art edges.

STEP 2

Create a new layer named "Hair," and drag it above the Skin layer. This will cover any overlapping skin tone. Laying flats like this means you can be quick and messy with the lower layers (especially if using a Brush or Lasso tool) in the knowledge that excess tone will be concealed later.

STEP 3

After placing all the flats on their respective layers, lock each one with the "Lock transparent pixels" icon. This will prevent rendering outside the flatted areas.

Flatting can be a monotonous and repetitive process, but it's important to get solid flats laid—and once they're down you know the fun part is about to begin!

RENDERING CEL-STYLE SKIN AND HAIR

To give your work an animation/cartoon look, use solid color tones for shadows and highlights. When placing shadows you need to be aware of form, of how light falls and of the shapes that are cast. Perhaps you're used to painting traditionally and placing shadows and highlights—if you aren't, observe from life, playing around with a lamp and camera and training both on different objects and people. Have a look at other artists' work, too, and see how they do it.

Once the relevant layers of your flats have been created and filled, take some time to consider alternative color options for each. Choosing colors can be difficult, but it gets easier with practice. The good thing with digital art is that you can always change the colors or hues later on, without hassle.

Here the light source from the top left is created in an airbrush style (left), then simplified to a cel-style (right).

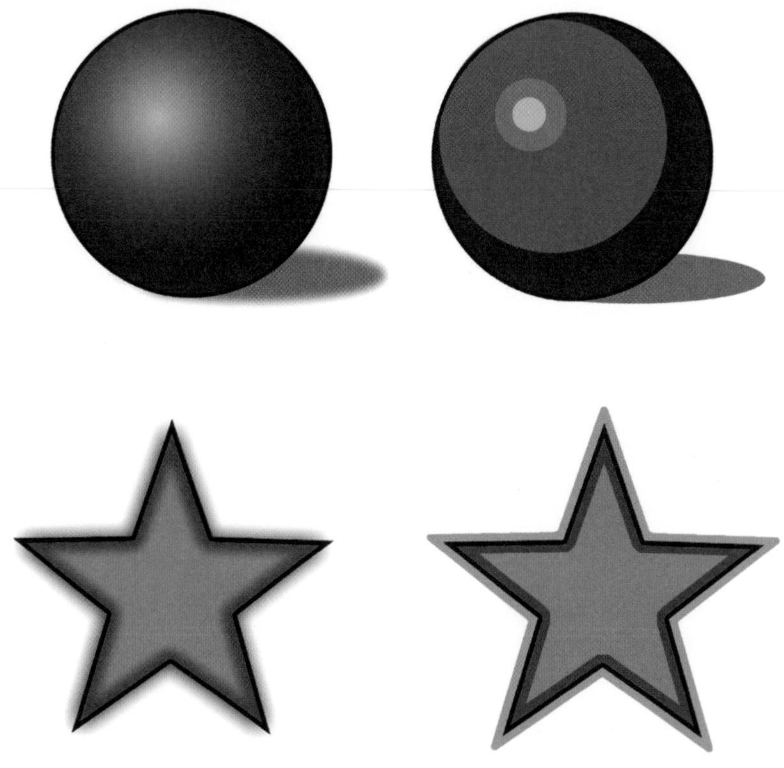

The central light source on an embossed shape (left) is simplified to cel-style (right).

STEP 1

Select the Skin layer (see opposite) and the Polygon Lasso tool. In addition to using Shift and Alt / Opt keys to add and subtract selections, you can use the square icons in the tool options bar (next to the Lasso icon).

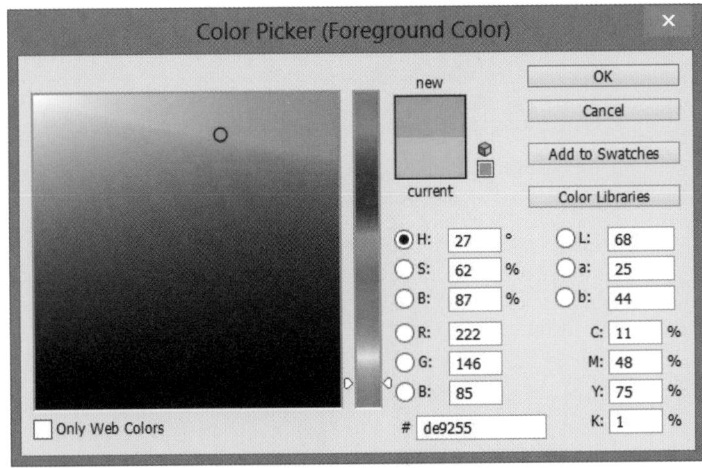

Choose a darker tone for the skin shadow via the Color Picker. With a left-hand light source in mind, begin to select where shadows form and are cast—they will be placed on the right-hand side of the character.

STEP 2

When a selection has been created, fill with the darker tone then deselect [Ctrl+D / Cmd+D]. If any shadows are too angular they can be smoothed out manually using the Brush tool. You can bypass the Polygon Lasso completely and shade with a brush if you prefer. If you do this, move the cursor quickly to avoid creating a lumpy edge where Photoshop picks up wobbles in your hand movements.

STEP 3

I thought some of the shadows were a bit overpowering, so I decided to trim them back. When tweaking a solid shadow tone it is useful to have the foreground color as your primary base tone and the background color as the shadow tone. You can alternate between these by using the shortcut key "X" on the keyboard. This makes adding or subtracting tone a lot easier.

For the darkest shadows, add a second selection that is smaller than the previous one and fill it with an even darker tone. Then, using a small brush, add a few small highlights of a lighter skin color to the cheeks and nose.

STEP 4

Moving on to the hair, use a brush with a darker tone selected to plan where the shadows will be. The hair looks pretty messy at this stage, so I need to go back to the Polygon Lasso to clean up the shadowed areas. Using the Polygon Lasso makes the creation of straighter lines and sharper points a lot easier than attempting to taper the lines with a brush and tablet pen. But it's fine if you feel more comfortable using just the graphics tablet brush strokes or the Polygon Lasso to shade.

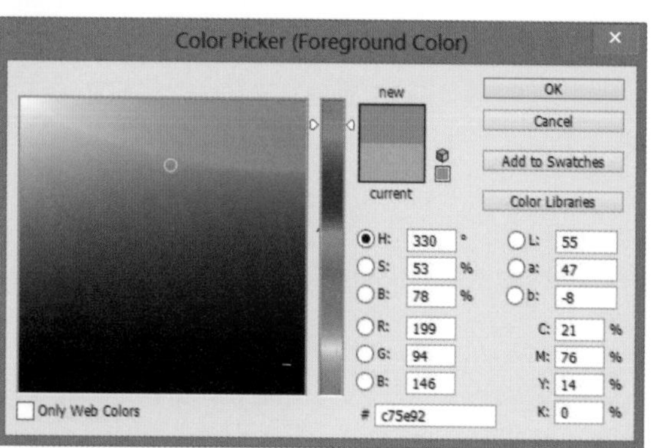

STEP 5

Add some white or lighter highlights to the hair to give some shine. Be sparing with highlights—less is more and too many can make an area look messy and overcrowded. As with the skin and hair tones, add shadows to the clothing and accessories.

STEP 6

Neaten the image by placing a simple background round it. The lighter gray square was created using the rounded Rectangle tool and the background was kept gray so that it didn't detract from the brighter colors used on the character. Take a final look at the image and adjust the hues on each layer if necessary. In Step 5 the skin looked a little too yellow so I adjusted it accordingly.

The Soft CG Figure

The cel style used in the previous chapter looks great, especially if you're into cartoons and anime (a vibrant style of Japanese animation). However, there's another cool style to try, which I call the "soft CG" look. This closely mimics the more smoothly blended shading you would expect from a traditional airbrush. The added realism and silky-smooth effects of this style can really enhance your character art.

Brightness/Contrast
Brightness:
25
OK
Cancel
Contrast:
0
Auto
Use Legacy
Preview
Ben's Workspace
Filter
3D
View
Window
Help
Mode:
Strength:
50%
Sample All Layers
Finger Painting

SKIN AND SHADING

This standing pose of manga girl Nikki is used to illustrate the airbrush technique. The design has been kept fairly simple to allow you to concentrate on rendering larger portions of skin tones and hair.

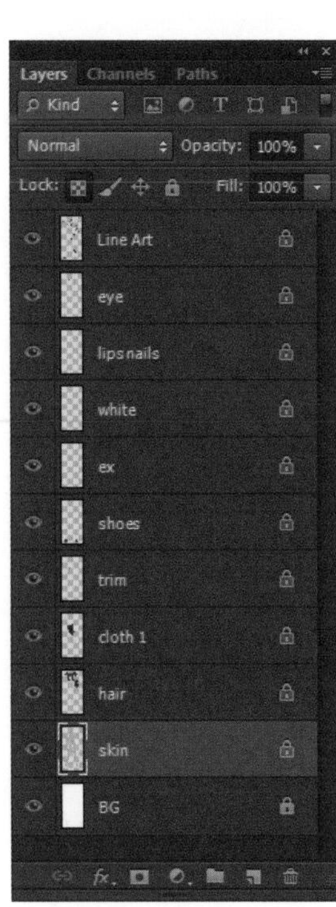

Whether I intend to use standard daylight lighting or something a little more fancy and colorful, I always start with a neutral range of tones that I can adjust as I progress. For example, you should flat a Caucasian skin layer using a peach tone, which is a light, desaturated orange—see the Color Picker (left).

STEP 1

As with cel-style coloring (see pages 160–163), start by laying each flat color on its own layer, labeled for future reference.

STEP 2

As with cel-style shading, choose a skin tone a little darker and slightly more saturated for the shading. Do this by clicking the foreground color and sampling the original skin tone via the Color Picker, then selecting a tone with a little more saturation, black and red. In this example, the flat peach skin has the hexadecimal value of "#eebd8b" and my darker shading tone has the hexadecimal value of "#cf8961."

Select the Brush tool and via the Brush options bar set it to 0% hardness. The brush size should be quite large to start with—in this case, 200–600 pixels.

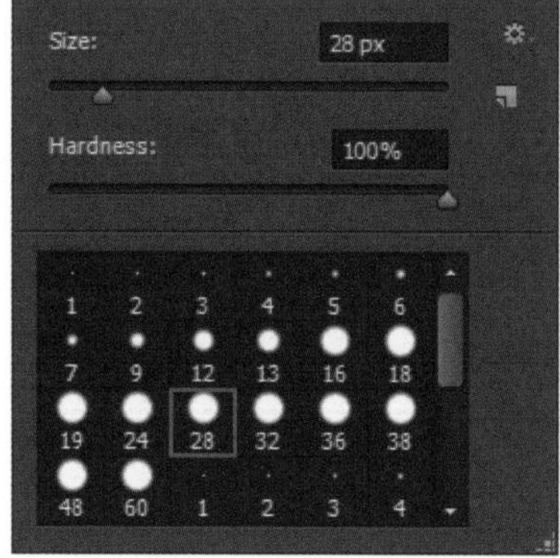

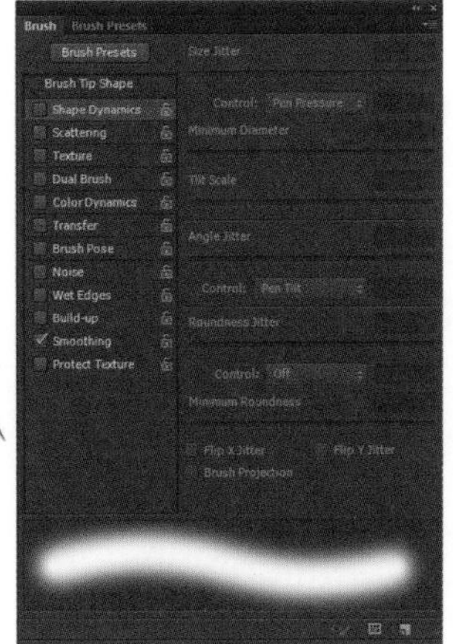

Keep the flow percentage low, at between 5% and 10%, to allow greater control; this creates smoother, more graduated shadows and tones. Apply an initial wave of airbrush shading around the edges of the Skin layer by using the outside edge of the brush—see the cross-hair on the image (left). To guarantee a more uniform tone, make sure Shape Dynamics is turned off via the Brush panel (F5 on the keyboard). Turn it on if you want to control the brush size with tablet pen pressure.

STEP 3

Use the Color Picker to select an even darker skin tone, and apply a second wave of shading. This is where you begin to define the off-center light source. Throughout the process of adding shading, zoom in to the image and decrease the brush size to tackle smaller areas. In the event that a small brush has left clumps of shadow which look a little messy, increase the brush size, lower the brush flow percentage and paint over this area to blend out any unwanted marks.

STEP 4

Using a darker brown skin color, apply another round of shading. With this wave, try to smooth out the previous tones and add further definition. Sometimes during the coloring process certain parts of the line art do not look quite right. In this case, the shadow direction on the nose has been changed.

STEP 5

There should now be a good range of tone, although here the skin looks too dark and needs attention. Adjusting the brightness of the Skin layer can be done using Levels: Image –> Adjustments –> Levels [Ctrl+L / Cmd+L]. Experiment by moving the Shadows, Midtones and Highlights sliders underneath the Histogram. These are also represented by numerical values beneath.

The idea is to make the skin look natural while retaining a range of contrast. Moving the Shadows slider too far to the right can make the skin look saturated and muddy. Moving the Midtones slider too far left can make it look washed out, and moving it too far right results in oversaturating, as with the Shadows slider. Moving the Highlights slider too far left will result in the skin tone looking overexposed. Here the Shadows value is set at 20, Midtones at 1.03 and Highlights at 227.

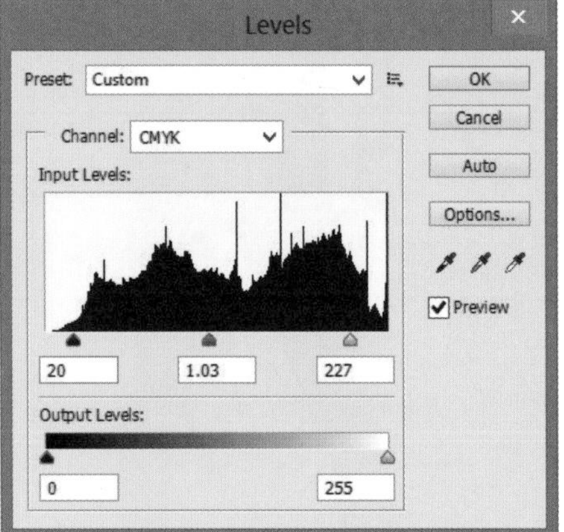

If the skin is still too dark or too light, make a final adjustment to the brightness: Image –> Adjustments –> Brightness/Contrast and set it to +25 or whatever value you think is necessary for maximum impact.

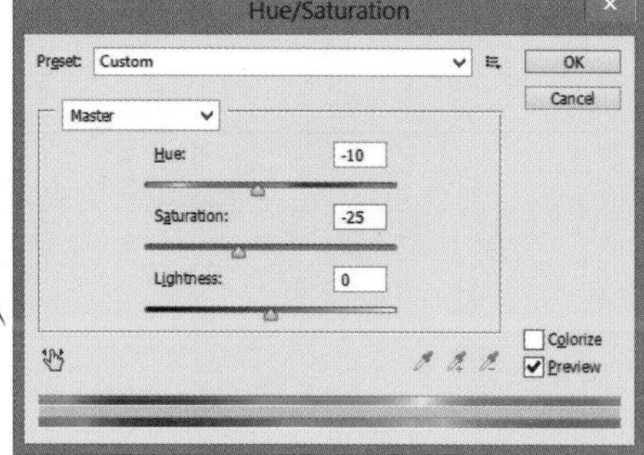

The next adjustment is Hue/Saturation: Image –> Adjustments –> Hue/Saturation. The Hue is set to –10 to make the skin a little more red/pink and less yellow, and the Saturation is set to –25.

Brightness/Contrast
Brightness: 25
Contrast: 0
OK
Cancel
Auto
Use Legacy
Preview

The last thing to do is to add a couple of small highlights to the cheeks. Sometimes it's nice to add small specular (white dot) highlights to the shoulders, elbows, and knees.

Shading Clothing

Next I move on to the clothing, returning to the hair layer afterward.

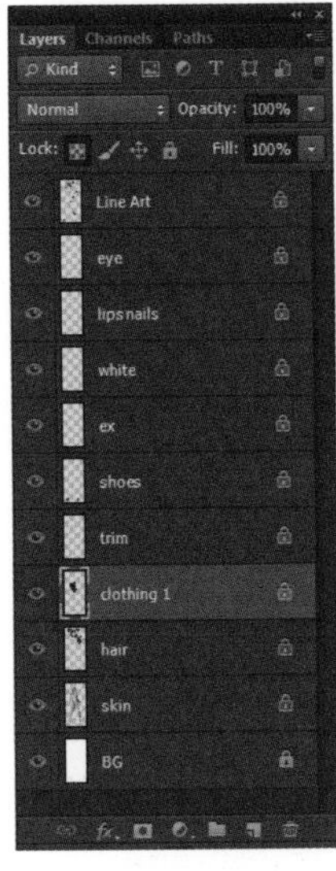

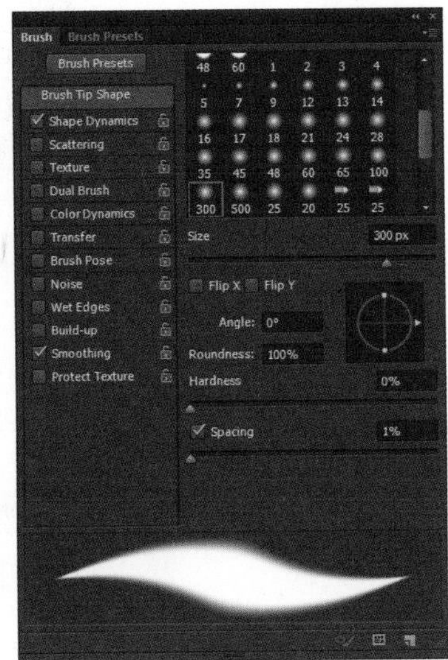

STEP 1

Select a clothing layer named "Clothing 1." Sometimes you may have a "Clothing 2" or "Clothing 3" layer, depending on the outfit, but this design is fairly simple, consisting only of a swimsuit.

As with the skin-rendering process, select the Brush tool and set it to a large, soft, 0% hardness brush. In addition to the Brush options bar, brush sizes, hardness and other settings can be changed via the Brush panel. So far as Brush Spacing goes, keep this low—1% spacing will create slightly straighter lines, but takes more computer power to process.

Using the Color Picker, choose a dark tone for the first wave of shading. Keep the shading primarily toward the outside edges of the swimsuit and underneath the breasts, but allow some of the darker color to bleed on to the overall area to produce a subtle graduation of tone (see above right).

STEP 2

Pick a darker tone and add a second wave of shading to the swimsuit. Switch back to a lighter tone and paint in creases and fold highlights using a smaller brush.

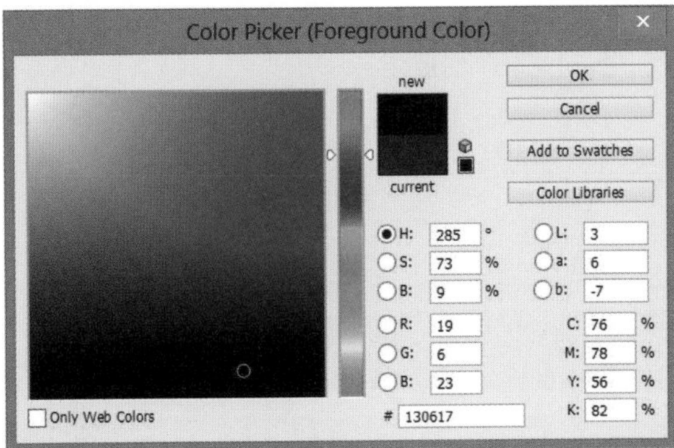

STEP 3

Reduce the outlines under the breasts using the Eraser tool on the Line Art layer. Remember to take off the transparent pixels lock and switch it back on again after editing the line art.

Tweak the Brightness / Contrast of the Clothing 1 layer, then add shading to the pink trim layer, including the bracelets and earrings.

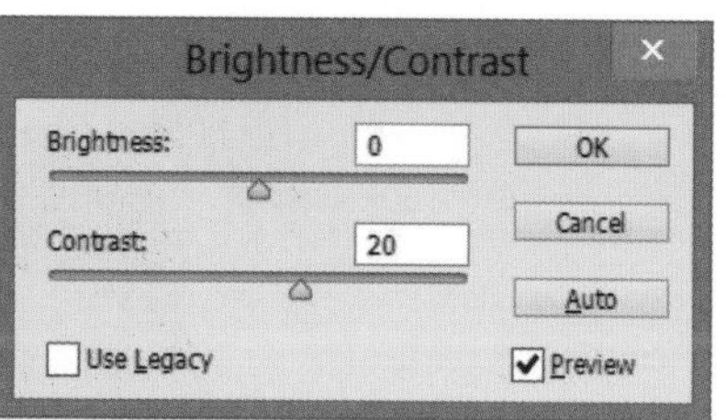

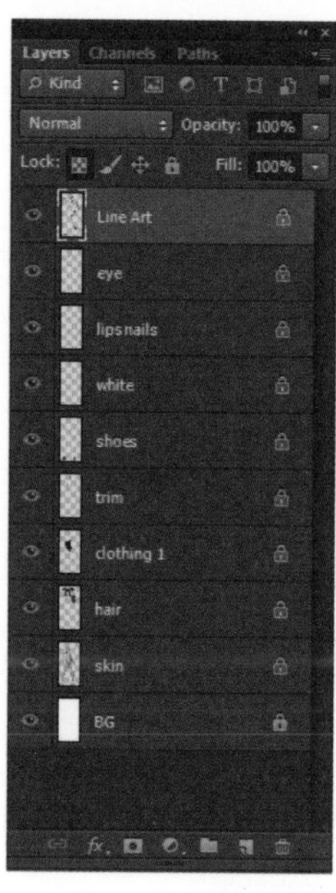

SHADING HAIR

Shiny, glossy hair can help make a manga character stand out. For a great effect, use white highlights and increased contrast levels.

STEP 1

Select the hair layer. As this is brown, choose a darker tone with more black for the first wave of shading. Start adding form to the bangs and ponytails. With manga style, the idea is to group portions of hair together rather than attempt to paint individual strands.

Use the Rotate tool to angle the canvas and create a long, continuous curve that follows the direction of your wrist movements. Aim to place the darkest tones toward the edges and alongside the outlines.

STEP 2

With yet another darker brown color, begin to define the hair even more. It can be difficult to achieve long, smooth strokes of shadow, especially with the way hair bends and curls. You can use the Smudge tool to blend. On the tool options bar, try setting the Smudge strength to around 50% and adjusting it if necessary.

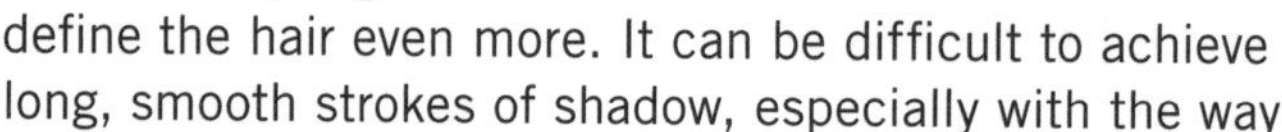

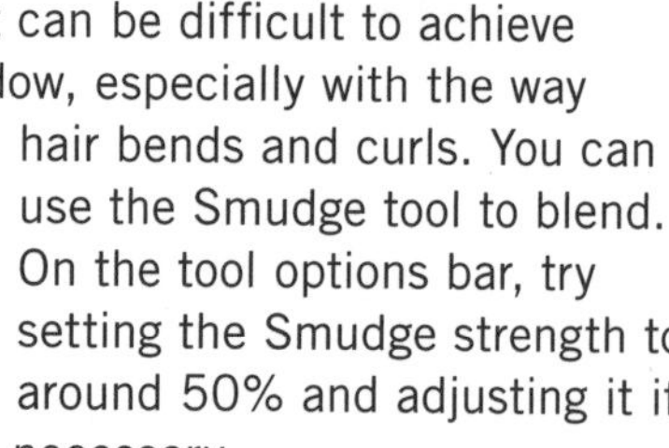

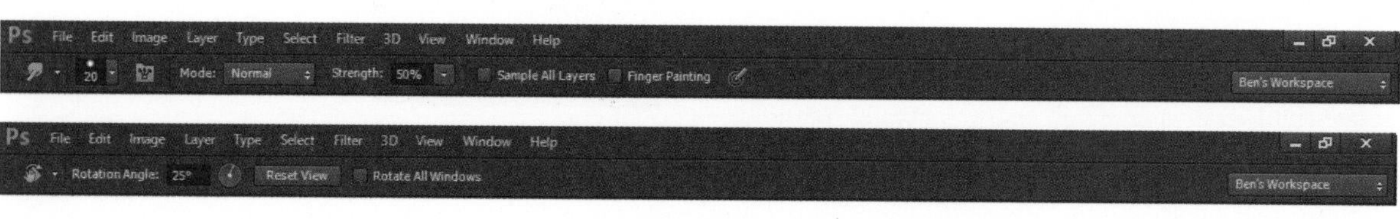

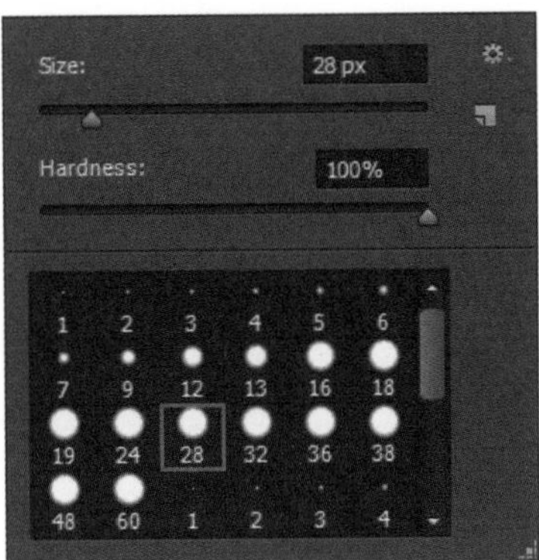

STEP 3

Add in shiny highlights on the hair, using a small, harder brush.

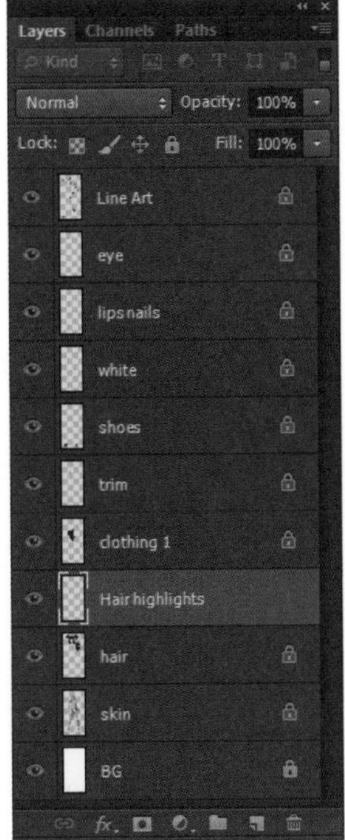

STEP 4

Use the Smudge tool to neaten the highlights so that they are smooth, blended, and tapering downward. If you're concerned about messing up the hair layer, add the highlights to a separate new layer above and refine them using the Smudge tool. Merge this layer with the hair color by clicking the Layer menu icon in the top right of the Layer panel, then select Merge Down [Ctrl+E / Cmd+E]. Alternatively, right-click the layer you want to merge, then select Merge Down from the Context menu.

STEP 5

Adjust the hair contrast using the Levels or Brightness/Contrast adjustments to produce a high-impact glossy look. Sometimes using the Dodge and Burn tools over the top of highlights can add extra color variation and style.

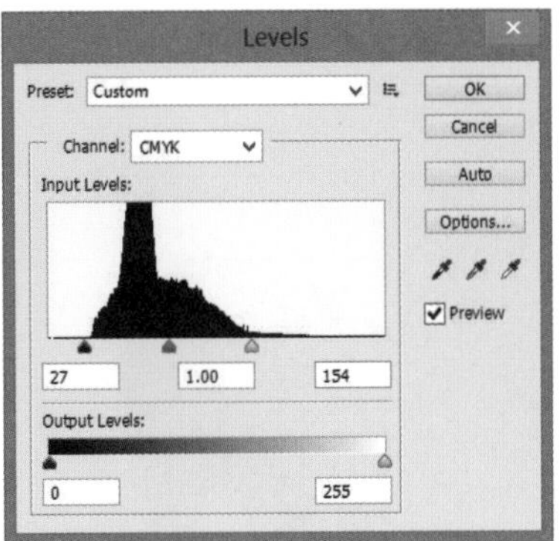

FINISHING OFF

Using the techniques you have learned so far in this chapter, put the finishing touches to your character.

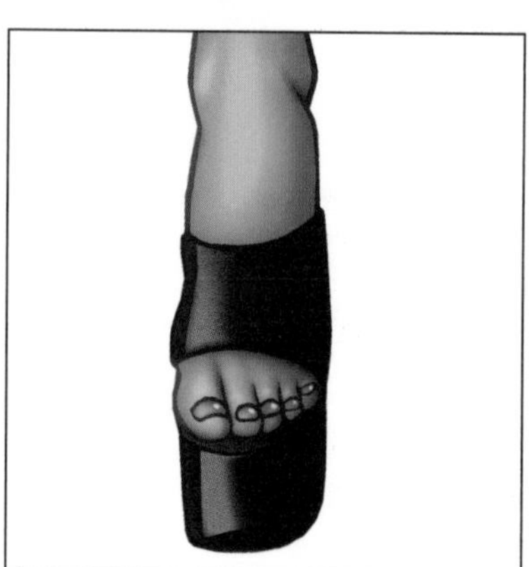

STEP 1

Shade the shoes using darker tones. Create a new layer above the Shoes layer and name it "Shine." With the Shine layer selected, add a white highlight to the shoes to create a gloss effect. The reason for doing this on a new layer is that the opacity can be adjusted and toned down if the white is a little too strong. In this case, the opacity of the Shine layer has been reduced to 65% via the Layers panel.

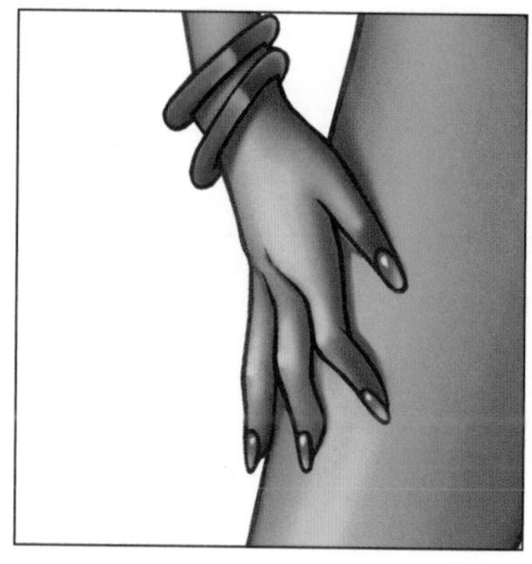

STEP 2

Zoom in to shade the lips and nails. Sometimes you might decide not to match these and to color the lips a different hue. As they are both on the same layer, it's possible to isolate the lips by using the Lasso tool to create a selection around them. Then tweak Hue or Contrast.

STEP 3

Next, shade the whites of the eyes and the teeth. I always use a gray or off-white for these. Then color the irises. With green eyes, I usually add a lime or yellow highlight toward the bottom of the iris and keep the top part of the iris dark to blend into the upper eyelashes and add more contrast against the white eye highlights.

STEP 4

Now color the line art. With the Line Art layer selected and the transparent pixels locked, use a brush to paint on to the lines themselves. This helps to merge the lines and colors into a cohesive image. Use different colors for different parts of the image—for example, dark brown around the skin and dark purple around the pinks. It's a subtle effect, but softens the overall artwork and looks great.

LAYER SHADING SUMMARY

- Lay flat color
- Apply a wave of shading using a soft, large brush
- Apply more waves of shading with increasingly darker tones and smaller brushes for details
- Adjust contrast levels if necessary

ALTERNATIVE VERSIONS

There are infinite variations and techniques you can use to give artwork a different look and style. Here are a couple of alternatives for the same line art, one of which uses a higher-contrast, over-exposed range of values while the other is lower contrast, with a warmer tone to it.

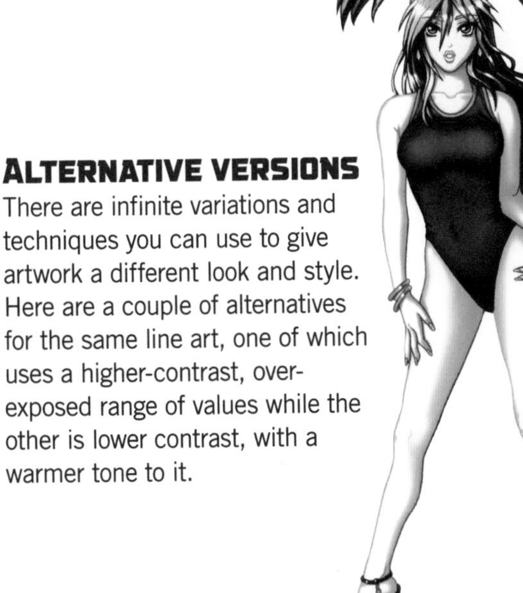

A BODY SKETCH USING REFERENCE

I'm going to draw a full-length character and show you how to use a photo as reference. First, source a dynamic jumping pose. You might want to search the internet for royalty-free stock images, look in magazines or books or take photos of your friends or yourself in the mirror. In this example I just wanted a pose to work from, but you might look for a photo with stronger shadows or better lighting which can be useful if you go on to color in the artwork.

STEP 1

As with the previous sketch, start by setting up an A3 canvas at 300 dpi (which works out as 3508 x 4961 pixels). Drag the stock image from the computer desktop on to the Photoshop canvas, then use the corner nodes to resize its dimensions and click the little "check" icon on the Properties bar or press Enter to confirm. The photo is now placed on a new layer as "Smart Object." This means that the image can be resized later without potential quality loss, though the layer is not fully editable. However, you can Rasterize the layer at any time, converting it to a fixed pixel dimension object which can then be fully edited like any other layer. To do this, right-click the stock pose layer and select Rasterize. Alternatively, the reference image can be opened directly in Photoshop and copied and pasted onto the new canvas.
From here the photo's brightness or contrast levels can be increased to make the details easier to pick up when tracing. Select Image –> Adjustments –> Brightness/Contrast [Ctrl+B / Cmd+B] and play around with the sliders, with or without Legacy mode, until you are satisfied with the result, and then click OK.

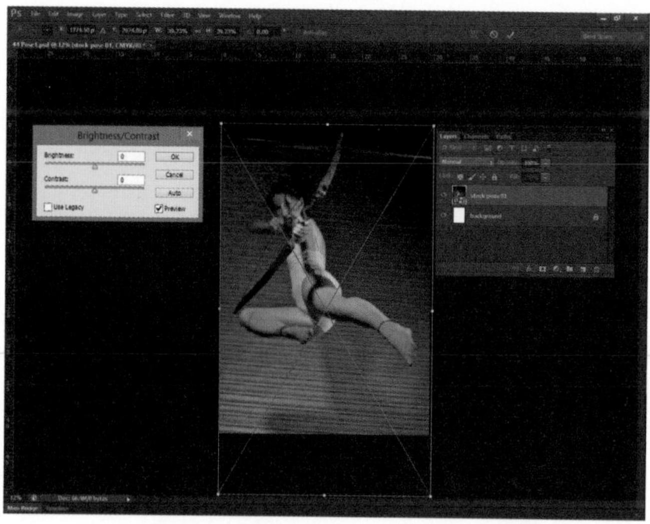

STEP 2

Adjust the stock pose layer to around 25% opacity and create a new layer at the top called "line art;" this will be your "tracing paper" layer. This time I'll be working onto the line art layer only, but you can use a blue or light gray brush as before to mark in the proportions and anatomy, and then refine. Try to keep the tracing light and sketchy as the photo is only a rough guide.

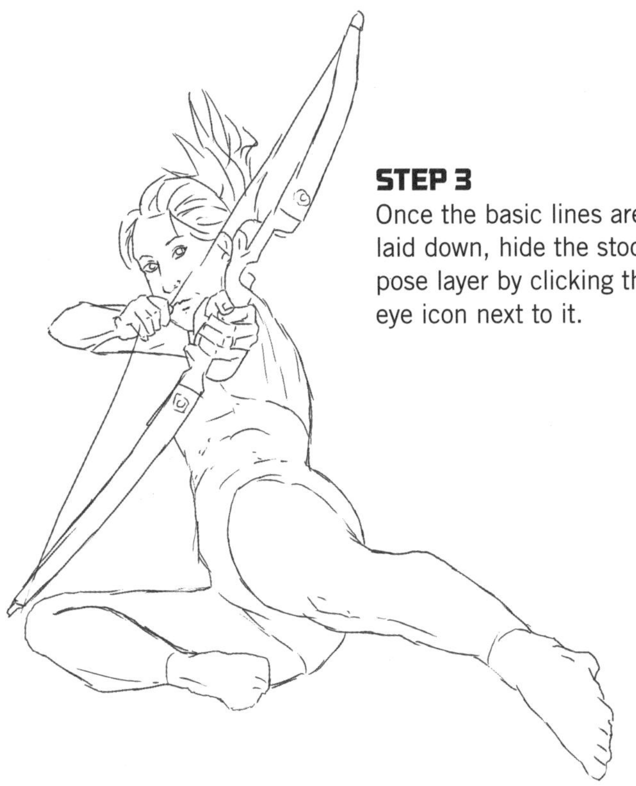

STEP 3

Once the basic lines are laid down, hide the stock pose layer by clicking the eye icon next to it.

STEP 5

Continue to tweak and add clothing details to the rest of the image until the sketch is complete. This one would be well suited to a fantasy RPG-style game or story. Save your work as a PSD file. If you want to post your artwork on the web later, it can be scaled down and saved in a JPEG format.

STEP 4

Next, begin to refine and add details, zooming in and out as needed. I decided to move the character's head up slightly so that it's not obscured by the bow.

DIGITAL INKING

To bring line work to the next level, you can ink the artwork digitally using the Pen tool for precision lines (instead of the freehand style mentioned on page 149). For this example I've sketched a scarred samurai—the kind of lone *ronin* you might find featured in martial arts manga. You can work from a digitally created sketch as before, or from a scanned drawing.

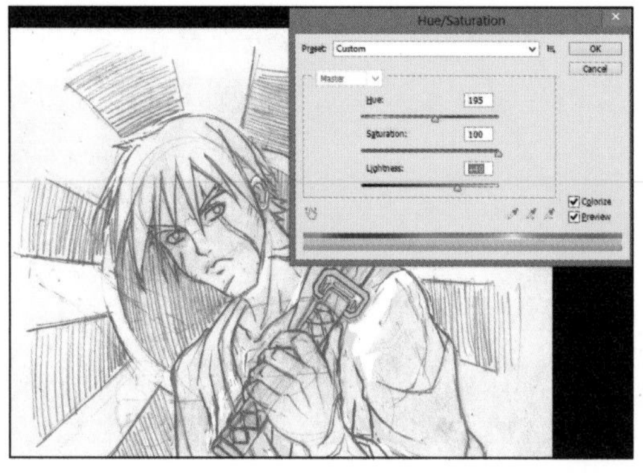

STEP 1

Set up the canvas and layers as usual, then create a clean layer for adding the inked lines. The scanned sketch layer is underneath. Convert the gray pencil lines to blue. To do this, go to Image –> Adjustments –> Hue/Saturation, then check the Colorize box before moving the color slider to blue. You could also drop the sketch layer to a lower opacity, such as 50%, to fade out the sketch so that it will interfere even less with the inking process. Give the sketch layer a "Lock All" lock to prevent accidentally drawing on it. Create a white background fill layer at the bottom of the Layers palette, also applying "Lock All."

STEP 2

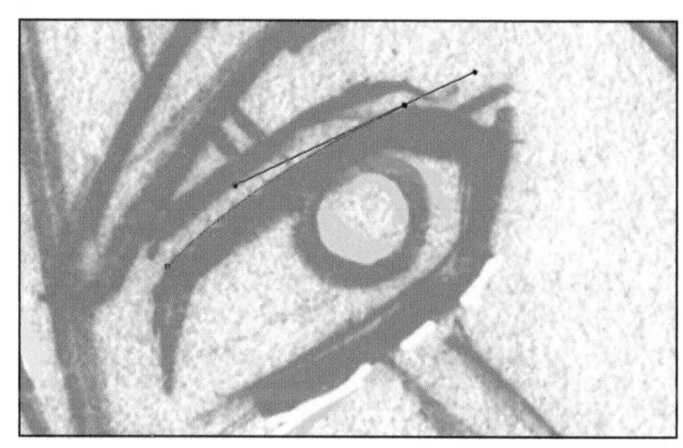

The Pen tool is used by placing anchor points around or along lines, to create paths. These paths can then be filled, resulting in digitally perfect lines. Zoom in to the image—it's essential to work on a large scale for best results. Select the Pen tool, then via the tool options bar set the pen to draw a path rather than a shape. Figure out where to begin—I usually start with an eye. Click the canvas to place the first anchor point (represented by a small square), then click a second time where you want the path line to finish. Before releasing the second click, you can drag the cursor to create a slight curve.

Continue clicking around the sketchy line and adjusting the curves until you end up back at the beginning, completing and closing the path. There will be a small circle next to the pen cursor to show you are completing the path. To edit nodes and curves created with the Pen tool, hold down Ctrl/Cmd, select an anchor point, then drag to move the anchor point location or click one of the curve points to adjust the curve. Hold the Alt/Opt key and select an anchor point to edit individual curve points.

STEP 3

With the Lines layer selected, right-click the path and select Fill Path. I'll fill it with my black foreground color. I can now remove the path by pressing delete, leaving nice crisp lines.

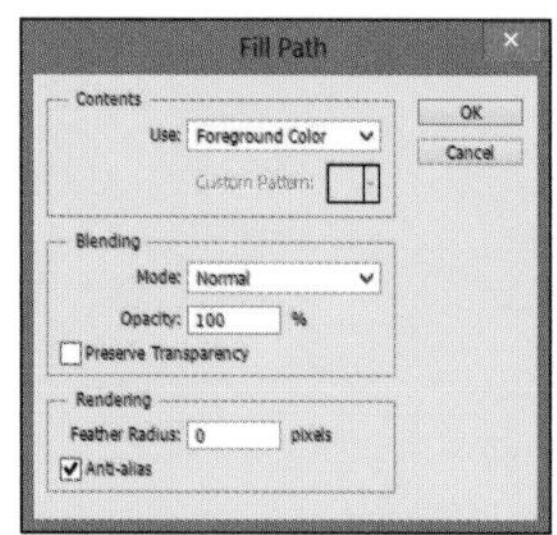

STEP 4

For the eyelid, I want to draw a single line, rather than fill in the area. First, I need to set up my Brush tool to a hard, 5-pixel diameter. Go back to the Pen tool, right-click the eyelid path, and select Stroke Path. Then choose Brush from the drop-down menu. Checking the Simulate Pressure box will taper the ends of the line. You can adjust the amount of tapering beforehand via the Brush setting menu.

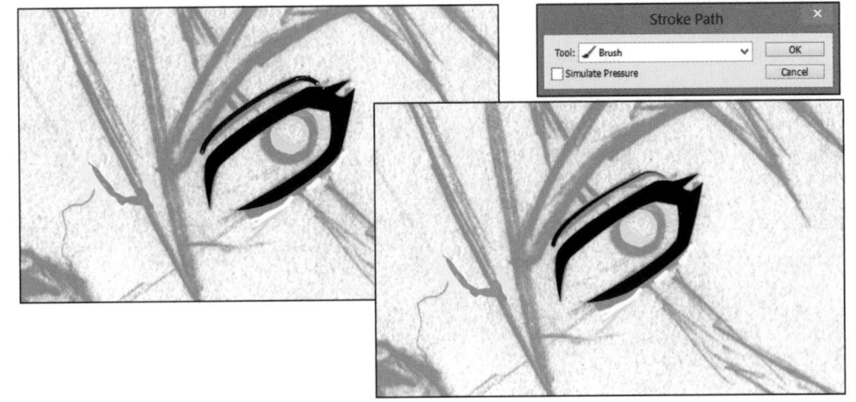

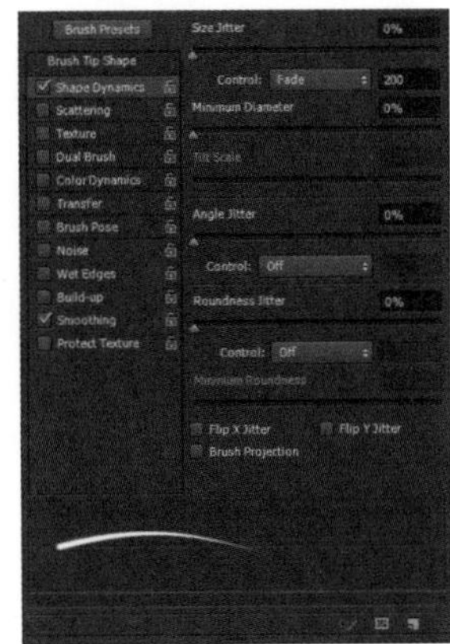

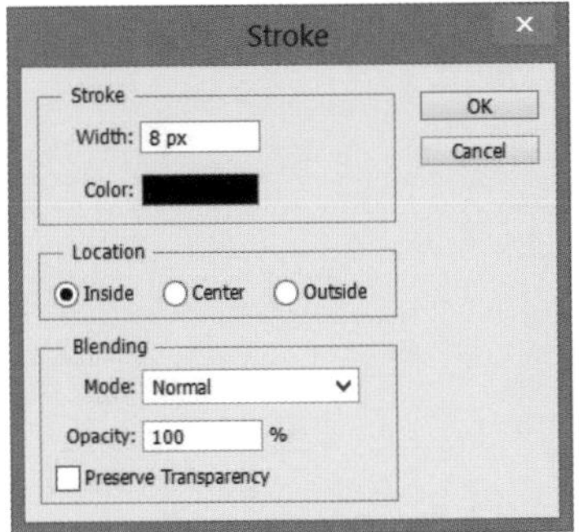

STEP 5

For circles, such as the iris of the eye, I sometimes use the Elliptical Marquee tool. Draw a circle selection at the appropriate size, then right-click and choose Stroke. Stroking Inside a selection often yields better results than Center and Outside.

STEP 6

Either continue to line or fill paths over the top of the sketch until it is complete. Any unwanted overlapping lines can be removed with the Eraser tool. Finally, delete the sketch layer, leaving just the line art.

Color Choice

There is more to adding color and rendering than simply the placement of tones and hues. Color can represent a character's emotions, personality, and intentions. With digital artwork, it can be a challenge to get your colors looking the way you want for web or print. This chapter demonstrates various ways in which you can deal with coloring problems.

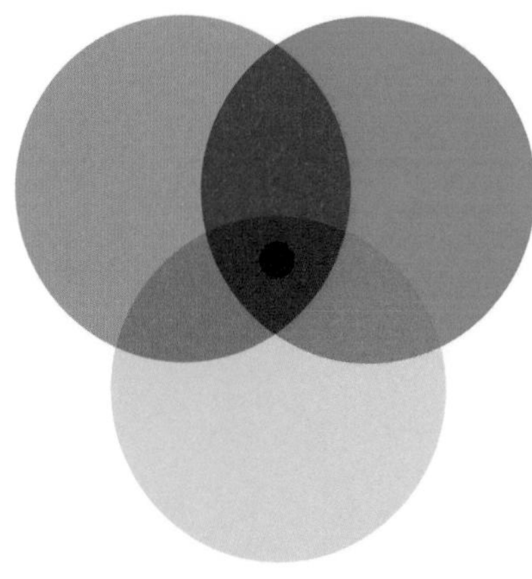

CONTRAST

Contrast isn't just the difference between light and dark—it includes warm and cool, and sharp and soft. The most effective images often succeed by maximizing contrast. The visuals here show the difference between high- and low-contrast treatments of the same image using Cybernetik girl and a stock photo background provided by Malleni-Stock.

I've used various techniques to increase contrast:

- More color saturation
- Increased values between the lights and darks
- A peachy-orange skin tone which complements the outfit's blue tones
- Blurring of the background to focus on the character details
- Warm tones in the background on the right to complement the blue wires on the left

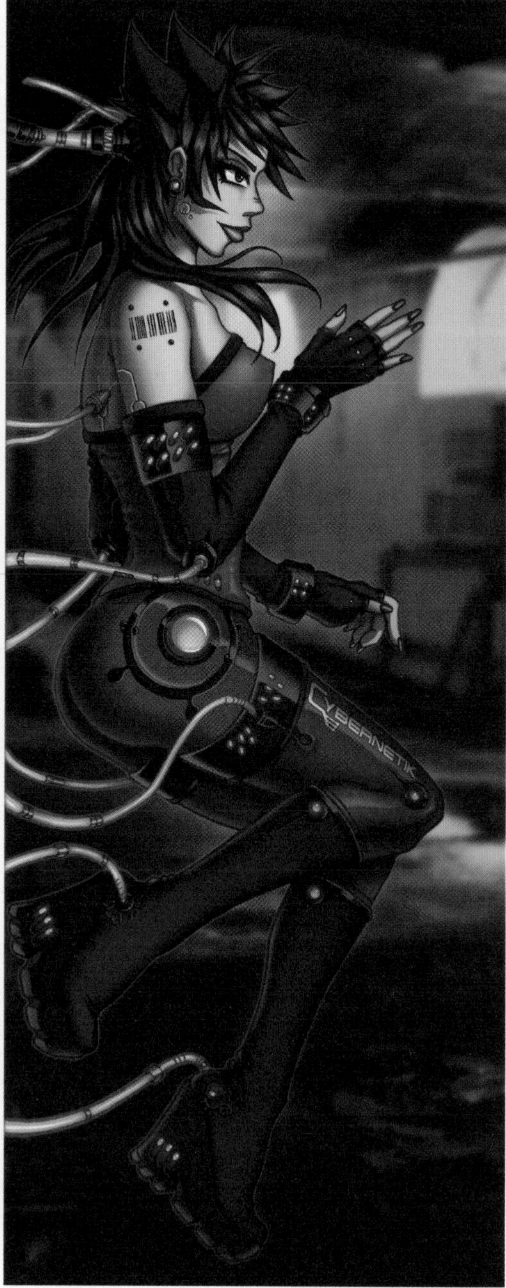

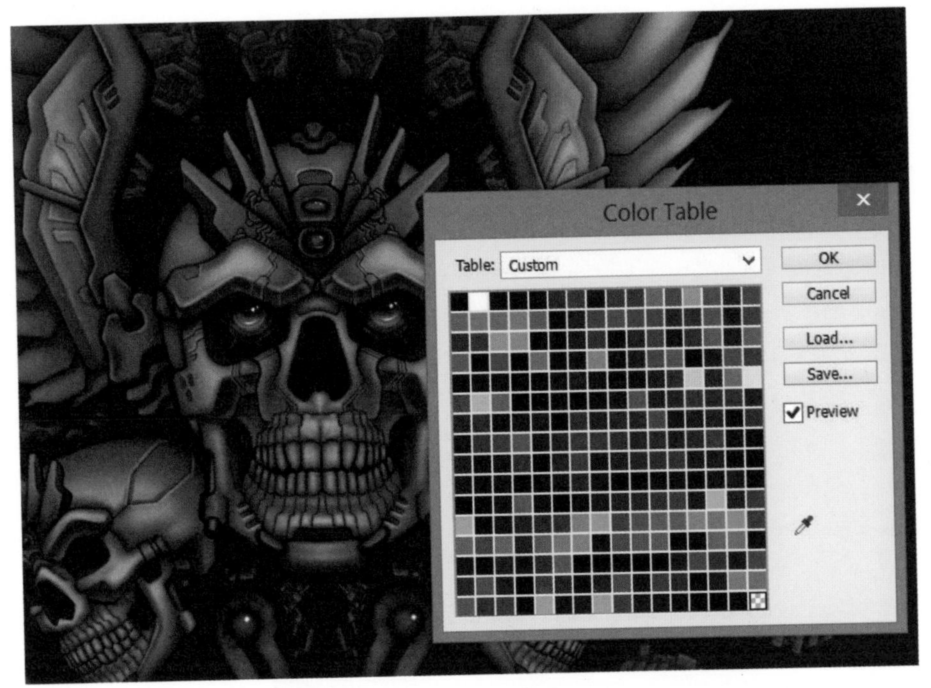

MONOCHROME

Sometimes hues can get in the way of understanding the power of values and contrast. Try experimenting with black, white, and grays. It's important to use a full range of lights and darks to achieve maximum impact.

THE INFLUENCE OF LIGHT

Different types of lighting affect the colors of objects. It's rare for a white piece of cloth to be pure white, for example. If placed outside on an overcast day it appears more gray, while inside, under a lightbulb, it takes on a yellow or orange tinge.

FOCUS

Make the focal point—the area you most want to draw the viewer's attention to—the lightest and brightest part of an image. This might be a character's eyes, for example, or their magical weapon. If you are adding a background, keep the character as bright as possible while dulling down the scenery around it.

COLOR PALETTE

A color palette is another way of describing the collection of colors used in your image. In Photoshop, you can create a palette based on your work so far; this way you can control your colour range and maintain continuity in your artwork.

Convert your image to Index Color: Image –> Mode –> Indexed Color. Set the number of colors you want in your swatch (256 is sufficient) and click OK. Then click Image –> Mode –> Color Table. From here you can click to save the palette as an ACT file. Go to the Swatches table and click the Menu icon toward the top right. Choose "Replace Swatches" and locate your previously saved ACT file. Make sure the ACT file type is selected via the drop-down option so that it shows the "CLUT" icon in your browser. Also remember to "Undo" to revert your image to RGB or CMYK from Indexed Color.

Color Examples

While it might be tempting to go wild with a huge variety of colors, it's generally preferable to limit your palette and use a specific color scheme. This is often how the most effective stand-alone pieces of character artwork are created. For optimum results, use colors adjacent to one another on the color wheel (these are known as analogous colors).

The sci-fi character artwork shown here demonstrates the use of different color schemes. "Bengosha" (left) illustrates the use of blue tones with an orange secondary color, while "Elise" (right) uses analogous pinks and purples.

TECHNICAL COLOR ISSUES: SCREEN VS. PRINT

There are a number of different ways in which you can set up your work and optimize it for print- and screen-based media.

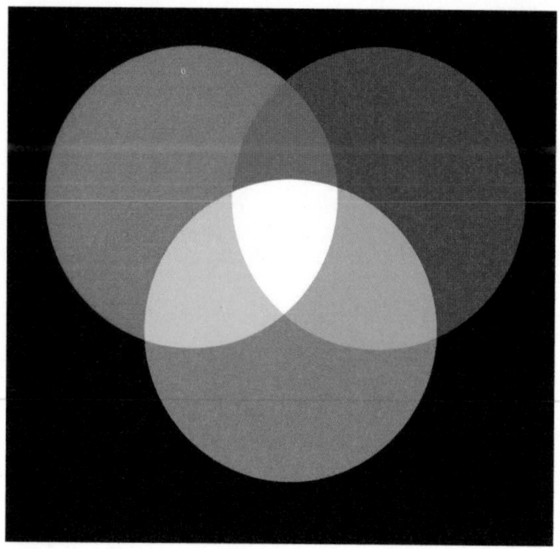

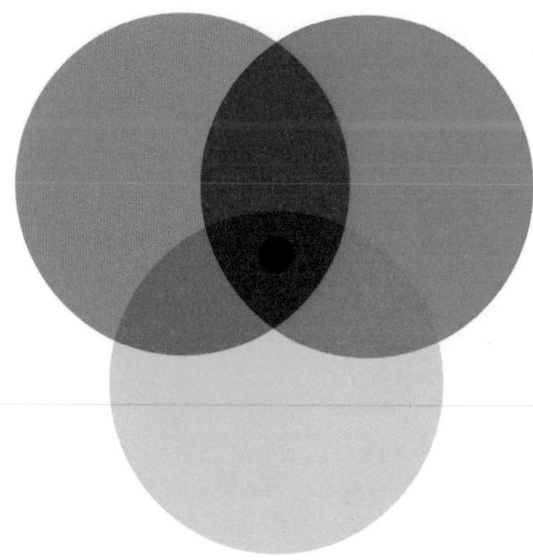

COLOR SETTINGS

RGB stands for Red, Green, Blue. It's a color scheme associated with electronic displays such as LCD monitors, cameras, and scanners and it works by combining these three colors to produce a range of hues and tones. RGB is an additive color model—colors come from a source which emits light (the screen), and light colors can be mixed together until white light is created. When all three colors are combined and displayed to their full extent, the result is a pure white. When all three colours are combined to the lowest degree, or value, the result is black. RGB offers the widest range of colors, allowing vivid hues such as lime green and turquoise to really pop.

CMYK is a process used for printers. It stands for Cyan, Magenta, Yellow, and Black. Using these colors in various amounts creates all the necessary hues and tones for printing images. CMYK is a subtractive color model—the colors come from inks (or paints, or dyes) that are overlaid until they shut out wavelengths of light and produce different colors. A CMYK file is larger than an RGB file because it has four color channels (referred to as "plates" in lithographic printing).

Setting up an artwork canvas as CMYK means that the colors seen on screen match more closely to printed color. However, if you are likely to work on digital comics, books, games, or with animation or film artwork, you might be better off sticking with RGB. This will give you the benefit of vivid RGB colors and the ability to use extra filters and image adjustments in Photoshop; you can then convert to CMYK, if necessary.

CONVERTING RGB IMAGES TO CMYK

Converting modes to make a print can be a complex task. Occasionally RGB images contain colors that are "out of gamut," which means they contain colors that CMYK cannot reproduce. To check for this, click View –> Gamut Warning [Ctrl+Shift+Y / Cmd+Shift+Y]. Colors that turn gray are incompatible with CMYK mode. Photoshop can replace these colors with what it calculates as the next best color, or you can manually use the color replace tool to select the closest matching color and Preview the CMYK mode via View –> Proof Colors.

After converting your RGB artwork using Image –> Mode –> CMYK, you can save it immediately or you can tweak adjustments such as Levels and Hue/Saturation to shift your colors closer toward the original tones. However, I find that the conversion from one color mode to the other is barely noticeable.

From a Fantasy World

Every character you create may require a slightly different approach and range of techniques. The first character in the line-up here is Japanese warrior girl Yuki. I will use her to show the ways in which you can make skin look more interesting. I'll also demonstrate how to create two-tone hair colors and a patterned material overlay while retaining the shaded areas beneath for a seamless, 3D finish.

Layers
Channels
Paths
Kind
Opacity: 100%
Normal
Fill: 100%
Lock:
ol
pupils
white
mouth
jewelry
details
glove
ribbons
swords
obi
trim
sleeves
jacket main
dress
boots
hair
skin
Size:
100 px
Hardness:
100%

CHARACTER RENDERING

I want to give this artwork a soft, airbrush feel. I've started with solid cel-style shadows then softened out the shadowed edges later. This helps me to plan my light source and figure out what shadows will be cast, so that my shading looks solid and bold.

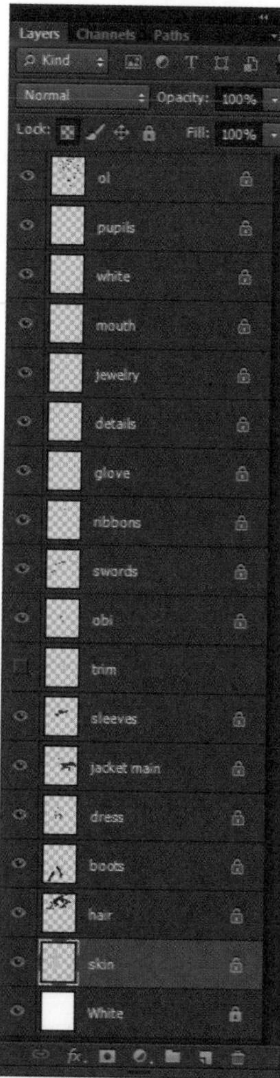

STEP 1

The first stage is to create the Line Art layer. I want Yuki to be a Japanese-inspired demon hunter warrior with a fantasy twist and a kimono-style outfit. I inked the artwork digitally.

STEP 2

I laid the flat tones (see pages 158–163), and Yuki was ready to color. At this stage, don't be overly concerned about color choice. You can alter the colors a little later on.

STEP 3

I blocked in a first pass of shadows using a hard brush for each individual layer. I chose a center-right light source, so my shading is mostly placed toward the left.

STEP 4

With a soft, low-flow percentage brush, I softened the image and blended in some smooth shading. I started with the skin, increasing vibrancy and contrast using the Levels or Brightness/Contrast adjustments. Adding a secondary light source and shadow conditioning (with additional tone or desaturated shadows and shaded areas) can help make the image look more realistic and dynamic.

With warm tones, such as skin, I like to add a colder gray, blue, or purple shadow color or secondary light. This can be done now, but I prefer to leave it until I'm happy with how the natural skin shading looks.

STEP 5

Now select a blue, purple, or gray tone via the Color Picker and set up a larger, soft, low-flow brush, setting its mode to "Color." Use this to shade the darkest parts of the skin, toward the left-hand side edges and shadowed areas.

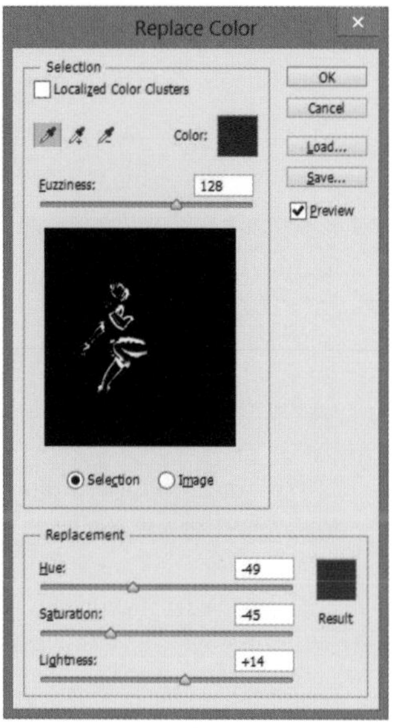

STEP 6

To replace shadow color, go to Image –> Adjustments –> Replace Color. Use the eye dropper to select the darkest brown color on the skin layer. Adjust the fuzziness to your liking; this affects the tolerance and spread of the color to be replaced. Then adjust the Hue, Saturation, and Lightness sliders accordingly.

STEP 7

On the Hair layer, set a large, soft, low-flow brush mode to Multiply. This will darken existing shades and multiply the amount of dark on the base tones. Use this brush to give form to the hair by shading toward the ends and edges. Use the [and] keys to adjust the brush sizes and reach narrower sections of hair.

STEP 8

Further refine the hair using a smaller, lighter brush with a normal blending mode. Use the Smudge tool to taper out clumpy rendering and brush strokes. When adding highlights, it's a good idea to create a new, separate layer so you can edit this without affecting the surrounding hair shading. Use a hard white brush to rough out where you'll be adding areas of shine.

STEP 9

Now use a combination of the Smudge tool and Eraser to sculpt the highlights into more defined shapes. In this instance, I faded them out by adjusting the layer's opacity to 60%. Merge the highlights and hair layer, then use a brush set to Color Dodge blending mode, and apply to the highlights to increase their glow and intensity. A few small tweaks to the layer contrast and use of the "replace color" technique and the hair shading is done.

STEP 10

Colorizing parts of the hair and adding colored highlights can be great fun and adds to your character. Create a new layer called "H color." Create a selection encompassing the existing hair layer boundaries by clicking the Hair layer while holding down Ctrl / Cmd on the keyboard. Choose a second hair color, in this case, blue. With a soft, low-flow brush, paint in the second color toward the tips of the hair. Change the H color layer to the Color blending mode. Optionally, add an additional third color toward the ends of the tips.

STEP 11

Work through rendering the remaining layers using the techniques mentioned so far until the clothing and accessories are complete.

STEP 12

The next step is Pattern Overlay. Source a suitable pattern for the clothing. Make sure the image dimensions are as high as possible to ensure the best quality. I've chosen a floral stock image tile for the kimono-style outfit.

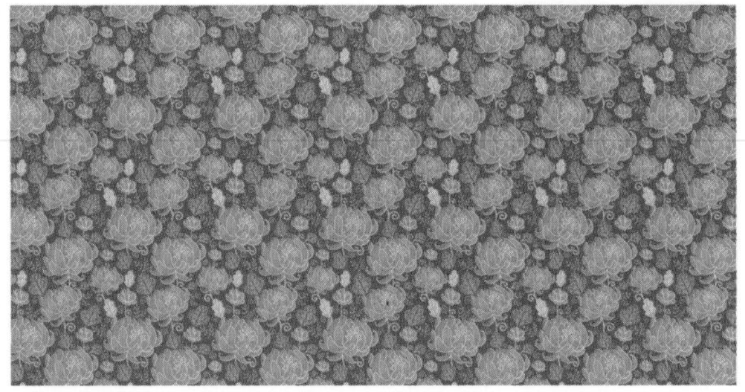

STEP 13

Open the pattern image, then duplicate and tile it. To do this, enlarge the canvas using the Crop tool or Image –> Canvas Size [Alt+Ctrl+C / Opt+Cmd+C]. Make the image layer editable. Duplicate the layer and place a tile next to it. Holding Shift while dragging the image into position keeps the layer contents parallel. Adding a Snap [Ctrl+Shift+; / Cmd+Shift+;] will help arrange these to fit perfectly next to each other.

Merge the layers, then duplicate and place next to the existing layer content. Repeat this process to build up a series of tiles next to one another.

STEP 14

Copy the pattern to the character image by selecting the pattern layer content [Ctrl+A / Cmd+A] then pasting it on to the Yuki canvas [Ctrl+V / Cmd+V]. Now position this over the Kimono layer. Select the Kimono content by clicking the layer on the layer panel while holding Ctrl / Cmd. Invert the selection: Select –> Inverse [Shift+Ctrl+I / Shift+Cmd+I] then press delete on the keyboard. Deselect the selection [Ctrl+D / Cmd+D].

STEP 15

Set the Pattern Overlay layer to a blending mode called Overlay. Tone it down a little by reducing the layer's opacity to 80%. Rather than using Overlay, experiment by toggling through the different layer blending modes and you might find an interesting effect you hadn't planned on.

STEP 16

Because of the crimson tone underneath, some of the yellow and purple tones of the pattern are lost. To combat this, select the crimson Kimono layer and desaturate it: Image -> Adjust -> Desaturate. Tweak the Levels to lighten and increase contrast—I've set Shadows to 5, Midtones to 1.2, and Highlights to 120. Adjust the Hue/Saturation level. I've set it to "Colorize" and changed the Hue value to 330, Saturation to 20, and Lightness to –5.

STEP 17

Repeat the Pattern Overlay process to add any other trim patterns or details—in this case I've added some patterning to the belt. Finish by adjusting any layer colors, contrast levels or settings until you're happy with the resulting image. After merging all the character elements, I added a subtle inner glow in white.

UNDER ARREST!

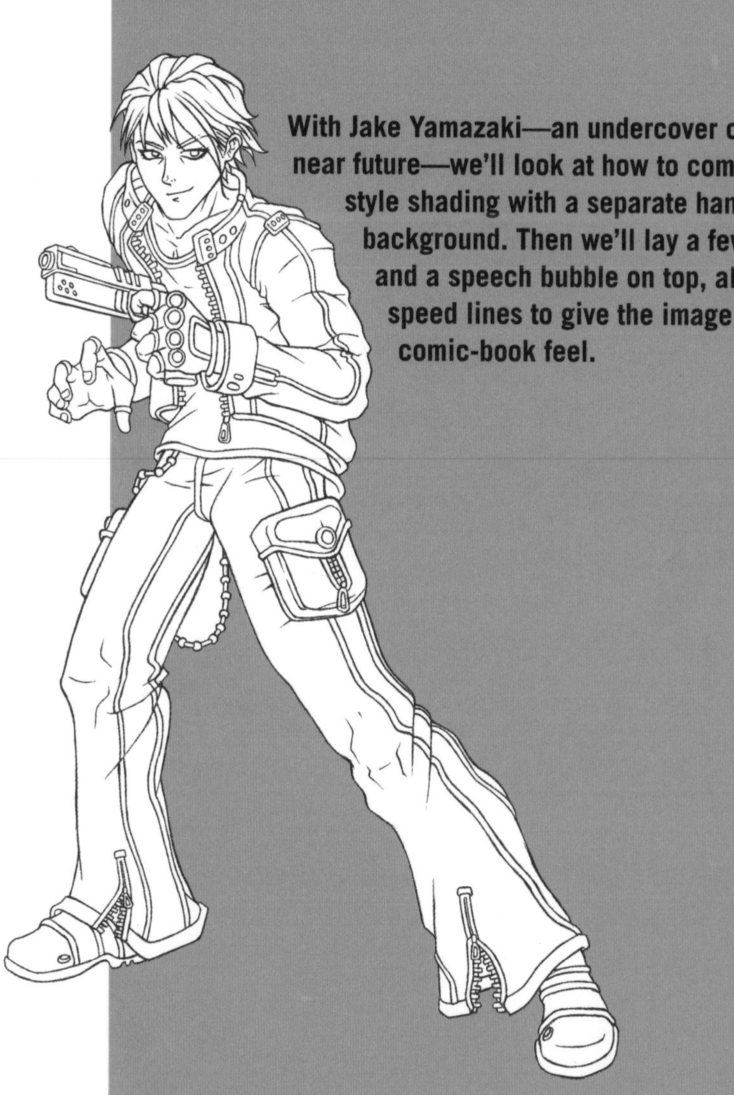

With Jake Yamazaki—an undercover cop of the near future—we'll look at how to combine cel-style shading with a separate hand-drawn background. Then we'll lay a few sound effects and a speech bubble on top, along with some speed lines to give the image a manga-style comic-book feel.

Layers
Channels
Paths
Kind
Normal
Opacity: 100%
Lock:
Fill: 100%
ol
gun ex1
trims 2
trims
shirt
trousers
jacket gloves shoes
hair
eye w
skin
BG

ADDING A BACKGROUND

Sometimes it's good to keep the character artwork and background separate. This makes coloring background elements easier because you don't have to mask off or work around the character. It also makes it easier to tweak perspective, styles, and color schemes.

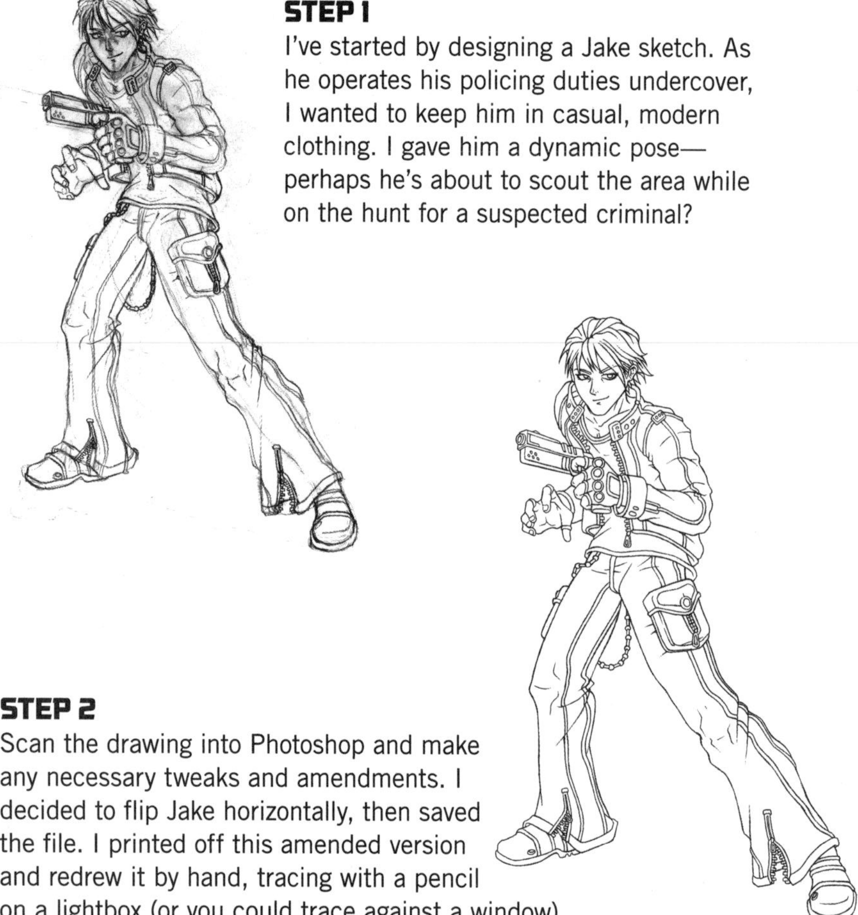

STEP 1
I've started by designing a Jake sketch. As he operates his policing duties undercover, I wanted to keep him in casual, modern clothing. I gave him a dynamic pose—perhaps he's about to scout the area while on the hunt for a suspected criminal?

STEP 2
Scan the drawing into Photoshop and make any necessary tweaks and amendments. I decided to flip Jake horizontally, then saved the file. I printed off this amended version and redrew it by hand, tracing with a pencil on a lightbox (or you could trace against a window). Once redrawn, I scanned the image into Photoshop and cleaned it up.

STEP 3
Next I hand-drew a city alleyway for the background. Keep in mind how big you want the character to be when drawing the perspective of the buildings. Scan the image into Photoshop and save it.

STEP 4

With the background image opened, open the character sketch to plan where you want to place him. Copy the character to the background image and place him on a layer above it. Using the Transform tool, make him bigger or smaller and position him so that he is in proportion with the background. The blue image shows an ideal placement. The red one could also work, although it's a little too small for this drawing unless you decide to crop the background image.

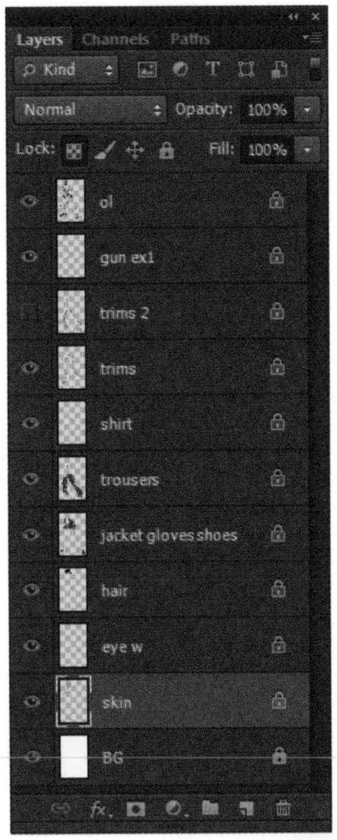

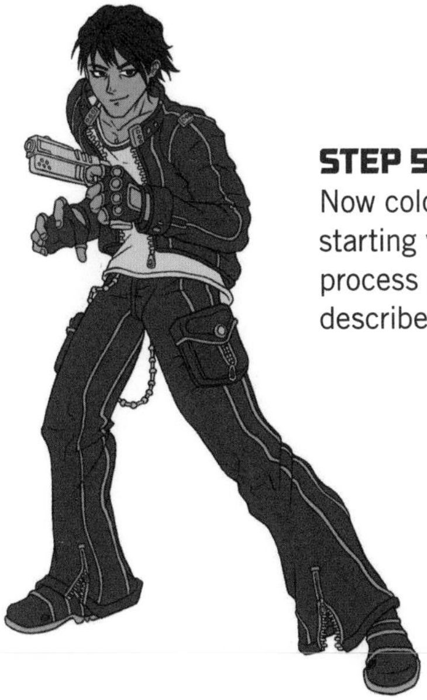

STEP 5

Now color Jake, starting with the usual process of flatting described earlier.

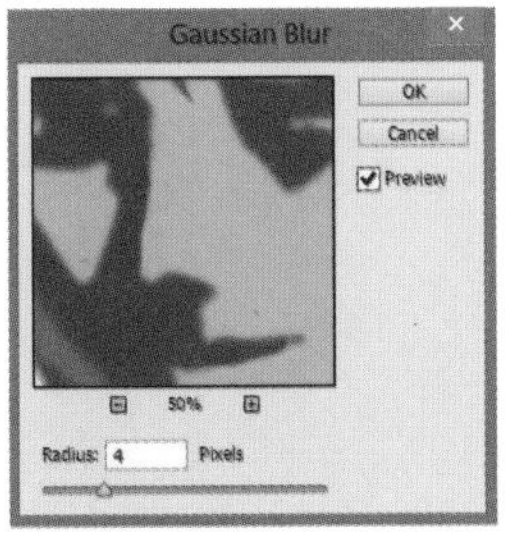

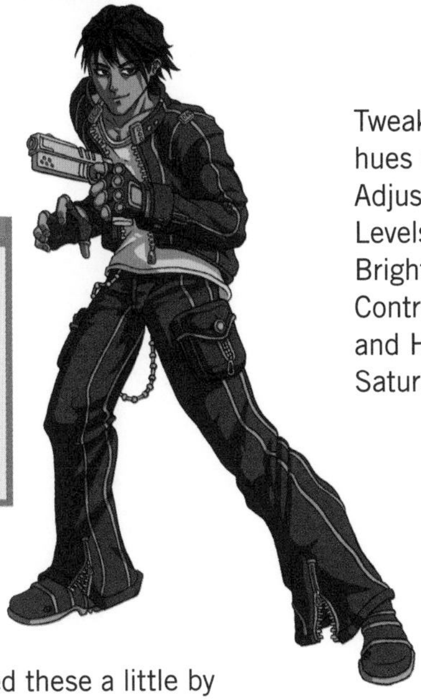

I've chosen a cel rendering with a single pass of shadows and softened these a little by using a blur filter with a radius of 4: Filter –> Blur –> Gaussian Blur.

Tweak the hues using Adjustments: Levels, Brightness/Contrast and Hue/Saturation.

STEP 6

Using gray hues for the background, create a "value study" (a high-contrast monochrome image, see left) to make sure the lights and darks are in the right place. To give the background a rough, textured look, use a thick, heavy brush from the Brush Presets menu (right) and a few Googled images for reference (photo elements have been added in the distance).

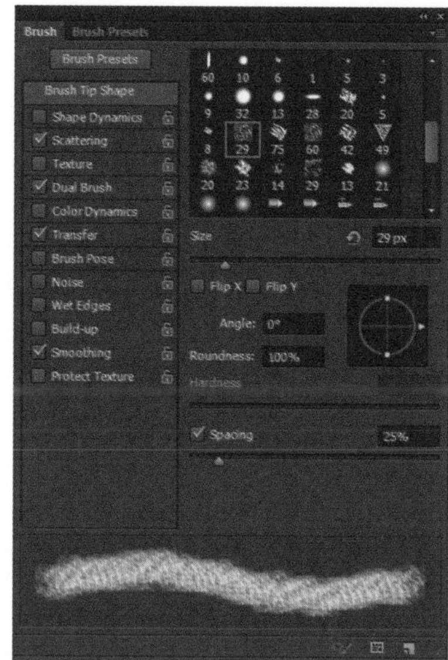

STEP 7

Add color to the background by creating a second layer and setting its blending mode to "Color." The trick is to keep it simple, like a speed painting. Merge this color overlay with the rendered layer beneath and name it "Background."

STEP 8

Using the plan in Step 4, merge the Jake color layers to a single layer by going to the Layers panel menu and selecting Merge Visible [Shift+Ctl+E / Shift+Cmd+E]. Copy Jake to the colored background image on a layer on top and name it "Jake." Use the Transform tool to adjust him to the appropriate size.

STEP 9

To tie his color tones in with the background, add a color overlay. To do this, add a new layer on top named "Overlay." Ctrl+Click / Cmd+Click on the layer thumbnail for Jake. This will create a selection covering all colored pixels. With the Overlay layer selected, fill it with a solid blue. Deselect the selection [Ctrl+D / Cmd+D]. Lock the transparent pixels on that layer and use a brush to add in secondary yellow light. Adjust the opacity to help you see where the secondary light will fall.

STEP 10

Set the blending mode of the Overlay layer to "Color" and reduce the opacity to 40%.

STEP 11

Create a layer between Jake and the background called "Shadow." Use a dark blue or black with a brush to add shadow on the ground underneath the character. Set the opacity of this layer to 50%. The ground shadow layer will look something like the image above (minus the character silhouette, of course).

ADDING SOUND EFFECTS

As well as using onomatopoeia—"boom," "swoosh," "pow," and so on—the Japanese manga industry uses sound effect words to express certain actions or emotions. There's pretty much a sound effect for every occasion.

STEP 12

Create a sound effect to denote tension by making a new layer between the background and character layers. Name it SFX. Click the eye next to each layer, excluding the SFX layer, to make it easier to see what you're doing. Select a hard brush and draw a blocky back-to-front C shape with two little accents to the right. This is the Japanese symbol "Go." It is used as a sound effect to indicate rumbling and to add tension to a scene.

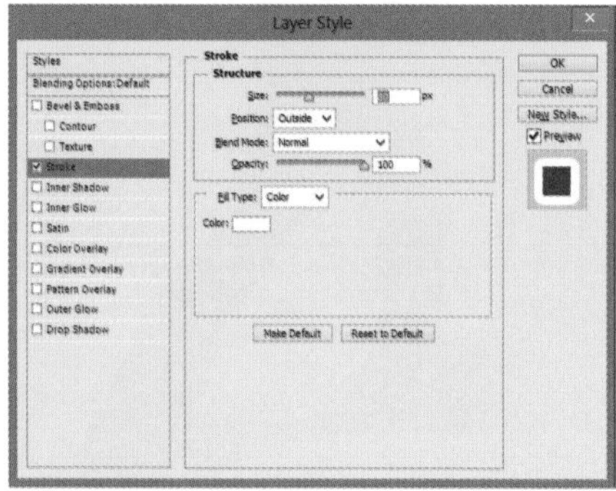

STEP 13

Duplicate the layer [Ctrl+J / Cmd+J] and free transform [Ctrl+T / Cmd+T] the second symbol to make it a bit smaller, rotated clockwise a little, and moved to the right. Repeat twice more so that you end up with an arc of text.

STEP 14

Position the sound effects behind the character and add a gradient to each symbol by using the Gradient tool or a large, soft brush. Right-click the SFX layer and click Blending Options. Add a white Stroke to create a white outline around each symbol.

STEP 15

Create a new layer at the top called "Bubble 1." Use the Elliptical Marquee tool to make a circular selection. Create a spike using the Polygon Lasso tool while holding down Shift to add to the selection. Fill the selection with white. Add a black Stroke to the bubble, making sure the Stroke position is set to "Inside" for a crisp outline.

STEP 16

Select the Type tool and click inside the bubble. Type the required text. Adjust the font size then go back to the bubble layer and adjust, if necessary, for a better fit.

Final Touches

STEP 17

To add action/speed lines, create a new layer on top named “Lines.” Select the Line tool and set the line weight (thickness) in the tool options bar.

Find a central point on the image where the lines will meet. Draw a line from this central point to the edge of the canvas. Repeat until you have created enough action lines in a spider-web pattern, increasing the weights of some of the lines, then use the Eraser to rub out and taper lines toward the middle. The action lines can be either white or black. I’ve used black for a more subtle effect and adjusted the layer opacity to 50%. I’ve finished the image with an orange overlay layer.

Futuristic Fighter Pilot

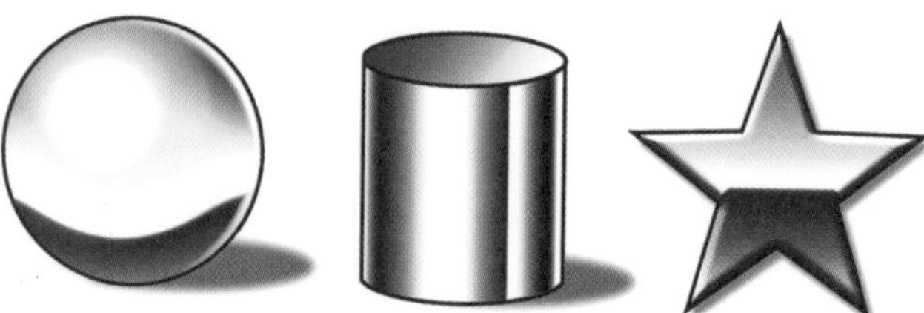

Technology and sci-fi are the staple diet of many Japanese manga fans. With futuristic fighter pilot Mizuki, you will discover how to use symmetry flip, duplicate finished character artwork to create an army, and add a vertical reflection. There are also tips on creating metal elements, neon glows, and shines.

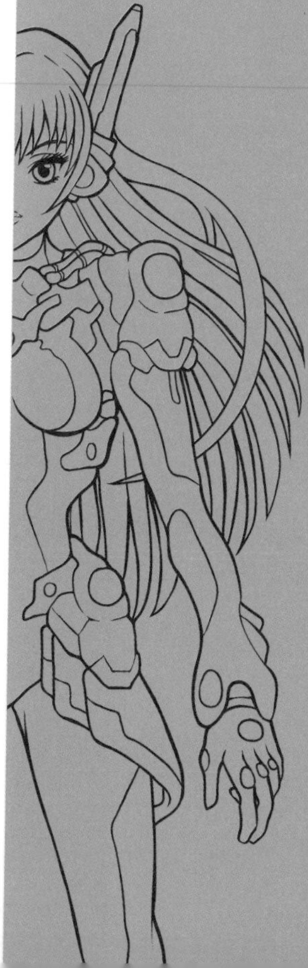

Layers
Channels
Paths
Kind
Normal
Opacity: 100%
Lock:
Fill: 100%
ol
eye
eye w
ex1
outfit 2
outfit1
hair
skin
w

Symmetry

Flipping artwork is a huge timesaver, as you only have to draw one side of a character. You can then duplicate and flip it to create the whole design.

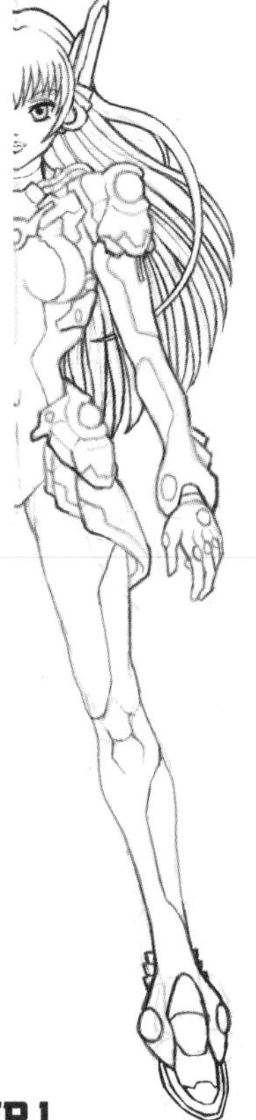

STEP 1
Start with a tablet-drawn sketch. I've decided to give Mizuki a tight-fitting outfit with armored areas on the shoulders and hips. I imagine she would be a pilot for some kind of giant robot/mecha.

STEP 2
Digitally ink the design and prepare it for color. Keep some outline overlap toward the center of the image.

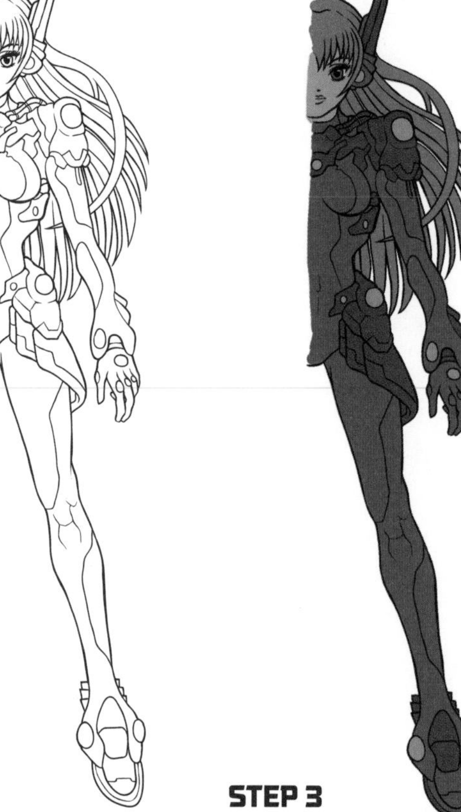

STEP 3
Add flat tones to the character.

STEP 4
Add rendering, shading, and highlights. Keep a neutral, central light source so that once this half is duplicated, the second half won't look out of place by using conflicting light sources.

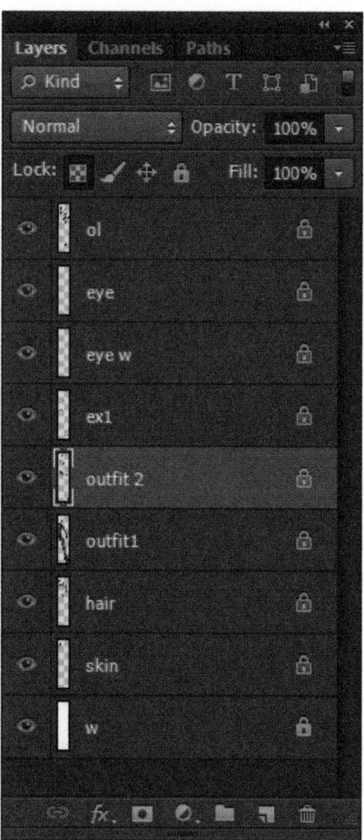

STEP 5

Once the skin, hair, and outfit layers are complete, move on to the Armor layer. Rendering and shading metal requires a high contrast between the light and dark areas. Metal can also become reflective depending on how shiny the surface is. Extra reflection detail is particularly required when creating a chrome look.

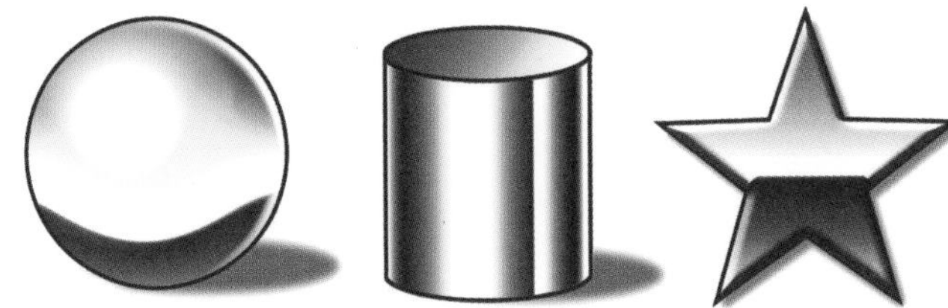

STEP 6

Add a first pass of shading over the armor.

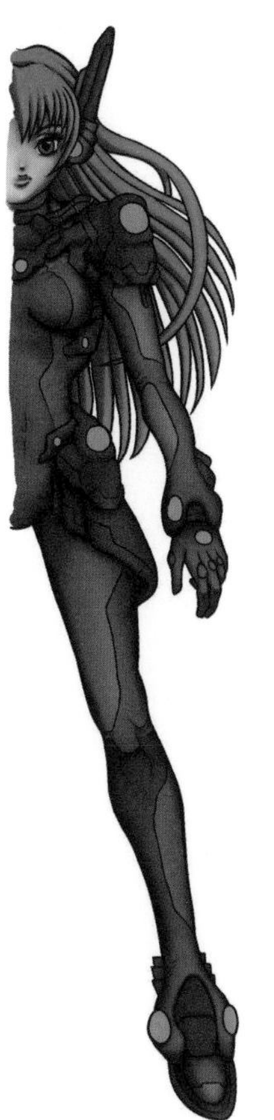

STEP 7

For the armored parts, the dark tone needs to butt up against a highlight tone toward the edges of each facet, bend, or fold.

Use the Levels adjustment to raise the contrast of the armor. If the tone becomes too saturated with color this can be altered via the Hue/Saturation adjustment. It's also possible to play around with the Brightness/Contrast adjustment sliders.

Once a high-contrast tonal level has been achieved, add some subtle purple into the mix to denote a degree of reflection from the purple outfit. This can be done by using a brush with its blending mode set to "Color" via the tool options bar. The purple is added to the edges of the armor next to purple parts of the outfit.

For this stage, it may be worth duplicating the Armor layer. Working on this duplicated layer means you can delete it if you make a mistake or overdo any Levels adjustments. Also, if the purple color on the armor is too strong it can be toned down by adjusting the duplicate layer's opacity setting and blending it in with the original Armor layer beneath.

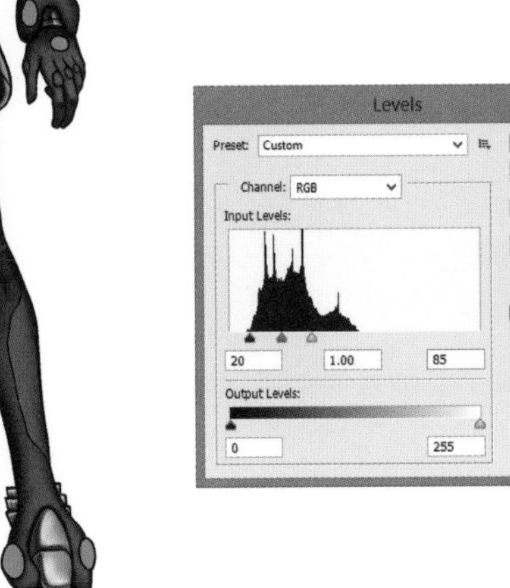

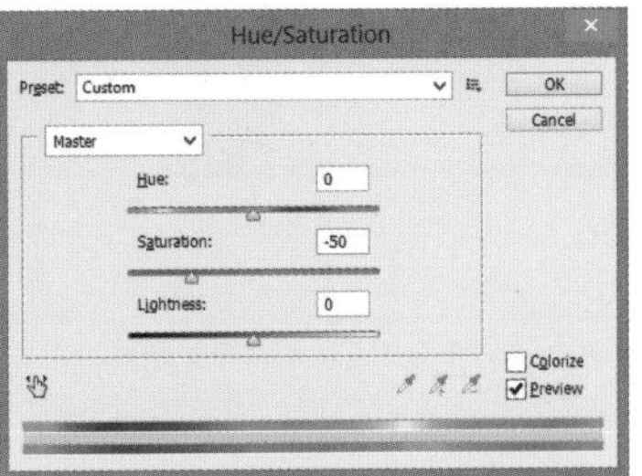

GLOWS AND ORBS

Neon glows are used in sci-fi to symbolize energy-powered equipment or circular orbs that can be used to fire laser projectiles. Mizuki has several circular orbs on her outfit. Restrict these to a single color to help limit the palette and tie the design together.

STEP 8

To create glows, start with a blue base color and add a lighter, whiter blue value toward the center of the circles using a low-flow brush. Click the small FX icon at the bottom of the Layers panel and select Outer Glow. From here, change the blending mode from Screen to Normal, Opacity to 70%, add a blue-colored glow, and adjust the glow strength using the Spread and Size sliders. In this instance, Spread is set to 15% and Size to 130 pixels. Click OK when you are happy with the result.

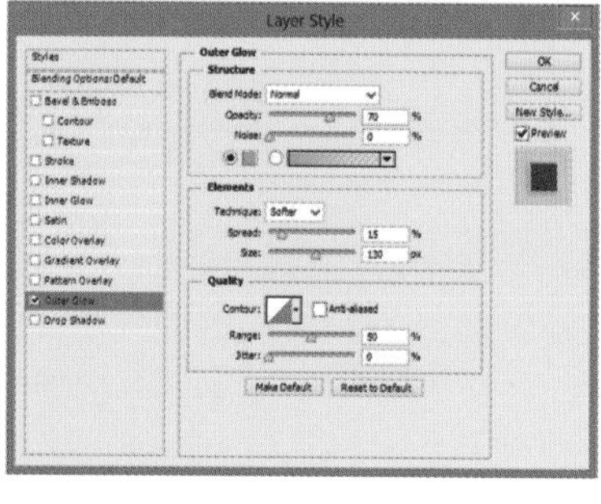

To complete the effect, select the Outline layer, make sure its transparent pixels are locked, and color around the circles using a blue tone and brush tool.

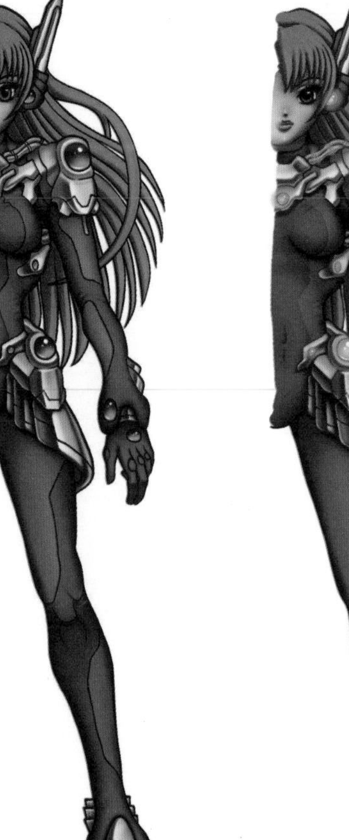

STEP 9

For shiny orbs, create a gradient from dark blue or black at the top to lighter blue at the bottom. On a new layer above, use a hard white brush to paint in the highlights. This is similar to rendering the eyes of a character. I usually place these "shines" toward the top left or top right for best effect, but placement also depends on where your light source is. To keep the light source consistent, the shines will need adjusting after the character half has been duplicated and flipped.

You can combine the glow method with the light shines to create a glowing, glossy orb. Then colourize outlines to finish this character half.

Duplicate and Flip

STEP 10

Once the coloring process is complete, use the Crop tool to enlarge the canvas or go to Image –> Canvas size and double the width. Merge all layers except for the white background and name this new layer "Right Half."

STEP 11

Make a copy of the Right Half layer. Name it "Left Half" and make sure it is above the Right Half in the layers panel. Flip the contents of this layer: Edit –> Transform –> Flip Horizontally. Use the Move tool to drag the Left Half layer to the left. Hold down Shift while you do this to constrain the movement to a straight line and match this up with the Right Half layer.

STEP 12

The excess image overlapping needs to be removed. Use a soft Eraser to do this. Use the Brush tool to fix errors and hide any seams. Finish this step by repositioning the light on the eyes and orbs and adjusting the eye size and position, using a combination of Lasso selecting, Transform, and Brush touch-ups. Then merge the Left Half and Right Half layers.

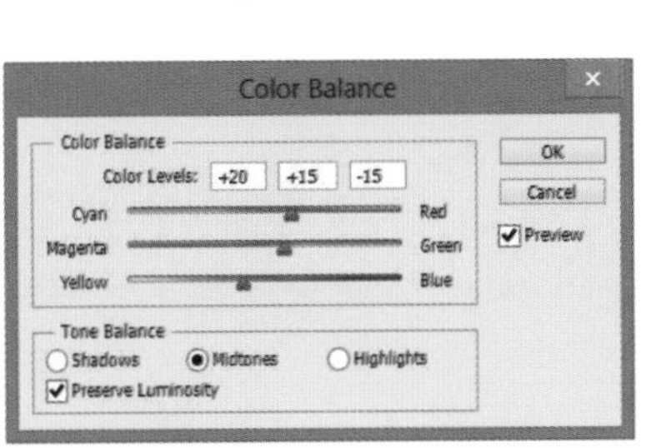

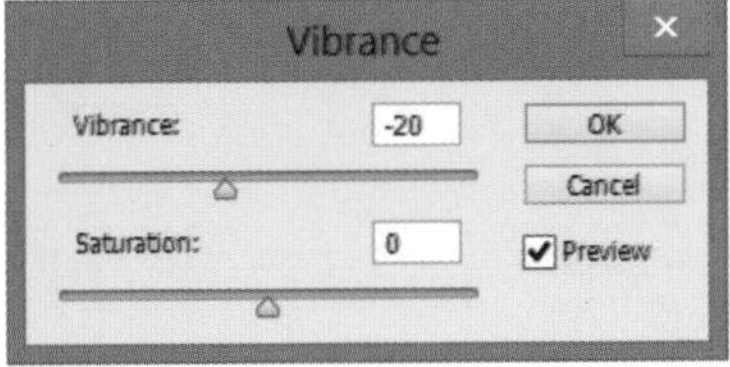

STEP 13

When finishing and merging color layers, spend time making some final adjustments to hues and tones.

STEP 14

For an army of Mizukis, increase the canvas size and duplicate the character layer as before. Move the second character copy beneath the first and use the Transform command to scale down the image. Position it above and beside the original character layer to create a sense of perspective.

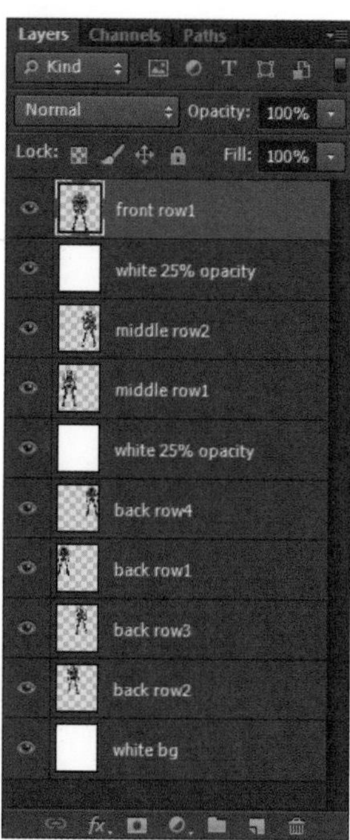

STEP 15

Repeat Step 14 for multiple lines of Mizukis. Between each row, add a new layer and fill it with white, then set its opacity to 25%. This will create some depth by fading out the Mizukis toward the rear of the art.

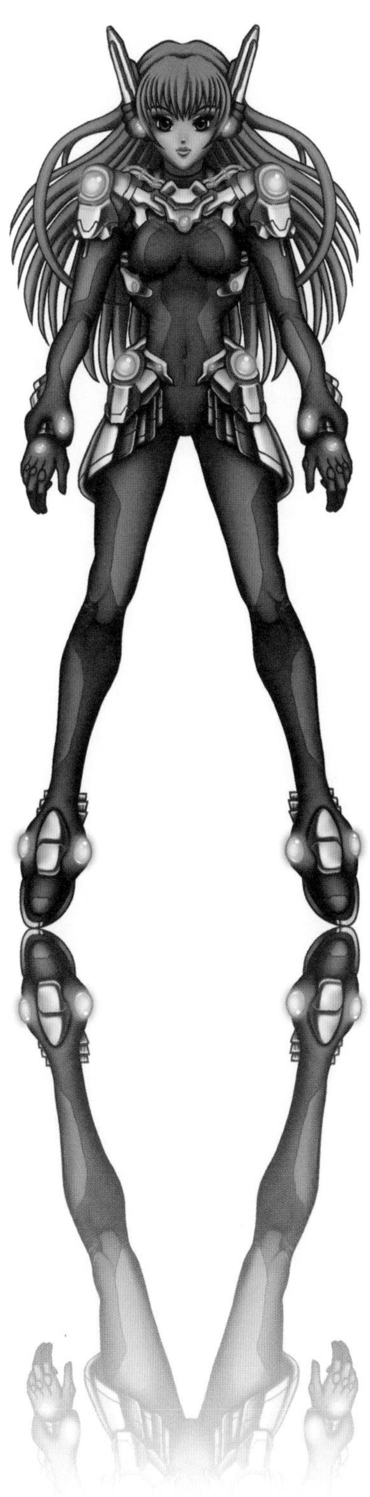

CREATING A GROUND REFLECTION

STEP 16

To create a ground reflection, double the canvas height, duplicate Mizuki and name the duplicate layer "Reflection." Flip the duplicate: Edit -> Transform -> Flip Vertically, so that the toe tips are touching. With the Reflection layer selected, click the "Add Vector Mask" icon at the bottom of the Layers panel. Make sure the Layer Mask thumbnail (situated to the right of the Layer thumbnail) is highlighted—this is indicated by the white corners. Add a black to white gradient fill on this Layer Mask, starting from the character's mid-point and dragging it up to the toes. Finish by adjusting the Reflection layer opacity to 80%.

WAR GAMES

The artwork for military commando Justin Silver reveals how to create seamless textures and patterns, and apply a range of camouflage styles. Military themes, soldiers, and guns dominate much of the video game industry and feature in many manga stories, so it's useful to learn how to apply these character elements and shortcuts.

Ps File Edit Image Layer Type Select
Pattern
Mode: Normal

RENDERING

Justin—an elite military commando fighting battles in a futuristic era—doesn't always play by the rules, but he always gets the job done.

STEP 1

Start with a pencil drawing and scan it into the computer. The line art is fairly neat to make it easier to follow at the inking stage.

STEP 2

The drawing is digitally inked for crisp, clean lines. I made a few small corrections to some of the lines at this stage.

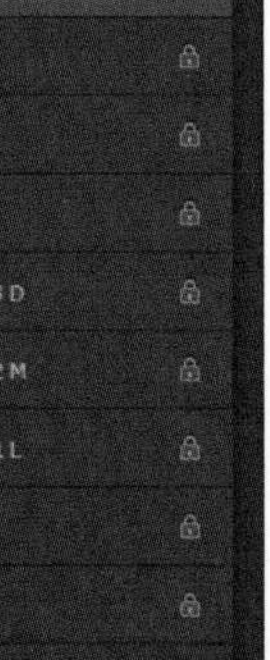

STEP 3

The flats are laid as usual on their respective layers.

I was undecided about outfit colors, so I broke up various elements into different gray shades: Layer "Cloth 1 L" for the light gray used on the main clothing; "Cloth 2 M" for a mid-gray used on boots and straps; and "Cloth 3 D" for a darker gray used on gloves and pouches, with a much lighter gray for "trims."

STEP 4

With a left-hand light source in mind, I began to plan out where shadows should go, using a hard brush to create a cel-style effect.

STEP 5

Using soft, round brushes of varying flow between 5% and 100%, soften the edges and add extra shadow where necessary. As with earlier examples, this step is a case of:

- Zooming in and out of the image to focus on adding various details (most often working in a zoomed-in state)
- Constantly increasing and decreasing brush sizes to fit the areas to be shaded
- Occasionally making use of the Smudge tool to create tapered shadow or highlights
- Sometimes setting a soft, low-flow percentage brush mode to Multiply to further darken areas with existing shadows
- Tweaking each layer's contrast after completing the rendering using Levels and Brightness/Contrast adjustments
- Coloring the Line Art layer

ADDING CAMOUFLAGE PATTERNS

As with the Yuki tutorial, adding a camouflage overlay to Justin's uniform can be achieved by sourcing textures and patterns from the internet and from stock image web sites. Patterns can also be created from scratch in Photoshop, then repeated or tiled on to a layer or selection using the Paint Bucket tool or layer effects.

STEP 6

To create a pattern, open a new canvas of equal dimensions, such as 1000 x 1000 pixels. Use the Brush tool to paint your design, using reference material if needs be.

STEP 7

To turn this pattern into a seamless texture or tile, go to Filter –> Other –> Offset. Set the Horizontal value to 200 and the Vertical value to 100, with undefined areas set to “Wrap Around.” Now you are presented with a tile where the shapes on the right margin will marry with those on the left margin and the top edges will marry with those at the bottom.

Go to Edit –> Define Pattern and name the tile “Camo 1” in the dialog box, then click OK. This will now be saved in the default Photoshop Patterns library and can be accessed and made use of later as an automatically repeated/tiled pattern.

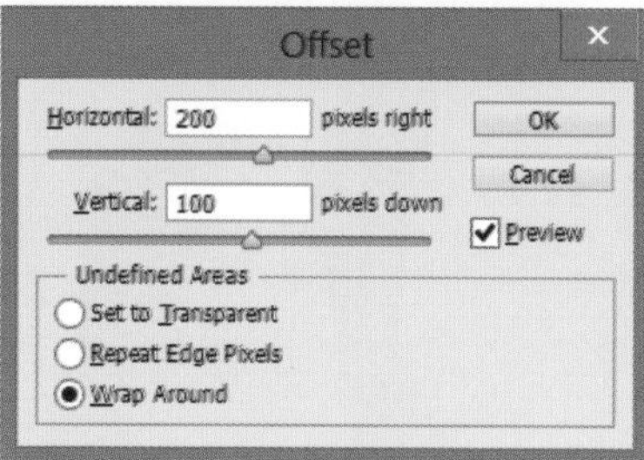

STEP 8

There are obvious straight-edged seams toward the top and left edges. Use the Brush tool to cover up and blend away these seams, but be careful not to take the brush up to the edges of the tile while doing this.

STEP 9

Adding a layer mask enables you to hide unwanted portions of underlying pattern and preserves the pattern as a whole. Go to Edit –> Presets –> Presets Manager, select the "Patterns" Preset Type from the drop-down box, then click "load." You should be able to select the PAT file you pasted to the appropriate directory earlier.

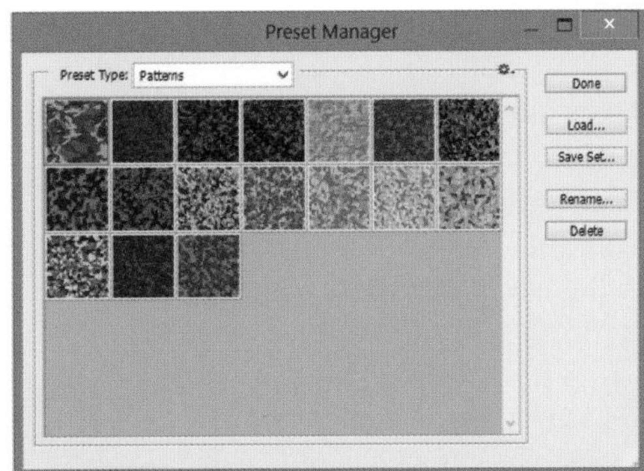

Create a new layer above the "Cloth 1 L" layer and name it "Camo Pattern." Select the Paint Bucket tool and change the fill mode from "Foreground" to "Pattern."

Next to the Fill mode option is a drop-down panel which houses various preset patterns. If the camo pattern you want to use is there, click the thumbnail to select it. If not, you may need to locate the relevant pattern by clicking on the small settings cog icon at the top right of this panel and choosing the required pattern library from the list.

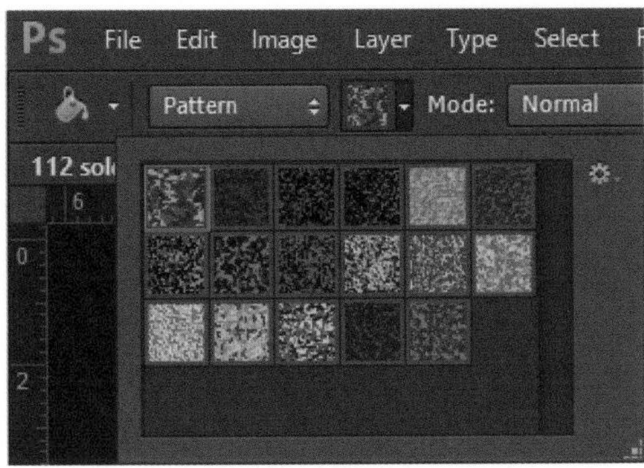

Next, click Append or OK to add these patterns to the pattern drop-down panel.

STEP 10

Click the canvas with Camo Pattern selected to fill the layer with a tiled pattern. Ctrl+Click / Cmd+Click the Layer thumbnail for "Cloth 1 L." This will bring up the "marching ants" selection around the elements on this layer.

With Camo Pattern still selected, click the Add Vector Mask icon. As with the Mizuki ground reflection tutorial, you'll notice a second black-and-white Layer Mask thumbnail image next to the first Layer thumbnail, with a chainlink icon between.

STEP 11

Set the Camo Pattern layer blending mode to Overlay. Tone it down a little by reducing the layer's opacity to 90%. Steps 9–11 can be repeated for layers "Cloth 2 M," "Cloth 3 D," and "Trim."

With the Mask Layer thumbnail selected, use a black brush to add to the mask (or white, to subtract). This can be used to erase any camo pattern not required on parts of the image.

STEP 12

Swap Camo Pattern layers and adjust some of the tones to create combat gear suitable for various environments. For the first example I used a "US woodland" style of pattern. You might want to test out digital urban, desert or arctic warfare styles too.

Logos and Finish

Logos can be created separately and applied toward the end, which means they can be manipulated or duplicated without interfering with the rest of the artwork.

STEP 13

To add the skull and swords insignia to the outfit, create a duplicate of the image before merging all layers except for the white background. Use the Lasso tool to create a selection around the logo, then cut and paste it to a new layer, and name the layer "Logo." If you want to put the logo in several places on the outfit, duplicate the Logo layer and hide the duplicate—it can be un-hidden and used or re-duplicated later on.

With the Logo layer selected, go to Edit -> Free Transform [Ctrl+T / Cmd+T] and begin to position, rotate, and resize the logo to fit over the soldier's left shoulder.

Use the Transform commands Warp and Perspective and adjust the corresponding anchor nodes to shape the logo, making it more spherical and 3D to fit on the round part of the shoulder.

STEP 14

Add a little shading to the logo, using a brush set to Multiply. Trim off any overlapping excess parts of the logo. Add a dark outer glow layer style to finish it off.

STEP 15

For the finishing touches:

- ▶ Add gun barrel smoke with a brush, reducing the smoke layer opacity to make it more transparent
- ▶ Add a ground shadow with a soft black brush
- ▶ To add a photo background, see pages 224–5 for instructions
- ▶ A blue gradient layer overlay ties things together; set the blending mode to pin light and the layer's opacity to 60%.
- ▶ Adjust hues, values, and tones where necessary

GOTHIC LOLITA

In Japanese manga, the term Lolita refers to "cuteness," "elegance," and "modesty;" it doesn't have the sexual connotations suggested by the name in Western culture. Gothic Lolita demonstrates how to add clothing trim and accessories, alter color combinations, use color overlays, and create an illustration by adding a photo-manipulated background.

Hue/Saturation
Preset: Custom
OK
Cancel
Master
Hue: -160
Saturation: 0
Lightness: 0
Colorize
Preview
Layers Channels Paths
Kind
Overlay
Opacity:
Lock:
Fill: 100%
ov colour
ov light
ov dark
bow collar
Effects
Stroke
bow s r
Effects
Stroke
bow s l
Effects
Stroke
bow d 4
Effects
Stroke
bow d 3
Effects
Stroke

GOTHIC LOLITA STYLE

Gothic Lolita style is based on Victorian-era clothing with a dark edge, on the "visual kei" genre, and on Goth rock bands. With some color alterations, you will be able to mimic other fashion variations too.

STEP 1

Start with a pencil drawing and scan it into the computer. The intention is to go for a sort of baby doll, "Alice in Wonderland" look.

STEP 2

To make things clean, clear, and easier to color, digitally ink the artwork.

STEP 3

Lay down flat tones. Lay an extra flat for the legs and hide the layer. You will use this for socks/tights on alternative versions of the image at a later stage. Also, optionally, divide the skirt into three layers (one for each row of folds) to make the shading more manageable.

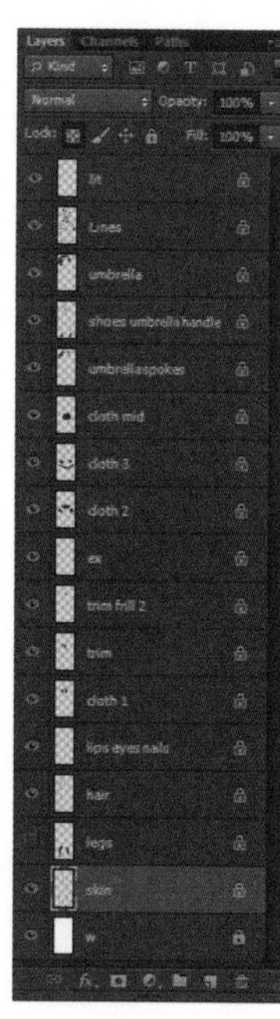

STEP 4

Add shadows and any necessary highlights. Keep the light source in mind—it will be coming primarily from the right-hand side. Use the methods explained on pages 160–3 to create an anime cel look.

ADDING ACCESSORIES

You can add photographic or predrawn objects and elements to an illustration, just like making a collage.

STEP 5

For the bow, source a stock image or photo. Open it in Photoshop and unlock the flattened Background layer by pressing Alt and double-clicking it in the Layers panel. Cut out the bow from the background using the Magnetic Lasso, found in the Lasso tool's flyout menu. Dragging it round the edges of the bow works well on an image where the contrast between object and background is high. Right-click the lassoed selection, choose Select Inverse, and press delete on the keyboard to remove unwanted background.

Use the Hue/Saturation adjustment to color the bow. Adjust the Brightness/Contrast levels.

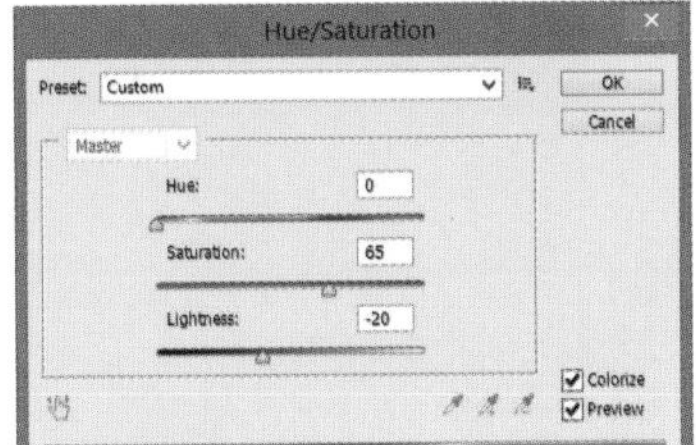

STEP 6

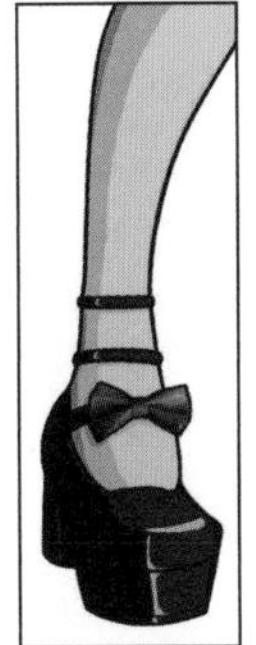

Copy and paste the bow on a layer above the Line Art layer and name it "Bow." This layer can now be duplicated as necessary and each bow layer can be positioned, resized, and rotated to fit on to parts of the image using Free Transform. You can also use the Warp and Perspective Transformation commands to manipulate these images further.

Place a larger bow around the belt area, a few on Lolita's dress, one on her collar, and one on each shoe. Add a 4–6 pixel-width black Stroke layer effect to each of the bows to mimic the outline around the rest of the image.

Add some shading to the bottom left portions of these bows to indicate cast shadows. This can be done with a brush and black on a new layer, with its blending mode set to Soft Light.

STEP 7

Source a sample of lace trim, edit it, and paste it on to a new layer on the image in the same manner as the bow.

STEP 8

Duplicate the lace layer and position over each hand. Shrink the sample down using Free Transform, then use the Eraser to rub out any excess to create a fingerless glove.

Use another lace layer to create a trim on the skirt. This can be done by positioning several lace samples next to one another. Use Warp Transform to curve the trim so that it follows the hem of the skirt.

Add some lace trim to the umbrella and a rose to Lolita's hairband at the side, using the same techniques.

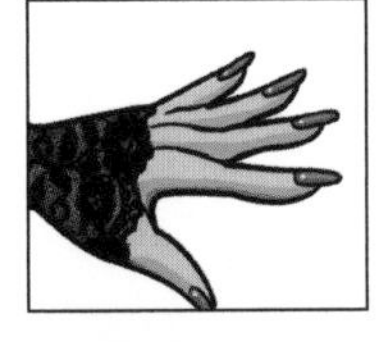

ADDING OVERLAYS

There are countless effects you can add to enhance illustrations. The following steps show just one way of adding overlays.

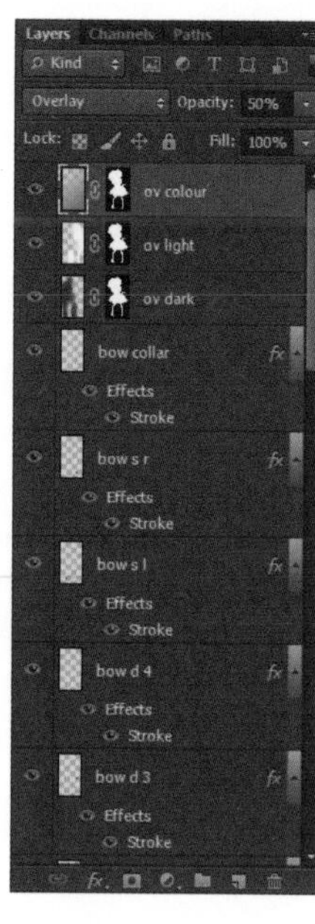

STEP 9

Further define the left-hand light source by adding a light overlay coming from the right. To do this, pick a large, soft 50% opacity brush and select a white foreground color. Add a loose spread of white tone around the right edges of the figure. Set the layer blending mode to Soft Light and the layer opacity to 35%.

STEP 10

Further define the shadows by adding a dark overlay toward the left. Add a gray spread of tone coming from the left. Set the layer blending mode to Vivid Light and the layer opacity to 35%.

STEP 11

Add a colored light source from the bottom right. To do this, select the Gradient Fill tool and drag a red to transparent tone over the image, starting in the bottom corner. Set the layer blending mode to Overlay and the layer opacity to 50%.

To stop the excess tone on these overlays from interfering with the background image, which will be added in Step 14, create layer masks (see pages 142–3). I also changed the eye color to brown.

Adjusting Colors

As well as "Gosu rori" (GothLoli), there are various Lolita sub-categories. To name but a few: Kuro Loli (all black), Shiro Loli (all white), Sweet Lolita (pastels and/or cute prints), Classic Lolita (Rococo, Regency, and Victorian influences), Country Lolita (gingham patterns and straw baskets), Punk Lolita (chains, safety pins, and tattered fabric) and Wa Lolita (traditional Japanese clothing styles).

Using the Hue/Saturation sliders and Levels adjustments, it's possible to create alternative outfits easily in minutes. Before starting an alteration process it's a good idea to save and work on a new copy of the file, or go to Image –> Duplicate to begin working on a second copy while retaining the original.

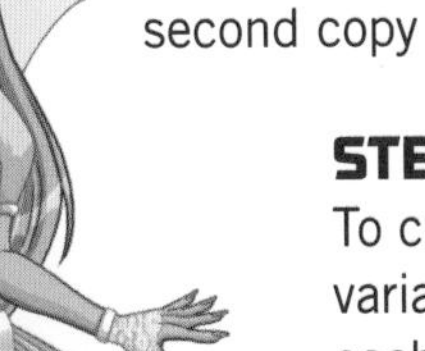

STEP 12

To create a pink Sweet Lolita variant, systematically go through each layer applying adjustments to the different outfit elements. The main colors to change are shown in the panel on the right.

For lace gloves and skirt trim: Image –> Adjustments –> Invert [Ctrl+I / Cmd+I]. Then add a red stroke at 50% opacity via the Layer FX icon.

To give Sweet Lolita a pair of tights, unhide the leg flats layer created earlier, color it a light gray and set its layer blending mode to Hard Light. Particularly when working with light or pastel tones, it looks best to color the line art also.

Layer/s	*Level adjustments*	*Hue/Saturation adjustments*
Dark clothes, shoes	Shadows: 0 Midtones: 1.30 Highlights: 80	Hue: 350 Saturation: 70 Lightness: 70 +check Colorize box
Umbrella	Shadows: 0 Highlights: 25	Hue: 360 Lightness: 60 +check Colorize box
Bows and reds	Shadows: 0 Midtones: 1.20 Highlights: 25	Hue: 360 Saturation: 60 Lightness: 60 +check Colorize box
Lips and nails	N/A	Saturation: 0 Lightness: 40

STEP 13

Now merge all outfit layers. To do this, exclude skin tones, overlays (and perhaps hair, eyes, lips, and bow colors) and create a new color version by editing multiple outfit parts in one hit. In this case, I've changed to a blue Sweet Lolita color scheme by adjusting the Hue level to –160.

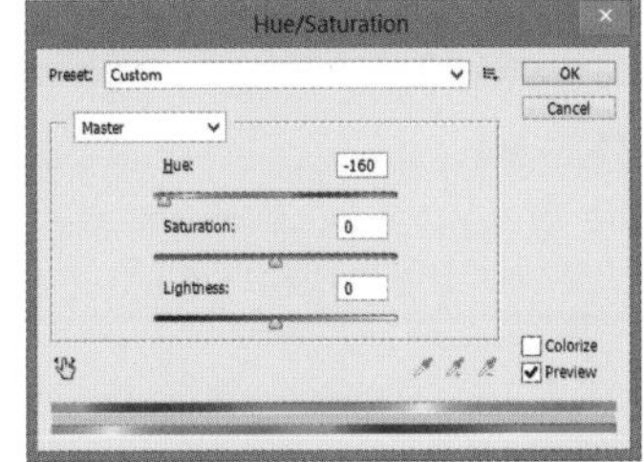

ADDING A PHOTO BACKGROUND

Just dropping a photo in to a piece of character artwork doesn't usually add a lot to the piece—it can overcomplicate and detract from the figure and illustrative elements. To integrate photos into an illustration, consider correcting the positioning and making sure the perspective used in the photo matches the artwork. If you blur the image, creating just a suggestion of background, it will make the character a focal point and stop the photo from looking out of place against the artwork style.

Try tweaking the colors and contrast. High contrast helps to create a more abstract background. The photo's tones should mimic or complement the illustration.

STEP 15

With the Photo layer selected, go to Filter –> Blur –> Gaussian Blur. Set the blurring to 20 and click OK. To blur out distant objects even more, use the Square Marquee tool, setting its feathering to 600 pixels via the tool options bar. Create a selection covering the top two-thirds of the canvas. Add a second Gaussian Blur set to 40.

STEP 14

Take or source an appropriate photo. In this case, I've used a Tokyo street scene.

Copy it to the Lolita art and name its layer "Photo." Use the Crop tool to enlarge the canvas to an appropriate size. You can also go to Image –> Canvas size and type in specific new dimensions. Position the background so it fits with the character's perspective.

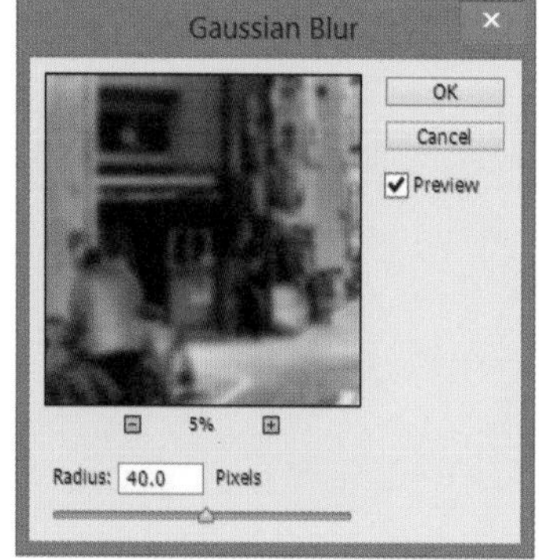

STEP 16

Increase the background contrast, create a shadow layer for the ground, and add any additional overlay tones. Once all visible layers have been merged [Shift+Ctrl+E / Shift+Cmd+E], play around with adjustments such as Color Balance, Hue/Saturation, Variations and Curves—this can be a lot of fun and will give your artwork a totally different look.

BEASTS

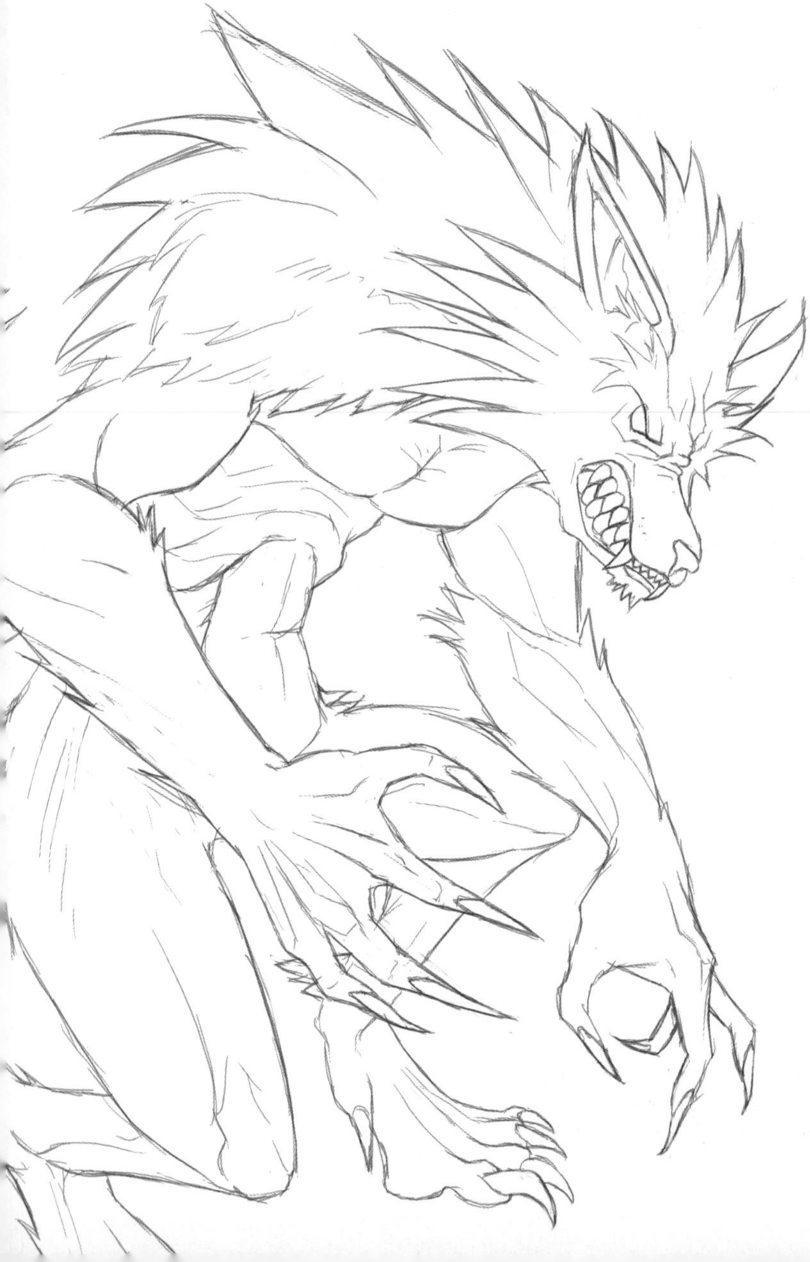

Working on non-human characters can be a lot of fun. This chapter explains how to achieve different textures and effects using photographic overlays and a variety of custom brush types on monster designs, including an eye-catching mutant zombie, a terrifying werewolf, and a serpent-headed Leviathan.

Size:
111 px
Hardness:
111 111 100 104
50 20 60 118
118 64 20 25
60 49 50 41
60

MUTANT ZOMBIE

Draw the kind of guy you might have to fight off in a survival horror video game. This involves drawing a front-view figure, then adding some wacky proportions and other mutating monstrous details.

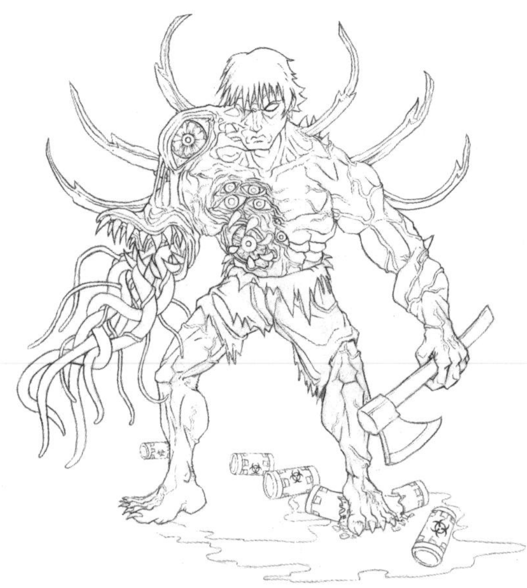

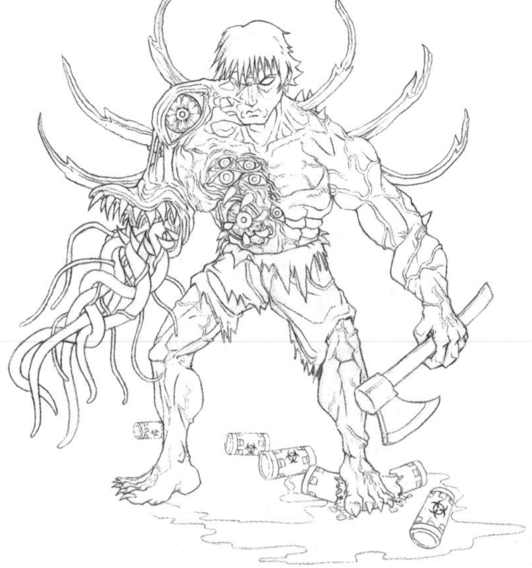

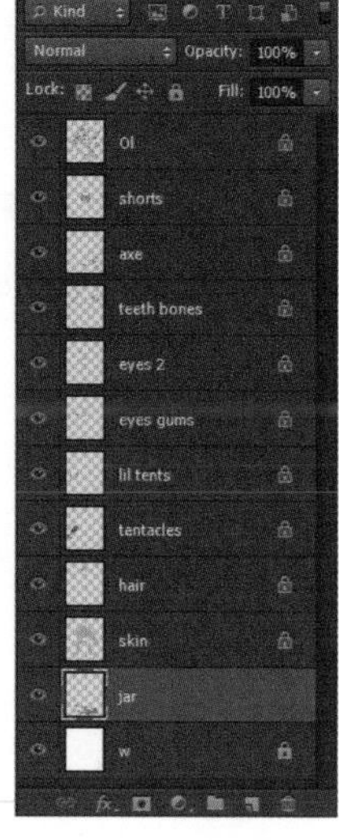

STEP 2

First, lay down your flat tones.

STEP 1

Make a pencil drawing and scan it in to the computer. Adjust the Levels to get rid of paper grain and smudges and use the Eraser or a white brush to delete any unwanted marks. The line art does not have to be vigorously cleaned up or digitally inked, as this is not necessary for rough-textured monster designs.

STEP 3

With a central light source in mind, add soft shading and rendering to the character, bringing together all the shading techniques you have learnt in earlier chapters. Keep the skin and clothing fairly dull, as the intention is to make the bright, creepy eyes and tentacles pop more. I set the Brush mode to "Color" to add some pink to parts of the gray-green skin and blue to the tentacle tips.

STEP 4

With subjects such as monsters, a dark background is required. Use the digital drawing method to add some background elements with blue lines—in this case, oil drums and barrels (nothing too detailed.) Then, using the background painting method explained in Jake's tutorial (see page 198), paint in some tone shading. Select "Thick Heavy" or "Natural Media" brushes of various opacity and flow percentages for added texture. Lay the ground shadow underneath the monster.

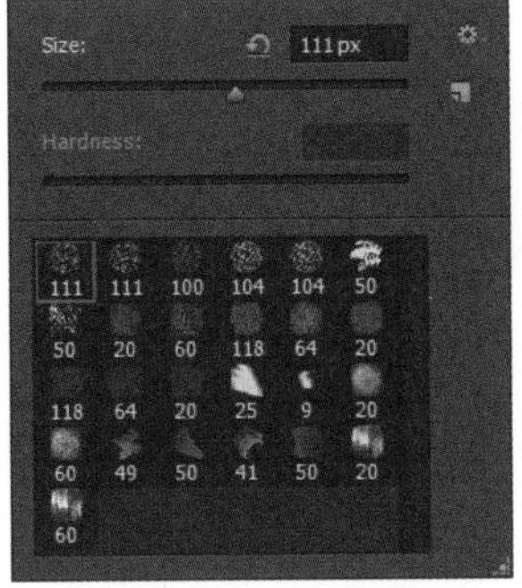

STEP 5

Now add some rain. Create a new layer on top in the Layers panel and name it "Rain." Fill it with black then go to Filter –> Noise –> Add Noise. Adjust the Amount slider to around 150%, check the Monochromatic box, then click OK.

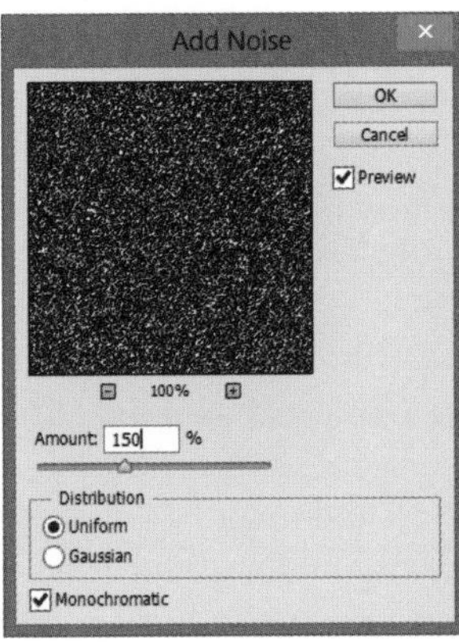

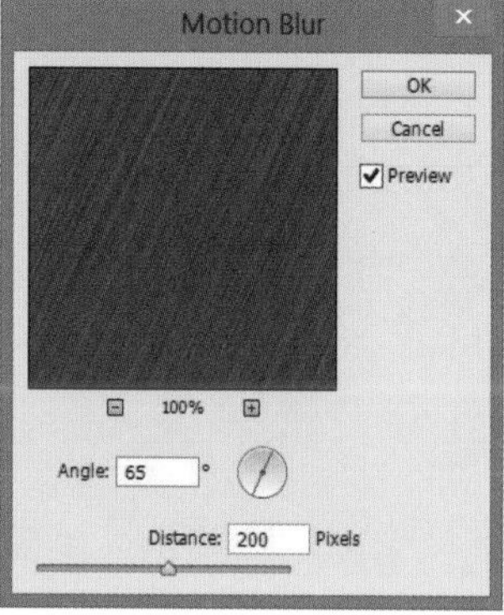

STEP 6

Go to Filter –> Blur –> Motion Blur and set Distance to around 200 and Angle to 65.

Enlarge the content of this layer using the scale Transform to around 150% to lengthen the rain and get rid of edges created with the filter. Now set the Rain layer's blending mode to Screen. Use the Levels adjustment and/or Curves and Brightness/Contrast to achieve a fine layer of rain overlay.

The effect of wind means that rain does not always fall in a single direction. So duplicate the Step 5 process, but with a slightly different blur distance and angle. Then place this layer toward the bottom, behind the character, and in front of the background.

STEP 7

Where the rain hits surfaces, it causes splashes and drips. To create random splashes, bring up the brush palette and select a small 5-pixels hard brush. Under "Brush Tip shape" set Spacing to 750%. Under Scattering, check "Both Axes," 1,000% scatter, set Count to 3 and Count Jitter to 20%.

On a new top layer, draw in the splash dots around the character's edge. You could paint these dots on to any surface facing the direction of rain, such as the barrel tops, bushes and ground, but keep them minimal or you will obscure too much of the character design and lighten the piece too much. Next, go to Filter –> Blur –> Gaussian Blur and set Blur Amount to 3.

STEP 8

For the finishing touches, add saliva to the tentacles. Add a green Screen overlay for the ground slime and a red Overlay layer toward the left. Make final adjustments to hues, values, and tones.

WEREWOLF

Draw a werewolf using digital techniques to create fur and atmospheric details such as fire and smoke.

STEP 2
Lay down the flat tones. In this case they're very simple—just fur, eyes, claws, and teeth.

STEP 1
Start with a tablet-drawn werewolf.

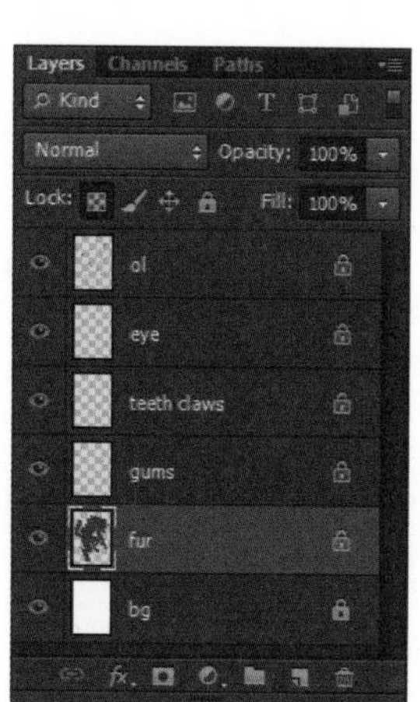

STEP 3
Add a wave of semi-soft shading.

STEP 4

With a selection of new brushes installed in the appropriate directory, add them to the Photoshop workspace by clicking the small cog icon in the top right of the Brush palette and selecting Fur Brushes.

Open a new canvas and experiment with the brushes to see the various textures you can create.

STEP 5

Return to the werewolf image and create a new layer above the Fur shadow layer named "Fur Texture." Select an appropriate brush and apply fur using black and brown tones. Temporarily hiding the Fur shadow layer may make it easier to see where the new fur texture is being added. Keep the direction of fur consistent, following the body's form and musculature. Refine the fur by selecting a smaller brush size and creating a series of short gray brush strokes over the top.

STEP 6

Set the Fur Texture layer blending mode to Vivid Light. Duplicate the layer. Set the duplicate layers blending mode to Hard Light. This will create more contrast as these layers overlay the original Fur shadow layer beneath.

STEP 7
Make final adjustments to the character. Replace the color of the darkest shadows and set them to a less saturated blue tone; adjust the contrast; clean up excess texture using the Eraser tool; color parts of the line art; add a little more shadow under the arm and neck with a purple color and brush set to Multiply; create the ground shadow.

FIRE AND SMOKE

You can add fire and smoke to illustrations by using manipulated Photoshop filters or custom brushes, or by cloning stock photos from the internet.

STEP 8
To make the image more interesting, add a fire effect on the lefthand side of the wolf. Insert a stock fire or flame photo, resize it to fit, then set its blending mode to Screen. The darker the character or background behind the fire, the more the flames will stand out.

STEP 9

To increase the amount of fire, add additional photos of flames of different sizes. A smoke image can also be added using the same process. The smoke can be inverted using Image –> Adjustments –> Invert [Ctrl+I / Cmd+I], then setting that layer to Multiply mode rather than Screen for dark rather than light smoke.

Finish by adding an orange overlay layer to the lefthand parts of the werewolf to denote glow from the fire. Darken the background and, after merging all visible layers, tweak the color balance and levels to achieve the desired effect.

LEVIATHAN

Draw a mythical sea creature using digital techniques to add scaly skin, ocean waves, and an otherworldly glow.

STEP 2

Lay the flat tones. I've alternated the front body scales on two separate layers as I want them to be slightly different colors.

STEP 1

Start with a pencil-drawn leviathan, a dragon-like creature. The idea is to situate him in water once he is colored.

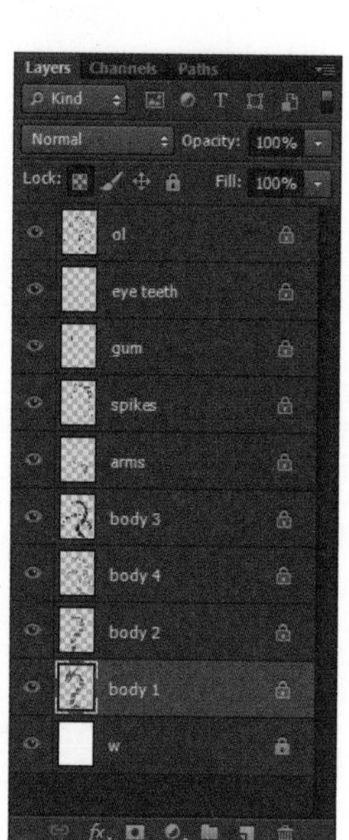

STEP 3

Add a soft shading to each layer.

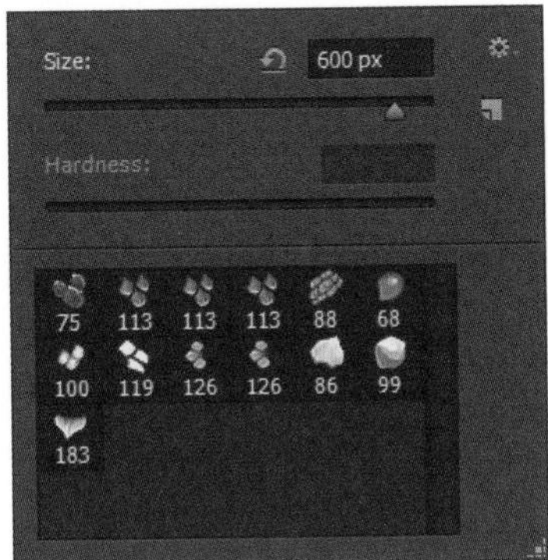

STEP 4

Add a selection of installed scale brushes to the Brush palette. Open a new canvas and experiment with the brushes to see how they work, then return to the leviathan image.

STEP 5

Create a new layer on top of the rear body layer and name it "Scales." Select an appropriate brush size and white foreground color then, starting from the head, draw a line of scales to follow the shape of the body. A second or third line may be needed, depending on the size of the brush. As with fur, make sure the scales follow the same direction. Check against a photo of a fish to make sure this is correct.

STEP 6

Create additional layers and repeat Step 5 to add scales to other parts of the leviathan. Use different scale brush types as necessary. Set the blending mode of these scale layers to "Overlay."

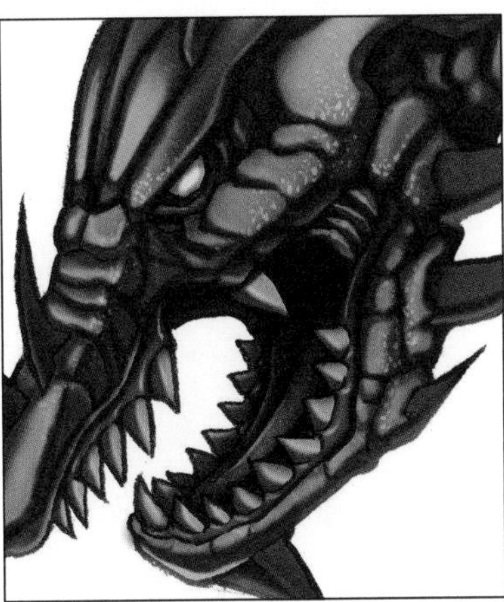

STEP 7

Another way to create scale-like texture is to use Cuts. Create some small circular selections with the Lasso tool on the leviathan's face. Then, on a new layer, use a soft brush with white to dust over the selections. Deselect [Ctrl+D / Cmd+D], then set this layer's mode to Overlay.

STEP 8

Next, add water. Enlarge the canvas, particularly at the bottom, to make space. Create a layer at the top of the Layers panel named "Water." This will be used to cover up the messy excess on the lower body. Replace the white background with a second Water layer—use a slightly lighter blue tone and brush to fill the bottom two-thirds of the image. Create a layer and name it "Sky." Fill this layer with a lighter blue tone.

Install custom water brushes and use these with white as the foreground color to build up overlapping splash effects. It's a good idea to place each splash like a stamp on its own layer so it can be tweaked and transformed independently before being merged with the Water layer. Try mixing different splash brush types, angles, sizes, and opacities.

STEP 9

Source an appropriate image for the sky and add it to the Sky layer. Perform the usual adjustments to make it fit and blur it out. Remember water often reflects the same color as the sky, so, for example, a purple sky means adding purple tone to the water color.

STEP 10

Now make your final touches. Adjust Contrast; add a little more shadow to the leviathan using black on a layer set to Multiply; add an inner orange glow; and add orange overlay layers to draw focus toward the face and add contrast against the purple sky.

DIGITAL DOS AND DON'TS

I hope by now you will have gained an understanding of what it takes to create characters and rendering to a professional level. In this chapter I've highlighted a few common mistakes you need to avoid and given reminders of techniques that will make your artwork even more successful.

NIKKI
GR

COMMON PITFALLS

Working digitally is not an excuse to be lazy with your art, nor is it a way of escaping the amount of time and effort it takes to develop general drawing and painting techniques concerning proportions, perspective, light, shadows, and composition.

PRACTICE MAKES PERFECT

No matter what level you're at, it's great to see any aspiring artist giving it a go and having some fun experimenting with digital art. Over the years I've seen hundreds of novice digital artists present samples of their work. Understandably, first attempts usually need a lot more attention. Here are some examples of what can go wrong.

ATTEMPT 1

There are a lot of problems with this image. The initial flats were not all placed up to the edges of the lines—notice where the skin meets the outline. During the flatting process, double-check that you have expanded all selections by 3–10 pixels before filling in with a color, especially if you're working with light colors on a white background.

There is a light source here from right to left, but it's much too subtle, especially on the skin tone. The aim is to show form—that the head is round and not flat and that overlapping or raised elements cast shadows. The hair is simply a light to dark gray uniform gradient with a blob of white highlight—this should be manually shaded with a range of values and tones for each section of hair. The top lip should be shaded darker than the bottom one, and the highlights in both eyes should reflect light coming from the same direction. The background is muddy, caused by mixing black into a light color.

ATTEMPT 3

This is more like it! The previous skin and hair tones have been neatened up and blended out to give a softer look. The eyes are now more detailed. Shapes have been added to the background to stop it looking flat and plain.

ATTEMPT 2

This is looking better, but it's still bland and uninspired. While simply adding darker shading around each line helps, it looks a little messy and rushed. Using a lower-flow, soft brush would enable these lines to be blended out so that they appear less blotchy. To make the work jump out, it needs more contrast and tonal range as well as details such as shine on the hair and skin and shading in the irises of the eyes—arguably the most crucial part of any figure.

ATTEMPT 4

Finally, some extra cast shadows and a few color overlays have been added. The skin tones in the previous attempt look nice and might be to your taste, but I like a high-contrast effect such as the one here as it creates more impact and has a glossy look to it.

TROUBLESHOOTING

If you've followed the book this far, you'll know what to do when using Photoshop. However, there are a few points, including the misuse of Photoshop tools, that are worth taking a further look at.

DODGE AND BURN

Some new artists try to rely on these tools for everything. While they have their place, Dodge often leaves artwork looking washed out, while Burn tends to make colors appear muddy.

LENS FLARE

Located within the Render category, this filter is often wrongly used to give a glow effect. It doesn't have a place in digital artwork.

THE OVERUSE OF FILTERS

While Photoshop has many effective filters that can be applied to artwork, they should be used for a specific purpose and to achieve a certain look. If they are overdone, they are distracting and the image can look tacky.

UP-SCALING

Once you've created your artwork you will be unable to increase its size without losing quality. Make sure you start out using the largest possible image dimensions your computer can comfortably handle.

LAZY/RUSHED INKING

This can spoil an otherwise great design. Common mistakes include lines that should be parallel but aren't, lines that do not meet at the ends where they should, and lines that wobble. An unvarying line weight is another problem—typically, fiddly details should use a thinner line, while bold shapes, outlines or objects closer to the viewer look best with thicker lines. Lines that do not connect to other lines should often taper to a point for best results. Drawing with wide, sweeping motions often helps to eliminate a lot of inking errors.

UNSUITABLE BACKGROUNDS

A great character illustration can be let down by a poor background. Sometimes a full-on, detailed background isn't required, but if you're using a color, pattern, or tone instead of white, make sure it complements the character and existing colors. Stay away from garish colors like flat red or saturated green and don't resort to using cheap-looking patterns of stars, circles, or clip art for a background. If you're creating an illustrative background to give some kind of context to the character, spend some time on it and try to make it look as impressive as your character art. Remember to add shadow to the ground to stop your character looking as though he or she is floating.

MISUSE OF THE GRADIENT FILL TOOL

The Gradient Fill tool is sometimes used instead of a brush to create shading, as seen in Attempt 1 on page 242. The Gradient Fill is great for enhancing artwork by creating overlay gradations, but it is not a substitute for manually placing shadows with a brush.

JAGGED STROKES

When using a hard brush, minimize brush spacing from the default 25% to 1% to avoid jagged strokes, if moving the pen slowly on a graphics tablet.

IMPATIENCE

You don't need to invest 100 hours in making a sketch perfect, and I certainly don't advocate putting in so much time and effort on an artwork that you stop enjoying the process. However, if your portfolio of best works consists of images that were created in an hour or two or demonstrates that you weren't willing to put in the time to correct mistakes or learn appropriate techniques to get the job done, then you're doing yourself a disservice. Learning new software and becoming the amazing artist of your dreams is something that is going to require hours of work, but the end result will be worth it and the journey can be a lot of fun.

LOSS OF WORK

It's obviously necessary to save your work regularly, but it's not uncommon for people to get so engrossed in their artwork that they forget to do so. You never know when Photoshop might crash or some other operating system error might occur. You could even experience a power cut. It's also worth backing up your Photoshop art files on a separate drive or location in case of hard disk failure. Photoshop CS6 and CC feature a customizable auto-save feature: setting auto-save to every 5 minutes may help to recover your latest work after a software crash.

When it comes to digital art, if you rush things and aren't interested in learning and improving you'll be stuck producing artwork you're not happy with. Always take the trouble to go back and fix things you know aren't right.

Finished Works

This section includes some of my finished works. It contains images that demonstrate the range of techniques discussed so far, and hopefully will give you some inspiration to draw on. It's worth building your own library of favorite artwork to refer to as you develop your desired style.

The most important thing is to have fun and enjoy the process of learning and growing as an artist. I hope this book has provided you with the tools you need to create your own incredible manga-style artwork.

DESCENT
PLAZA

MANGA FANTASIES

The designs on this pages started in sketch form; I redrew and neatened them up before coloring.

ZOMBIE LOVE (OPPOSITE)

This is my piece for an "art trade," where two artists agree to draw each other's original character for fun. The girl is manga artist Nayume's character. Apparently Nayume has a fear of zombies, so I thought it would be cool to have one creeping up behind her. Perhaps he's in love with her . . . or with her brain!

SOSUKE YONG KIM

I wanted to create a character who can kick some butt as well as being a person I can relate to—an artist! This Japanese-Korean character has a lot of frustrations in life and vents his feelings through fighting (of course!) and his art, using a variety of media to get the job done.

GOTHIC HALLOWEEN

This character was originally drawn for an anime calendar. The artwork needed to feature a "babe," something connected with the month of October, and had to reflect the theme "journeys." I chose a modern-Gothic witch girl to represent Halloween and showed her riding on a broomstick. The background was drawn and added separately.

CYBER POLICE

Natsumi is a rising star of the Japanese cyborg police force. She fights in the future against cyber criminals and monsters. She's a cyborg with a body designed for speed and endurance.

ETERNAL DESCENT

Drawing backgrounds adds context to characters and can make a massive difference to the overall effect of a piece. I created these three artworks for the album *Losing Faith* by the heavy metal band Eternal Descent. They represent city scenes from the album's narratives and were used on packaging and animated on an interactive web site.

GYNOID

This female humanoid robot was initially inspired by the original manga android, Astro Boy. I love Tron-style neon trim, so I had to get a bit of that in there! I wanted her hair and skin to look like plastic, which was a little different, and I added some color effect, such as the orange glow, in at the end.

FIRE-FIGHTING FEMME FATALE (OPPOSITE)

This character was created for a client interested in seeing his glamorous *Strike Force* action women take a manga form. My usual process is to send an initial pencil drawing to the client. This is either approved or marked for revision. After the revision, I'll have it digitally inked. The final aim is to bring it to a new level with Photoshop coloring.

Art Questions and Answers

› How long should I spend on a picture?

It depends on the size, amount of detail and your general drawing pace. Speed is usually determined by consistent practice and experience. I spend extra time on my own work to get rid of the brush strokes, ink bleed, and stray pencil marks.

Don't be afraid to work on a drawing for more than an hour. If you want to progress, take time to make sure everything looks real and, if you're adding a background, don't rush it. If you're doing manga or comic sequential pages, be prepared to spend between three and twelve hours penciling alone. Be patient with your picture. If you feel tired, leave it for a while and come back to it later.

› I REALLY wish I could draw, but for the life of me I can't. Does anyone else feel this way?

Don't worry—all artists have at times felt limited by a lack of ability. Drawing is something that takes time and practice. For some people, it might be a matter of weeks before they start to see improvement, while others might need longer. Resist the temptation of comparing yourself with other artists, just do what feels right for you.

› How long will it take me to become a master artist?

It's said that it takes 10,000 hours of practice to master any skill. Clocking up the hours will increase your skills as your brain begins to retain the knowledge and experience that comes from each new drawing session. You will learn from each image you produce as you try out ideas and create the types of characters or artwork you enjoy.

› I'm struggling with too much detail. What can I do?

Simplify your art to match your level. Beginners might find some of the final images in this book too complicated at first, so try cutting back on details. For example, clump hair into fewer spikes, remove the trim or fiddly detail on clothes, leave out some of the fabric folds, and concentrate on basic body shapes. Take it all step by step—work on stick figures and basic shapes first so that you don't feel overwhelmed by the final image. Lastly, be patient. Take your time—you'll learn to speed up as you improve.

› Should I post my artwork online?

Putting your work on the web is a great way of getting feedback. Online art communities provide a platform where you can show what you've created and gain constructive comments from other artists. It can be daunting, however, because you may get your feelings hurt by a negative evaluation of your image. However, most artists want to help others and can impart invaluable insights.

› How can I draw THAT?

If there's a particular area you're having trouble with, such as buildings, people, or animals, for instance, the best thing to do is find reference material from the web or take some photos to draw from. If you've never drawn a cat, for example, try doodling a few sketches of cats from a photo, so you get used to how they look and move. The more you practice any single object, the easier it is to draw it again next time.

› Where's the best place to draw?

Any place you feel comfortable. Some people set aside a room in their house for the purpose, some use their bedroom, others take their sketchbook to the local café. I've been known to sit around the house in different rooms with a clipboard and paper, or draw at a library, a pub, a coffee shop, waiting for a train, and so on. However, I spend most of my time creating artwork in my studio. If you're likely to be drawing frequently, a dedicated workspace is essential for long-term comfort.

› I want to sell my work – what should I charge?

Pricing your work is never straightforward; there are several factors to take into consideration. Some of the main ones are:

- What is your work worth to you? All work takes time, effort and skill.
- How does your work compare to that of professionals?
- Who is paying and what will the work be used for? This is very important, as individuals will only pay so much for a private commission, whereas companies looking to use your character in a game or as a mascot are usually willing to pay much more.

Starting up as a commercial artist is hard at first because you need to understand business as well as how to draw well. Be strict with your pricing and don't undersell yourself, but be careful not to overcharge either or you'll never get customers! It's a tricky balancing act.

› Are there any universities that teach manga and anime?

Most countries have educational institutions that run a range of illustration and animation courses. Research what is available in your locality. Since the quality of education you can expect to receive will vary greatly from school to school, look out for reviews of establishments you're thinking of attending, or seek feedback from existing students. There are several online schools that offer art instruction and guidance. They may be focused on general art techniques or more specific courses such as animation, illustration, concept design, and comics. There are also a few schools that specifically focus on teaching manga.

› How can I develop and maintain a drawing style?

The more you practice the same style, the more it will lodge in your memory and become part of you. If you're like me, you'll constantly see other styles you like and want to imitate, so following one style can be hard. Style is something an artist will continue to develop and is something that comes naturally. Don't try to force a style—let it develop over time.

Glossary

Action lines Multiple, straight, parallel "speed lines" to denote movement, or a circular arrangement of "focus lines" to draw attention to an object, person, or element on a page.

Adjustments A Photoshop command/process carried out on artwork and layers to change color, contrast, and tone.

Adobe The company responsible for producing Photoshop as well as other multimedia and creativity software products.

Airbrush shading/soft CG A style of digital art which uses smooth, blended tones like those of a traditional airbrush.

Anatomy The structure of the body and how the various parts are in proportion with one another.

Anime A Japanese style of animation and artwork.

Background The area of an artwork that appears farthest away from the viewer; also, the area against which a figure or scene is placed.

Cel shading An artwork style like that of an animation still, which uses solid tones and shading.

CG An abbreviation of "computer graphics," often used to describe digitally rendered manga art. CGing is the process of rendering artwork digitally.

Chibi A small, cute style of character, often drawn with a large head and small body and limbs.

Color modes These allow different color ranges. CMYK is a mode suitable for art intended for print, while RGB is for art for screens and the internet.

Commission To request the production of a work of art. Artists interested in earning money from their artwork take on commissions from individuals.

Composition The arrangement of elements within a work of art to form a unified whole.

Contrast The range of light to dark areas in the composition. An image with high contrast will have a greater variability in tonality, while an image with low contrast will have a more similar range of tones.

Cosplay The act of dressing as one's favorite characters from anime, games, and movies, usually at comic conventions and events.

Custom brushes These can be downloaded or created for use with Photoshop's Brush tool. They come in a vast number of shapes and sizes, with different associated default settings.

Cuts A Western comic-book coloring technique that uses a combination of masks and selections along with airbrush shading to add highlights.

Digital inking Adding clean black outlines to an existing pencil or graphics tablet sketch using computer software.

Dojinshi A fan comic based on an existing story, setting, or characters.

File formats Artwork image files are typically PSDs (Photoshop files). JPEG, GIF, and PNG are used to compress files into a smaller size for web use. TIFF and BMP are occasionally used as flat files with low or no compression.

Flatting Or "adding the flats." The process of adding a solid, flat base tone to layers on an image, often within predrawn outlines and line art.

Foreground The area of an image that appears closest to the viewer.

Graphics tablet An input device that connects to your computer, allowing you to draw with a pen or stylus instead of a mouse. Often simply referred to as a "tablet" (not to be confused with a tablet computer.)

Inking Adding clean, black outlines to an existing pencil or graphics tablet sketch using traditional media or computer software.

Layers Most graphics software uses layers. These act like sheets of stacked glass—you can see through transparent areas of a layer to the layers beneath. You can move a layer and reposition its content, like sliding a sheet of glass in a pile. The opacity of a layer can be altered to make the content partially transparent.

Layout This is the arrangement of the elements within an image or comic page, such as the panels, speech balloons, and gutters or margins between elements.

Manga A Japanese style of comics and artwork.

Mecha An abbreviation for "mechanical." Mecha are machines (most commonly robots) as well as a genre of manga.

Medium The material used to create a work of art, for example, pencil, ink, acrylic. Digital is also a medium.

Middle ground The part of the picture that is between the foreground and background.

Monochrome Having just a single color.

Opacity Another term for transparency. Opacity percentages can be adjusted using Photoshop's tools, options, and adjustment settings.

Overlay An effect or color added to a layer that is situated on top of artwork or shaded elements. In this book, overlay refers primarily to the layer and effect. Photoshop also has a blending mode named Overlay.

Panel A single frame or drawing in the multiple panel sequence of a manga or comic-book page. It is an individual drawing depicting a captured moment in time.

Perspective A technique used to depict a 3D object or environment, as in an illustrated scene that appears to extend into the distance.

Photoshop CS & CC CS stands for Creative Suite; CC means Creative Cloud. Photoshop is one of several Adobe programs. The tutorials in this book are based on Photoshop CS6 and CC.

Reference Typically, images and photos that assist an artist with generating ideas or understanding what a subject or scene looks like in real life.

Render A term meaning "add shading" by, for example, adding shadow to depict the form and shape of an object.

Scanning Importing images and artwork into your computer and converting them to a digital format. An alternative to scanning might be to photograph artwork and transfer it to the computer.

Selection A selection isolates one or more parts of your image.

Shading Adding darker or lighter tones and values to create the effect of shadows, highlights, and 3D forms.

Shojo Manga for the teenage female demographic. Josei manga caters for older women.

Shonen Manga which caters for the teenage male demographic. Seinen manga caters for young and older men.

Stock image Usually, a photograph that is licensed for specific purposes. It is used to fulfill the needs of creative assignments instead of hiring a photographer or drawing parts of an image manually. Stock images come with terms of use. Royalty-free or no-charge images often require you to give credit to the owner or provide a link to the image source.

Tone A term used to describe a hue and the result of mixing it with any shade of gray.

Workflow The process an artist goes through to achieve his or her results from start to finish or from one step to the next. The more efficient your process, the better your workflow.